HISTORICAL DICTIONARIES OF RELIGIONS, PHILOSOPHIES, AND MOVEMENTS
Edited by Jon Woronoff

1. *Buddhism,* by Charles S. Prebish, 1993
2. *Mormonism,* by Davis Bitton, 1994
3. *Ecumenical Christianity,* by Ans Joachim van der Bent, 1994
4. *Terrorism,* by Sean Anderson and Stephen Sloan, 1995
5. *Sikhism,* by W.H. McLeod, 1995

HISTORICAL DICTIONARY OF SIKHISM

by
W. H. McLEOD

Religions, Philosophies, and Movements No. 5

The Scarecrow Press, Inc.
Lanham, Md., & London

SCARECROW PRESS, INC.

Published in the United States of America
by Scarecrow Press, Inc.
4720 Boston Way
Lanham, Maryland 20706

4 Pleydell Gardens, Folkestone
Kent CT20 2DN, England

Copyright © 1995 by W. H. McLeod

British Cataloguing-in-Publication Information Available

Library of Congress Cataloging-in-Publication Data

McLeod, W. H.
Historical dictionary of Sikhism / W. H. McLeod
p.   c. — (Religion, philosophies, and movements; 5)
Includes bibliographical references
1. Sikhism—Dictionaries. I. Title II. Series.
BL 2018.M38 1995 294.6'03—dc20 95-15853 CIP

ISBN 0—8108-3035-3 (cloth : alk. paper)

♾ ™ The paper used in this publication meets the minimum
requirements of American National Standard for Information
Sciences—Permanence of Paper for Printed Library Materials,
ANSI Z39.48—1984.
Manufactured in the United States of America.

To
Dr. Amrik Singh
in gratitude

CONTENTS

The Punjab

EDITOR'S FOREWORD

Due to the distinctive way most of them dress, Sikhs can be recognized not only on the Indian subcontinent where the largest communities dwell but also by a vast number of people throughout the world. Unfortunately, the overwhelming majority of those who can recognize them would be extremely hard put to explain the basic tenets of Sikhism. That could even apply to many of their neighbors on the Indian subcontinent, and all the more so to those encountering newer Sikh communities in Europe, the Americas, and Asia. That is a very unfortunate gap with regard to one of the world's more active and dynamic religions.

This *Historical Dictionary of Sikhism* helps fill the gap. It provides information not only on the religion, its principles, precepts, and practices, but also its history, culture, and social arrangements. Numerous entries cover the founder and early Gurus as well as Sikh leaders and groups of today. Others deal with events and conflicts that shaped Sikhism in the past and the problems and challenges that influence the directions it is taking into the future. Of course, there is also reference to how the Sikhs dress and why.

This book was written by one of the foremost authorities of the subject, W. H. McLeod. Dr. McLeod teaches at the University of Otago in New Zealand and was for five years Visiting Professor in Sikh Studies at the University of Toronto, Canada. He has lectured widely and written many works, including *The Sikhs: History, Religion, and Society*. Imparting knowledge that can be useful even to Sikhs who know their religion well, this volume is presented in such a way that outsiders can understand and thus overcome the gap referred to above. This, along with a copious bibliography, should stand all readers in good stead.

Jon Woronoff
Series Editor

ACKNOWLEDGEMENTS

I should like to thank the following organizations and individuals for assistance in compiling this *Historical Dictionary of Sikhism:* Singh Brothers, Publishers and Booksellers, Bazar Mai Sewan, Amritsar; Department of Guru Nanak Studies, Guru Nanak Dev University, Amritsar; Guru Gobind Singh Department of Religious Studies, Punjabi University, Patiala; Professor Surjit Hans; and Professor Pashaura Singh. Their help has been greatly appreciated. I should also like to thank Amrit Kaur Singh and Rabindra Kaur Singh of Wirral, Merseyside, for suggesting that the round shape on nineteenth-century nishans was actually a cooking vessel and that this shape later evolved into the quoit of the khanda. (See KHANDA.) Paula Waby has, as usual, fully shared in the production of the typescript, discharging her portion of the burden with the utmost patience and fortitude. Finally, I thank Margaret with love for all her help and tolerance.

ABBREVIATIONS AND ACRONYMS

AG   Adi Granth
ICS   Indian Civil Service
SGPC   Shiromani Gurdwara Parbandhak Committee

INTRODUCTION

Sikhism is a religion which has been little understood in the past. To a large extent, that lack of understanding can be explained. Although Sikhs are more numerous than is generally supposed, their prominence has been seen largely in terms of military activity or sports. Until recently they dwelt almost exclusively in northwest India, and few major events involving them enlisted the attention of the outside world. Moreover, Sikhs themselves have disagreed on the meaning of the faith which they affirm, some seeing it as a part of the wider field of Hindu India while others insisting that it is a separate faith. Westerners who knew a little about the Sikhs vaguely regarded the religion as a blend of Hinduism and Islam.

Today the Sikhs and their religion are at last receiving an increasing amount of interest and attention, reflected in the number of encyclopedias and dictionaries of Sikhism which are currently being produced. The world is slowly being made aware of the Sikh religion as a distinctive faith. This is a result both of the total number of Sikhs and the fact that they comprise a highly mobile community. Numbers are impossible to estimate with accuracy, but it seems that the figure is approximately 16,000,000 worldwide. Of this number, approximately one million live outside India, constituting a significant minority in the United Kingdom, Canada, and the United States. Many of them are highly visible, particularly the men who wear beards and turbans, and they naturally attract much attention in their new countries of domicile.

Less fortunately, the Sikh community has in recent years been the object of considerable interest to the outside world as a result of political differences with the Government of India. These led in 1984 to an assault by the Indian army on the Golden Temple of the Sikhs and to several years of serious disturbance in the Sikhs' home state of the Punjab. The situation has now quieted, but for many people the memory still remains, and not all those who still remember it are Sikhs.

One result of this confrontation with the Government of India has been a further emphasis upon the separate nature of the Sikh religion. This was claimed by some Sikh scholars at the end of the nineteenth century, and during the hundred years since it has won increasing acceptance. The recent troubles have further strengthened the conviction for many Sikhs.

Before beginning this brief survey of Sikh history and religion, there is one fact which, though obvious enough, still requires emphasis. For Sikhs history and religion are inextricably intertwined. It is quite impossible to study the religion of the Sikhs without reference to their history. Likewise it is impossible to study the history without frequent recourse to their religion. The religion was born in historical events and it evolves in intimate response to the unfolding pattern of those events. To some extent this can be said of any religion. It is abundantly true of Sikhism.

The teachings of Nanak

Sikhism traces its beginnings to Guru Nanak, born in 1469 and dying in either 1538 or 1539. With the life of Guru Nanak the account of the Sikh faith begins, all Sikhs acknowledging him as their founder. Stories of the life of Nanak abound, but they are related in hagiographies known as janam-sakhis, and very few of them can be authenticated. Many of them are, as one would expect, plainly impossible. All that is known with certainty concerning his life follows. Nanak was a Hindu, born in the Punjab village of Talvandi forty miles west of Lahore. He was sent to the town of Sultanpur where he was employed in the local ruler's commissariat. While there, he evidently underwent the experience which convinced him of his divine mission. For several years he journeyed around India and perhaps beyond, returning to the Punjab in the early 1520s. He spent his final years in the village of Kartarpur on the Ravi river, receiving there the people who came to hear the teachings which were winning him an increasing following. Beyond this there is little to add with any assurance, apart from the names of some of his relatives.

Although his life is sketchy his teachings can be positively known. This is due to the copious works which he has left and which have been treasured by his Sikhs as a part of the Adi Granth (the Sikh scripture). Nanak emerged as a religious teacher belonging to the Sant tradition of Northern India. The Sant tradition has commonly been treated as a part of the Bhakti movement, as indeed it was. It was, however, a very distinctive part. This was a religious tradition which drew most of its support from Hindus but which laid paramount stress on the conviction that the one God in whom they believed could never be represented in any visible form. Religion for the Sants was wholly inward, and inwardly they meditated on God. For them there could be no outward forms, no temple nor mosque, no holy scriptures, no sacred person such as a Hindu Brahman or a Muslim qazi. Idols were totally rejected, as were castes.

Most Sants were in fact low caste or outcaste, and in this respect Nanak was a conspicuous exception. Like all of the Sikh Gurus he was a Khatri, a highly-ranked mercantile caste. This made no difference to the message which he communicated, which was as rigorous with regard to caste as that of any other Sant. Caste was useless when it came to liberation, and the outcaste had just as good a chance of attaining it as the Brahman or anyone else. Meditate within, for by regularly so doing you will at last attain liberation from the bonds of transmigration.

For Nanak the key to liberation lay in the **nām** (the divine Name). All that could be affirmed concerning Akal Purakh (God) was an aspect of the **nām,** and the evidences of the **nām** lay all around and within a person. Akal Purakh was **sarab viāpak,** everywhere present, and the person who was spiritually attuned to Akal Purakh would increasingly comprehend the manifold presence of the **nām.** Meditate on the **nām** in all its aspects (**nām simaraṇ**), and the believer would progressively find liberation. By the regular practice of **nām simaraṇ** a person would achieve a final harmony of spirit in which the endless wheel of death and rebirth would be stilled, and the soul would find ultimate peace.

This was the message which Nanak communicated to all who would hear him. It was one which required no separation from the life of the world and which could be followed by any person, regardless of present caste or of past deeds. Above all it was wholly internal, a discipline to be followed without any assistance from sacred persons or sacred things. Regular meditation was the one requirement. **Nām simaraṇ** could consist of the simple repetition of meaningful words (words such as **sat nam,** 'true is the Name,' or the popular modern name for God, **vāhigurū**); it could be the singing of hymns which told of the glories of the **nām,** or it could be deep meditation within. These teachings were delivered with clarity, and the hymns which express them are noted for their beauty. As such Nanak is the pre-eminent Sant.

The origins of the Sant movement were to be found primarily in Vaishnava bhakti or devotion to Vishnu, with the all-important difference that Akal Purakh (unlike Vishnu in all his incarnations) was strictly without form (**nirguṇ**). The emphasis upon formlessness and the need for inner meditation evidently owe something to the beliefs of the Naths. The Naths (or the Kanphat yogis) were followers of the semi-legendary Gorakhnath (placed sometime before 1200). Nanak certainly was no Nath and is very outspoken in his criticism of them. The Naths, however, laid paramount stress on an interior discipline, and there are clear evidences of their influence on some other members of the Sant tradition (particularly Kabir).

To many in the West Nanak's teachings have been represented, as we have seen, as a syncretic mixing of Hindu and Muslim beliefs. This is not correct. An analysis of the works of Nanak reveals very little that can be traced to a Muslim source. The Sant tradition was a part of the wide area of Hindu belief, and any suggestion that it or the teachings of Nanak were syncretic is a mistake. Hindu and Muslim ways could be, for Nanak, either true or false. They were true if they upheld interior devotion, and they were false if they put their trust in exterior symbols such as temples or mosques.

Is Sikhism therefore merely one of the many examples of the Hindu tradition? For a modern Sikh the answer would usually be no. In Nanak's time the question would be unlikely to arise. The particular variety of teachings which he imparted would not have marked the Sikhs as significantly different from their Punjabi neighbors, though Nanak certainly distanced himself from those (whether Hindu or Muslim) who preached a conventional form of religion with its dependence on what would be regarded as external. In this sense the religion which he taught transcended both Hindu tradition and Islam.

The real difference came with the tenth and last Guru. At the very end of the seventeenth century Guru Gobind Singh formed the core of his followers into the Khalsa, and it is the Khalsa which thereafter assumes the dominant form of Sikhism. The Khalsa, though, was still regarded by most of its members as a special form of India's religious landscape without any clear sense of being a separate faith. At the end of the nineteenth century there developed the Singh Sabha movement, and as a result of the keen scrutiny of some Singh Sabha members there evolved the unambiguous conviction of Sikhism as a wholly distinct and separate religion. This conviction is now generally accepted.

All that lies well in the future. In Nanak's own time the person who accepted his teachings became his Sikh or 'learner,' and the community of his followers came to be known as the Nanak-panth, those who followed the way of Nanak. Later the name Nanak was dropped and the term applied to the Sikh community became simply the Panth. The word **panth** is commonly used in India for the disciples of a particular person or doctrine, but for the Sikhs it has a special meaning, and if written in English it is better spelled with a capital P. The Sikh community is the Panth, and the Panth it will be called hereafter.

Nanak was not usually called Guru by his early followers, the name Baba (Father) being preferred. To later generations of Sikhs, however, he was the one who had revealed the truth and enshrined it in works of great beauty. As such he was their Guru, and so too were his nine successors. It is believed that when the tenth Guru announced that with his death the line of personal Gurus would end the title passed to the Granth Sahib (the Adi Granth) which contained their teachings, and it thus came to be known as the Guru Granth Sahib.

The successors of Nanak

Nanak appointed one of his devoted disciples to follow him, a man called Lahina who became second Guru under the name of Angad (1538/39–1552). Guru Angad continued to direct the Panth in the manner of Nanak, but by the time he was succeeded by Guru Amar Das (1552–74) times were changing. To meet the needs of a Panth growing to maturity, Amar Das appointed his village of Goindval as a pilgrimage center, digging there a **baolī** or sacred well where pilgrims were expected to bathe. Devout Sikhs were appointed as manjis to engage in preaching, and particular days (notably Diwali) were designated festival days. On these days, Sikhs, when practicable, were encouraged to visit Goindval and receive the Master's blessing. The various hymns of his two successors were recorded, together with his own, in what came to be known as the Goindval Pothis (volumes).

To modern eyes it may seem as if Amar Das was steering the Panth away from the inward emphasis taught by Nanak, setting up a visible center of pilgrimage and recording hymns in a visible scripture. Amar Das, however, had to contend with a changing situation. The original Sikhs had joined the Panth from personal conviction and required little organization to hold them together. Now the Panth consisted of many who had been born into it, and it was also extending its geographical bounds as Sikhs engaged in trade carried their faith to distant places. A firmer organization was required, and Guru Amar Das was providing the Panth with a rudimentary one. It was, moreover, seen to be the actions of the first and only Guru. Sikhs believe that the ten persons who occupied the position of Guru were providing a habitation for the one eternal Guru. As ten torches can successively pass on the same flame, so the ten Gurus were really one. Decisions taken by Amar Das were therefore decisions which Nanak would have taken in the changing circumstances.

The fourth Guru was Ram Das (1574–81), the son-in-law of Amar Das, who moved the center of the Panth to the new foundation of Amritsar. His youngest son, Arjan, became the fifth Guru (1581–1606), and from then onwards all the Gurus were Ram Das's male descendants. Guru Arjan is important for two particular reasons. The first was the delivery to his Sikhs of a formal scripture, the Adi Granth, which built upon the extensive foundations laid by the Goindval Pothis. Later the Adi Granth was supplemented by the compositions of the ninth Guru. The scripture was installed in the central shrine of Amritsar known as Harimandir Sahib, the location which eventually was to be renowned as that of the celebrated Golden Temple. (At the death of the tenth and last Guru it came to be regarded, as we have seen, as the permanent habitation of the eternal Guru and is accordingly known as the Guru Granth Sahib.)

The second reason was the manner of Arjan's death, interpreted by Sikhs as the first martyrdom. North India was, at that time, ruled by the Mughal dynasty, and it seems clear that the Mughals were becoming concerned at the growth of the Panth. Arjan was arrested and died in Mughal custody.

This latter event produced a significant change in direction. Arjan was succeeded by his only son Hargobind (1606–44), under whom the Panth resorted to arms in order to protect themselves from Mughal hostility. This change has been interpreted as the introduction of **mīrī/pīrī** by Hargobind. As Guru he still maintained the emphasis on spiritual matters of his five predecessors (**pīrī**). The new element was the willingness to engage in worldly affairs and to physically fight for the Panth's preservation (**mīrī**). This was symbolized by the two swords of the Guru and by the erection of Akal Takht, the worldly counterpart to the spiritual quality of the neighbouring Harimandir Sahib.

Guru Hargobind was eventually compelled to withdraw from the plains of the Punjab and took up residence at Kiratpur on the edge of the Shivalik Hills overlooking the plains. His three successors all spent the greater part of their periods as Guru in the Shivaliks, generally safe from Mughal enmity. The seventh Guru was a grandson of Hargobind named Har Rai (1644–61), and he was followed by his son Har Krishan (1661–64). Har Krishan was a small child and died in Delhi of smallpox after only a short tenure. His dying words **bābā bakāle** were understood to indicate that his choice of a successor was a surviving son of Hargobind, at that time a recluse living in the Punjab village of Bakala. This was Tegh Bahadur (1664–75). In 1675 Guru Tegh Bahadur was executed by the Mughals in Delhi, thereby becoming the second Guru to be martyred.

Guru Gobind Singh and the Khalsa

When Tegh Bahadur was executed, his only son Gobind Rai (later Gobind Singh, 1675–1708), was still a young boy. The execution is said to have had a profound effect upon the child, as indeed it may well have done. Little is known of his upbringing in the Shivalik Hills. He emerges as the leader of his Sikhs, fighting to sustain his position as the ruler of a small Shivalik principality. In 1699, or shortly before, he took the most critical decision in all Sikh history. This was to establish the order of the Khalsa.

The Guru evidently already had a Khalsa which comprised those Sikhs under his direct supervision. Most Sikhs, however, were under the intermediate supervision of masands, men appointed to watch over the Guru's Sikhs and convey their offerings to him. The masands, first instituted by Guru Ram Das, had by this time grown corrupt and dangerously independent. Guru Gobind Singh therefore decided to suppress them and to have all his Sikhs join his own Khalsa.

This appears to have been one reason for the creation of the order, but there was clearly more to it than this. Those who joined the Khalsa were to adopt a highly visible identity which was to include uncut hair and the bearing of weapons. Just what the uniform precisely was is far from clear, but tradition is adamant that it included the Five Ks. These are five items, each of which begins with the letter 'k': **kes** (uncut hair), **kanghā** (comb), **karā** (iron or steel ring for the wrist), **kirpān** (sword or dagger), and **kachh** or **kachhahirā** (breeches which must not come below the knee). The Five Ks actually evolved during the eighteenth and nineteenth centuries, but on this point tradition brooks no doubt. The same applies to the Rahit or 'Code of Belief and Conduct' which the Guru is said to have delivered at the same time. It too evolved during the next century and a half in accordance with the pressures of the period (particularly the wars of the eighteenth century) from a nucleus imparted by the Guru.

The actual details are far from clear, but there can be no doubt that the Guru did inaugurate the Khalsa and that he summoned all who were committed to his cause to join it. This was done through a rite of initiation, each candidate swearing allegiance to the Guru's way. Each male added Singh to his name, and each female added Kaur. Many of his followers joined, particularly members of the Jat caste. Others held back, continuing to regard themselves as Sikhs but not as Sikhs of the Khalsa. Those who did join rendered themselves conspicuous by their appearance. It is said that the Guru vowed that never again would Sikhs be able to conceal their identity as they had done when his father was executed.

The inauguration of the Khalsa raises, of course, the fact that its emphasis on exterior symbols is the direct antithesis of Nanak's insistence upon the interior nature of religious belief. The answer lies in the same justification which has been applied to the changes introduced by Amar Das, namely that the decisions were taken by the one eternal Guru in accordance with the changed circumstances of the time. Belief in the one eternal Guru is fundamental for Sikhs. Gobind Singh faced differing circumstances which demanded the obligation to fight for justice against the forces of evil. It was to meet this demand that the Khalsa was created.

Serious trouble followed after the creation of the Khalsa. The Guru was besieged in his fortress of Anandpur by Shivalik enemies allied with Mughal forces from Sirhind. He was obliged to evacuate Anandpur in 1704 and to fight his way through to the safety of southern Punjab. In the process he lost two of his four sons to the Governor of Sirhind who put them to death by walling them up. The other two were killed during the escape. A defiant letter, the **Zafar-nāmā,** was despatched to the Mughal emperor Aurangzeb. In 1707 Aurangzeb died, and the Guru travelled south with his successor, Bahadur Shah, apparently in order to negotiate peace between the two. In the Deccan town of Nander he was assassinated by unknown assailants, probably agents of the Governor of Sirhind.

Subsequent Sikh history

Following the death of Guru Gobind Singh in 1708 the Punjab declined into almost a century of intermittent warfare. Sikh tradition represents it as a century in which a Sikh rebellion was followed by an attempt to exterminate the Panth. This was answered by heroic deeds, swinging the balance of power increasingly in favor of the Panth. Ultimately the century was crowned by the success of Ranjit Singh who emerged as Maharaja of the Punjab in 1801.

The rebellion against the Mughals was led by Banda Bahadur (Banda the Brave). Banda was a recluse who was selected by Guru Gobind Singh shortly before his death in Nander and who, after several years of mixed fortunes, was eventually captured and cruelly executed in 1716. The attempt to exterminate or (more likely) to bring the Panth under strict control was eventually marked by the appearance of the Sikh misls in the middle years of the century. These were territorial forces, each under the command of its own leader. The middle years of the century were also marked by the invasions of the Afghan ruler, Ahmad Shah Abdali. The Sikh misls gradually won the upper hand but used their success to fight among themselves. Eventually one of them was able to assert his hold over all the others, achieving his objectives by friendship, marriage alliances, and force. This was Ranjit Singh of the Shukerchakia misl.

The four decades of Maharaja Ranjit Singh's reign are regarded as a period of glory. Certainly Ranjit Singh extended the bounds of his kingdom in three directions, prevented from doing so in the fourth only by the arrival of the British. The Satluj river formed the border between the two. In one respect, however, Ranjit Singh's reign was not a success. He created a powerful army along European lines, but he did not succeed in creating a firm financial base for it. Moreover, Ranjit Singh did little to prepare his kingdom for the period after his death. When he died in 1839 the kingdom rapidly declined into confusion, and following two Anglo-Sikh wars it was annexed to British India in 1849.

The Sikhs were saved from a corresponding decline in morale by the appearance of the Singh Sabha movement. Founded in 1873 to arrest this decline, the Singh Sabha soon split into two major groups. One, centered in Amritsar, comprised the Sanatan ('orthodox') Sikhs, formed by old leaders (both social and religious) and some scholars who regarded the Panth as a special form of the Hindu tradition. The other, with its chief center in Lahore, was the Tat ('true') Khalsa. This comprised the majority of scholars and insisted that the Panth was clearly distinct from all other religious systems. Numerous other Singh Sabhas were formed in cities, towns, and even villages, each one usually in sympathy with either Amritsar or Lahore. A third extremist opinion found expression in the Bhasaur Singh Sabha.

After several decades of controversy, the Tat Khalsa emerged as virtually the complete victor, and ever since references to the Singh Sabha movement have assumed a Tat Khalsa meaning. By the end of the second decade of the twentieth century it was overtaken by the Akali Dal, a new political party which gave expression to the revived sense of Sikh identity. The Akali Dal immediately entered into a vigorous dispute with the British government of the Punjab for the control of the Sikh gurdwaras (temples), known as the Gurdwara Reform Movement, and in 1925 the passing of the Sikh Gurdwaras Act signalled their complete victory.

The Act also further strengthened the hold of the Khalsa on the Panth. It embodied a definition of a Sikh which leant strongly towards the exclusivist Khalsa view, as opposed to the broader inclusive view of those Sikhs who cut their hair and plainly were not members of the Khalsa.

When India won its independence from Britain in 1947, the Sikhs opted for India and a large-scale migration from Pakistan followed. Although the proportion of Sikhs in the much smaller Indian Punjab was significantly higher than in the total Punjab, they were still in a minority. After much agitation the Government of India agreed to Punjabi Suba (Punjabi State) in 1966, and those areas which had declared themselves to have a majority of Hindi speakers were separated from the Punjab, most of them to form the new state of Haryana. The Sikhs were now a majority in the Punjab, but this did not mean a stable rule for the avowedly Sikh political party, the Akali Dal. The Akali Dal represented a significant proportion of the Sikh land-owners, and the conviction rapidly grew that the central government was hostile to their interests.

In the early 1980s the militant Jarnail Singh Bhindranvale appeared as an uncompromising leader and, rapidly gathering strength in the Panth, occupied the precincts of the Golden Temple. In June 1984, the Government of India committed a serious mistake by sending the army into the Golden Temple area. Only after fighting against very heavy opposition did it manage to kill Bhindranvale. Several years of grievous disorder followed, with many Sikhs claiming that their only future lay in the creation of Khalistan or independent Punjab. In late 1992 the forces of the Government of India were eventually able to kill or capture most of the leading dissidents, and an uneasy peace has now returned to the Punjab.

This concludes the historical survey of the Panth. Two issues remain, one concerning Sikh identity and the other a problem of definition.

Sikh identity

One major point which is still largely misunderstood by the outside world concerns the identity of Sikhs. For the person whose acquaintance with the Panth is slight, a male Sikh is generally identified as having a beard and a turban. This is not always the case, particularly outside India. In dealing with the creation of the Khalsa, attention was drawn to those who joined rather than to those who held back. Those who joined the Khalsa adopted the Khalsa Rahit, whereas those who declined cut their hair and did not observe the Rahit.

This distinction identifies two main groups of Sikhs. Those who take initiation into the Khalsa are known as Amrit-dhari Sikhs, having received the **amrit** or water of baptism. For those who held back the name adopted was that of Sahaj-dhari Sikhs, a term which is variously construed.[1] Actually, three groups of Sikhs were indicated. Those who do not take initiation but who observe the fundamentals of the Rahit (particularly the uncut hair) are known as Kes-dhari Sikhs, those who preserve their hair (**kes**).[2] The Kes-dharis are normally indistinguishable from the Amrit-dharis and form a far larger group within the Panth. No statistics exist, but it is generally assumed that only about 15% are Amrit-dharis. The Kes-dharis as well as the Amrit-dharis are generally regarded as constituting the Khalsa.

These were the three main groups within the Panth until relatively recently. The overwhelming majority of Sikhs were rural, and the vast majority of them were generally considered to be Amrit-dharis or Kes-dharis (though the loyalty of many Kes-dharis to the Khalsa Rahit was distinctly shaky). The Sahaj-dharis were mainly urban dwellers belonging to certain castes, and their numbers are relatively few today.[3] Particularly amongst the migrants, however, there is a marked tendency on the part of Khalsa Sikhs to abandon their beards and turbans, with the result that those living in England or North America do not proclaim their identity and so remain invisible Sikhs. For this group no name exists, though they are certainly identifiable as a separate group in overseas countries. Coming from Khalsa families they are easily recognized by the fact that the men still have Singh as a middle or last name, and the women have Kaur.

Finally there are the Patit Sikhs. An Amrit-dhari who commits any one of four specified sins (notably the cutting of hair or the smoking of tobacco) is declared a Patit ('fallen') Sikh. Kes-dharis can also be regarded as Patits if they flagrantly disobey the prime Rahit. Few Sikhs are actually declared to be Patit, however, and the category exists more as a notional form, serving to assert the wrongness of falling away from Khalsa standards.

Concerning this Dictionary

Near the beginning of this introduction a basic fact was emphasized, namely the impossibility of explaining the Sikh religion without constant reference to Sikh history. There is one other point which also requires emphasis. This is the all-important meaning which should be attached to the words 'tradition' or 'traditional' and the part which they play in the interpretation adopted here for the explanation of various items.

With reference to Sikh history 'tradition' or 'traditional' means that which is handed down within the Panth. The material thus passed down has not been subjected to rigorous scrutiny, but for a traditionalist historian that is not necessary. It is known to be true because it is said to be derived from sources which are believed by the Panth to be absolutely secure. The janam-sakhis, for example, are traditionally known to be generally accurate because they deal with matters concerning the life of the first Guru, and they have been recorded by faithful followers of the Guru. Occasionally they may err with regard to detail, but they are substantially accurate. When the material derives from the Gurus themselves, or is intimately associated with them, it is treated as wholly and absolutely beyond reproach.[4]

This difference needs to be understood, for clearly there is a fundamental disagreement on this point. The disagreement here covers a whole range of historical method, but in the last analysis it comes down to the difference between two approaches. On one side stands the historian of religions who trusts traditional sources; on the other the one who views such sources with scepticism. Within each camp, of course, there are differences of opinion. Some of the traditionalists impart a degree of rigor to their research, while others view the traditions as true in all essential respects. Likewise, one expects degrees of scepticism from the other side, some giving traditional sources a measure of cautious trust while others are thoroughgoing in their criticism of them. But almost all fall within the territory marked out as either traditional or sceptical. The historian who can claim to have a foot in both camps is a very rare person indeed, though certainly that person may exist.

A major example which can be given concerns the Sikh scripture. In the case of the Adi Granth (the Sikh scripture) it means, according to the traditional view, that the text is beyond any investigation. The Adi Granth is perfect because it came to us through perfect men. As such, there can be no possibility of any research concerning it.

Not all adherents of the traditional school would carry the definition as far as that, but essentially they would agree with its substance. The general tenor of their interpretation makes this clear. Opposed to it are religious historians of the opposite camp, the historians who embrace the sceptical view with its rigorous examination of sources. For them the text of the Adi Granth is indeed open to investigation. The investigation must certainly be conducted in a reverential manner, for the researcher needs to be acutely aware that this is sacred ground which is being traversed. At the same time the Adi Granth must be available for research, for otherwise a highly important element in religious studies will not be understood.

Another example is provided by questions associated with the Singh Sabha period in Sikh history.[5] Whereas the traditional historian of religion will conduct research on the basis of a general acceptance of the truth of the Singh Sabha interpretation, the thoroughgoing sceptical historian will assume the reverse. Or at least the interpretation will be treated as the product of scholars who were themselves a part of the Singh Sabha movement (men such as Vir Singh or Kahn Singh Nabha) and will be set aside. Study is then conducted on the basis of modern historical research, with such skills as sociology and linguistics employed, and although some of the results may agree with earlier interpretations, others assuredly will not. An elementary difference will be a breaking open of the Singh Sabha movement and demonstration that it was the result of at least three major factions, one of which (the Tat Khalsa) was eventually to carry the day and assume the title of the whole Singh Sabha movement. This awareness makes an enormously important beginning to the task of interpreting the period.

No apology is given for this definition, because the meaning which it expresses is genuinely believed to be true. It means, however, that the explanations given for various features of Sikh history and religion (including some major ones) differ from those which readers will find in other dictionaries and encyclopedias. These occur, for example, in *The Encyclopaedia of Sikhism* which is currently being published by Punjabi University in Patiala. The *Encyclopaedia* is a work which is much larger than this *Dictionary* (the complete set will eventually run to four volumes), and much sound work has gone into its preparation. For these and other reasons it will be a useful tool to the person working on various aspects of Sikh history and religion. It is, though, based on a different understanding of the nature of religious truth. Whereas it takes its stand on the general reliability of tradition, this *Historical Dictionary* adopts the contrary view.

Needless to say, the interpretation reached by the sceptical historians of religion will not stand forever, each generation of historians finding new insights and in consequence producing new interpretations. But that is the nature of History, or at least of the sceptical variety. History is constantly being rewritten and no interpretation is forever fixed.

* * *

Note: Except where specifically mentioned, Common Era dating is used for all dates in the entries which follow.

In the Dictionary portion all names have been alphabetized according to Indian usage, i.e. by the first letter of the first name. For example, Vir Singh appears under V, not under S. This is because in India two-word names are invariably used and listed in this way. To expect any reader in that part of the world to look up Vir Singh under 'Singh, Vir' would be to invite some puzzlement. The natural place for such a reader to search would obviously be under V. Only where the individual uses a third name (which is generally a caste title) does India sometimes use the western method of listing according to the initial letter of the last name. In the Dictionary portion of this work it is not followed. Abdus Samad Khan, for example, is listed under A, not under K.

In the Bibliography portion, however, this practice has been reluctantly reversed. Many users of this bibliography will want to consult works held by western libraries and there they will find that the western method has been invariably used. Vir Singh is catalogued under S as 'Singh, Vir'. Because this is the situation in western libraries it has been adopted in the Bibliography portion of this work.

Notes

1. See below the item SAHAJ-DHARI.

2. The term is sometimes spelt Kesh-dhari.

3. This point can, however, be argued. There are many Punjabi Hindus who might hesitate to call themselves Sahaj-dhari Sikhs, but their devotion to the religion of the Gurus makes them in every way the same as the Sahaj-dharis.

4. See the entry TRADITION below.

5. See below the items SINGH SABHA MOVEMENT, SANATAN SIKHS, TAT KHALSA, and BHASAUR SINGH SABHA.

THE DESCENDANTS OF GURU AMAR DAS AND GURU RAM DAS

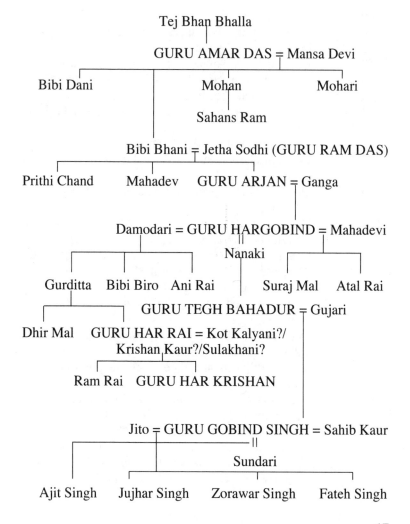

CHRONOLOGY OF SIKH HISTORY

1469	Birth of Guru Nanak.
1538/39	Death of Guru Nanak. Succeeded by Lahina who became Guru Angad.
1552	Death of Guru Angad. Succeeded by Amar Das.
1574	Death of Guru Amar Das. Succeeded by his son-in-law Jetha who became Guru Ram Das.
1581	Death of Guru Ram Das. Succeeded by his third son Arjan.
1603–04	Compilation of the Adi Granth.
1606	Death of Guru Arjan, in Mughal custody. Succeeded by his only son Hargobind.
1644	Death of Guru Hargobind. Succeeded by his grandson Har Rai.
1661	Death of Guru Har Rai. Succeeded by his second son, the child Har Krishan.
1664	Death of Guru Har Krishan. Succeeded by Tegh Bahadur, a son of Guru Hargobind.
1675	Execution of Guru Tegh Bahadur by the Mughals in Delhi. Succeeded by his only son Gobind Rai (later Gobind Singh).
1688	October 3rd: Battle of Bhangani between Gobind and Fateh Shah of Garhwal.
1699	March 30th: Probable date of the inauguration of the Khalsa.
1704	The great siege of Anandpur and its evacuation by Guru Gobind Singh on December 21st.
1708	Guru Gobind Singh's meeting with Banda at or near Nander in the Deccan. On October 7th, following an assassination attempt, the tenth Guru died. No successor was appointed, the role of Guru passing to the scripture.

1709–15	Rebellion against the Mughals in the Punjab led by Banda Bahadur.
1716	Execution of Banda Bahadur in Delhi.
1726	Zakariya Khan became Governor of Lahore.
1733	Land grant offered to the Khalsa Sikhs by Zakariya Khan. Accepted together with the rank of Nawab for Kapur Singh.
1738	Execution of Mani Singh.
1740	Massa Ranghar assassinated by Mahtab Singh and Sukha Singh.
1746	Yahiya Khan became Governor of Lahore. On May 1st the **Chhoṭā Ghallūghārā** ('Lesser Holocaust') occurred.
1747	The invasions of the Punjab by Ahmad Shah Abdali began. During the middle decades of the eighteenth century the Sikh misls developed.
1762	February 5th: the **Vaḍḍā Ghallūghārā** ('Great Holocaust') occurred.
1772	Death of Ahmad Shah Abdali.
1780	Birth of Ranjit Singh.
1799	Occupation of Lahore by Ranjit Singh.
1818	Occupation of Multan by Maharaja Ranjit Singh.
1819	Conquest of Kashmir by Maharaja Ranjit Singh.
1834	Occupation of Peshawar by Maharaja Ranjit Singh.
1839	June 27th: death of Maharaja Ranjit Singh. Succeeded as Maharaja by Kharak Singh.
1840	November 5th: death of Kharak Singh and Prince Nau Nihal Singh.
1841	January 20: Sher Singh succeeded as Maharaja.
1843	Assassination of Sher Singh and Raja Dhian Singh. Duleep Singh proclaimed Maharaja.
1845–46	First Anglo-Sikh War. Annexation of the Jalandhar Doab.
1848–49	Second Anglo-Sikh War and the annexation of the remainder of the Punjab kingdom to the British.
1873	First Singh Sabha founded in Amritsar.
1879	Singh Sabha of Lahore founded.
1898	Kahn Singh Nabha's *Ham Hindū Nahīn* ('We are not Hindus') published.

1902	Chief Khalsa Divan established.
1909	Anand Marriage Act passed.
1913	Rakabganj Gurdwara protest campaign.
1919	Central Sikh League founded, followed by the founding of the Akali Dal.
1920–25	Gurdwara Reform Movement.
1925	Sikh Gurdwaras Act passed.
1947	August 15th: Indian independence from Britain, followed by the partition of the Punjab. Mass migration of Sikhs and Hindus from Pakistan Punjab and of Muslims from Indian Punjab.
1966	Punjabi Suba ('Punjabi State') granted by the Government of India. A smaller Punjab was formed by cutting off those areas where a majority had declared their mother tongue to be Hindi.
1984	June 4th: the Government of India launched an attack on the Golden Temple and its environs. Jarnail Singh Bhindranvale and many others were killed. October 31st: Indira Gandhi was assassinated by one of her Sikh guards. This was followed by a massacre of Sikhs, particularly in Delhi and New Delhi. Rajiv Gandhi succeeded his mother as Prime Minister.
1985	July 24th: An Accord was signed between Rajiv Gandhi and the Sikh leader Harchand Singh Longowal, agreeing that the city of Chandigarh should be transferred to the Punjab, that the canal waters issue sue should be considered by a judge of the Supreme Court, and that other grievances of the Sikhs should be re-examined. August 20th: Longowal was assassinated. The terms of the Accord have not been fulfilled.
1985–92	Turmoil in the Punjab, with many casualties. Sikh underground movements exercised considerable influence. The police were accused of serious brutality. Sikh leaders during this period included Parkash Singh Badal, Gurcharan Singh Tohra, and Simranjeet Singh Mann. By the end of 1992 the Government of India had secured the upper hand, and an uneasy peace returned to the Punjab. The principal issues involving the Sikhs (investigation of the killings, the status of Chandigarh, canal waters, etc.) remain, however, unresolved.

THE DICTIONARY

A

ABDUS SAMAD KHAN. The Mughal governor of Lahore who in 1715 captured Banda (q.v.) and for the next five years continued to wage war against Khalsa Sikhs, driving them into hiding. Thereafter, with affairs more stable, he relaxed his firm policy. In 1726 he was transferred to Multan and was succeeded in Lahore by his son Zakariya Khan (q.v.).

ABILCHALNAGAR *see* NANDER (NANDED).

ABLUTION *see* ISHNAN.

ABORTION. Sikhs have no problem with abortion, though they are commonly reluctant to discuss it. In recent years, with advances in amniocentesis and particularly in ultrasound, the rate of abortions of females has increased amongst the Sikhs as with other communities in India. Boys are still greatly preferred to girls in India, and this preference is present in a large majority of Sikh families. Ultrasound permits the sex of the fetus to be ascertained while there is still time for abortion to take place, and if the fetus is female it is often aborted. This trend will produce problems of gender imbalance throughout India in future. The incidence is also growing amongst the Sikhs and other Indians of the diaspora.

ACHAL BATALA. A place near Batala in Gurdaspur District where Guru Nanak (q.v.) is said to have debated with Nath yogis (q.v.).

ADI GRANTH. The principal Sikh scripture. Anthologies of religious songs were common in late medieval India, and one had

21

already been collected during the time of the third Guru, Amar Das (q.v.). This three- or four-volume work was known as the Mohan Pothis or the Goindval Pothis (q.v.). According to tradition Guru Arjan (q.v.) was persuaded of the need to compile a definitive scripture because other claimants were circulating their own works, spuriously attaching the name Nanak (q.v.) to them. A substantial base was provided by the Goindval Pothis which contained all the works of the first three Gurus together with those of Sant poets (q.v.) and was ordered according to the pattern of raga and author which Guru Arjan followed. The task was carried out in Amritsar (q.v.) from 1603 to 1604, possibly based on an earlier draft which Arjan had prepared. To the Goindval Pothis he added the works of his father, Guru Ram Das (q.v.), and his own substantial array of compositions. This large manuscript, recorded by Bhai Gurdas (q.v.), is believed to be held in Kartarpur (Jalandhar District) and is known as the Kartarpur **bīṛ** ([q.v.] volume). The collection reached its final form with the addition of the works of the ninth Guru, Tegh Bahadur (q.v.) and later came to be known as the Adi Granth (the 'original' Granth) to distinguish it from the Dasam Granth (q.v.). There are thus three recognizable stages in its compilation: the Goindval Pothis, the Kartarpur recension, and finally the Adi Granth. The collection proved to be of crucial importance, particularly after the death of the tenth and last Guru when the sacred volume came to be accepted as the literal embodiment of the eternal Guru (q.v.). As such, it came to be called the Guru Granth Sahib (q.v.), 'the sacred volume which is the Guru.' The full title used today is Adi Sri Guru Granth Sahibji.

ADI GRANTH CONTENTS. Although it is a substantial collection, comprising 1,430 pages in the standard printed edition, the Adi Granth (q.v.) is remarkably consistent in terms of content. The message which it communicates is that spiritual liberation comes through belief in the divine Name (q.v.).

ADI GRANTH LANGUAGE. The Adi Granth (q.v.) has a reputation for wide-ranging linguistic variety. This is not correct. The Gurus, like their Sant predecessors (q.v.), used a simplified form of early Hindi known as Sant Bhasha or Sadhukari. This designates a language based on Khari Boli, the Hindi of the Delhi region, which was widely used for religious poetry before and during the time of the early Gurus. There are, however, variants in the different Gurus' usage. Nanak (q.v.) has a strongly Punjabi version whereas Arjan (q.v.) tends more towards western Hindi. Hymns for particular audiences take account of their particular language (for example Persian) without abandoning the Sant Bhasha framework. Because no term expressly denotes the language of the Adi Granth it is sometimes called the Sacred Language of the Sikhs (SLS). It was written in the Gurmukhi script (q.v.).

ADI GRANTH MANUSCRIPT 1245. Considerable interest has been raised by the purchase in 1987 of the manuscript numbered 1245 by Guru Nanak Dev University, Amritsar. Two scholars who made use of it were Piar Singh and Pashaura Singh, the first in a published book and the other in his PhD thesis for the University of Toronto. Although their use was responsible, the result was a storm of protest in the Panth. The alleged offenders were summoned before Akal Takhat (q.v.), and in 1993 Piar Singh was declared a tanakhahia (q.v.), compelled to recant and perform humiliating tasks as penalty. According to Pashaura Singh, who teaches in the University of Michigan, an analysis of the contents of the manuscript reveals that it can be placed historically in the period somewhere between 1595 and 1604, the years of the present Goindval volume 1 and the Kartarpur manuscript (qq.v.) respectively. As such it illuminates the textual process through which the evolution of the Adi Granth (q.v.) has taken place. His opponents argue that the manuscript is later than the Kartarpur manuscript and that it has a Mina (q.v.) provenance. *See also* GOINDVAL POTHIS; KARTARPUR BIR.

ADI GRANTH RECENSIONS. In addition to the standard Kartarpur text of the Adi Granth (q.v.), there also exists the Banno recension which differs from Kartarpur at three significant points and also incorporates some concluding works which Kartarpur lacks. One of the three textual differences is important. Banno includes a work said to be by Guru Arjan (q.v.) which appears in the Kartarpur version only as the opening couplet followed by a blank space. This hymn describes how traditional puberty rites were conducted for the future Guru Hargobind (q.v.), including the shaving of his head. This point has generated considerable controversy in the Panth (q.v.). The consensus still holds that the Banno version was amended later and that the text of Kartarpur still stands as the correct one. The dispute, however, continues. The recension is also called the Mangat or the Khari version, **khārī** meaning 'brackish' or (in this context) 'spurious.' Mangat is the village from which the copyist of the Banno recension is said to have come. Another tradition traces the orgin of Khari to Khara which was evidently an earlier name for the village. *See also* BANNO, BHAI; BANNO BIR; DAM-DAMI BIR; KARTARPUR BIR.

ADI GRANTH STRUCTURE. The Adi Granth (q.v.) is divided into three unequal parts. The introductory section (pages 1–13) contains liturgical works. It opens with the *Mūl Mantra* (the basic credal statement) and then records Nanak's *Japjī,* the *Sodar* collection of nine hymns, and the *Kīrtan Sohilā* group of five hymns (qq.v.). Then comes a lengthy section devoted to thirty-one rags (q.v.) or musical modes (pages 14–1353). Finally, there is the short epilogue consisting of miscellaneous works (pages 1353–1430). The middle section is subdivided according to rag, and then within each rag the text is further subdivided as follows. First there are brief hymns by the Gurus, comprising four verses and a refrain (**chaupad**). Secondly there are longer hymns by the Gurus, usually eight verses and a refrain (**ashṭapadī**). Thirdly there are long hymns by the Gurus, usually consisting of four or six long stanzas (**chhant**). Fourthly there are much longer works by the Gurus, such as Arjan's *Sukhmanī Sāhib* (qq.v.). Fifthly there is the distinctive Adi Granth form of the **vār** (q.v.). Finally there is the *bhagat bāṇī* (q.v.), the works of various sants (q.v.) whose compositions were in harmony with the message of liberation through the divine Name taught by the Gurus. Within the **chaupads, ashṭapadīs** and **chhants** there is a further classification, each one being grouped according to author. First come the **chaupads** of Nanak in a particular rag, then those of Amar Das, Ram Das, Arjan, and finally (if any) those of Tegh Bahadur (qq.v). This is followed by the **ashtapadīs** in the same order and finally by the **chhants**. There are no hymns (**shabads** [q.v.]) by Angad in the Adi Granth, only couplets or shorter works (**shaloks** [q.v.]) which are mainly included in the **vārs**. This intricate but generally consistent ordering of material is characteristic of other collections of scripture by religious groups in medieval and early modern India.

ADI GRANTH TERMINOLOGY. The compositions in the Adi Granth (q.v.) are almost all grouped according to thirty-one rags (q.v.) (**rāg**), a musical mode. A hymn in the Adi Granth is termed a **shabad** (q.v.). According to the teachings of Nanak (q.v.), the shabad is the vehicle of divine communication between God and man, and the term used for Word came to be applied to the composition which gave it expression. A shorter composition (usually a couplet) is called a **shalok** (q.v.).

ADI SAKHIS. A janam-sakhi (q.v.) which in its extant form dates from the late seventeenth century.

ADINA BEG KHAN (d. 1758). In 1739, during the rapid decline of Mughal authority in the Punjab, Adina Beg was appointed the governor of the Jalandhar Doab by Zakariya Khan (q.v.). Until he died in 1758 he served his own interests, variously supporting or opposing the Mughals, Ahmad Shah Abdali (q.v.), and the Sikhs.

ADULTERY. This is strictly forbidden by the Sikh Gurus. It is regarded as one of the four kurahits (q.v.).

AHLUVALIA. A small Sikh caste, originally Kalals or brewers of country liquor. The Kalals were very close to being Outcastes in status. It was, however, a small and tightly-organized caste, and late in the nineteenth century its leaders decided on a policy of determined elevation. They adopted for the caste the name of a famous Kalal, Jassa Singh Ahluvalia (q.v.), and rigorously followed a lifestyle conspicuously higher than was required of a low caste. So successful have they been that today their Kalal antecedents have been largely forgotten, and the Ahluvalias rank with the Khatris (q.v.) in caste status.

AHLUVALIA MISL. A small misl (q.v.) with a distinguished founder, Jassa Singh Ahluvalia (q.v.). Its territory was southwest of Jalandhar with its chief center in Kapurthala. Jassa Singh Ahluvalia, though not a Jat (q.v.), was regarded as the principal misl chieftain, and Ranjit Singh permitted his successor to retain his estates after the other misls had been extinguished. When the British took over the territory in 1846, it preserved its status as the princely state of Kapurthala.

AHMAD SHAH ABDALI (1722–72). Also known as Ahmad Shah Durrani, he was the ruler of Afghanistan who invaded the Punjab eight times between 1747 and 1767. Serious damage resulted, but each time he was compelled to withdraw to Kabul. During this period Sikh forces grouped as independent misls (q.v.).

AISSF see ALL-INDIA SIKH STUDENTS' FEDERATION.

AKAL BUNGA see AKAL TAKHAT and BUNGA.

AKAL PURAKH. The 'Timeless One'; God. A favorite term for God held by Nanak (q.v.) and other Gurus. Many other words are used in the attempt to encompass the infinity of God. He is **nirankār**, the Formless One. He is the Creator, Sustainer, and Destroyer. He is **abināsī** (eternal), **anādi** (without beginning), **achal** (ever constant), **nirañjan** (pure), **agam agochar** (inscrutable), **alakh** (ineffable), yet by his grace he is immanent to those who will but open their eyes and look around and within themselves. He is the Supreme Lord of the entire universe, knowable to those who meditate upon his **nām** (q.v.) which consists of everything that can be comprehended about him. *See also* GENDER OF GOD.

AKAL TAKHAT. Pre-eminent among the five takhats (q.v.) of the Panth (q.v.), Akal Takhat stands immediately facing Harimandir Sahib (the Golden Temple [q.v.]). Harimandir Sahib is the primary religious center of the Sikhs, and Akal Takhat is the primary temporal center where major decisions concerning the affairs of the Panth are made. Strictly speaking, Akal Takhat is housed in Akal Bunga, one of the numerous bungas (q.v.) which once surrounded Harimandir Sahib. The building stands near the Darshani Deorhi (q.v.) at a slight angle to Harimandir. During the eighteenth century the Sarbat Khalsa (q.v.) met in front of Akal Takhat, and today any decision of the whole Panth must be announced from it in the form of a hukam-nama (q.v.). It was in Akal Takhat that Jarnail Singh Bhindranvale (q.v.) was killed by Government of India forces in June 1984.

AKAL USTATI. "Praise to the Timeless One," an unfinished poem attributed to Guru Gobind Singh (q.v.) included in the Dasam Granth (q.v.). God is addressed as **Sarab Loh** (q.v.), the 'All Steel,' described in militant terms as absolutely supreme.

AKALI. 'A follower of the Timeless One [God].' Originally it was applied to irregular Sikh soldiers of the eighteenth/early nineteenth century who fought with reckless bravery on behalf of the Panth, acknowledging no leader who was not himself an Akali (also spelled Akalee). During the turbulent middle years of the eighteenth century the Akalis generally fought in the Shahid misl (q.v. misl). In the early nineteenth century there emerged the most famous of the early Akalis, Phula Singh (q.v.), the ill-disciplined but fearless warrior who with other Akalis under him fought for Ranjit Singh (q.v.). Following the death of Phula Singh in 1823, the strength of the Akalis dwindled, and the small remnants which still survive today are known as Nihangs (q.v.). The word has meanwhile assumed a different meaning. In 1920 radical Sikhs aiming at control of the Sikh gurdwaras (q.v.) formed the Akali Dal (q.v.) or 'Akali Army,' an explicitly Sikh political party. Ever since Akali has designated a member of the Akali Dal.

AKALI DAL. During the early years of the twentieth century devout Sikhs were concerned that many of their gurdwaras were in the possession of men who were not members of the Khalsa, nor even kes-dhari Sikhs (qq.v.). Since the turmoil of the eighteenth century the gurdwaras had been managed by mahants (q.v.) who frequently claimed to be Udasi Sikhs (q.v.) but lacked the visible marks of the Khalsa order. Under the British, who took over the administration of the Punjab in 1849, ownership of the gurdwaras was conferred on whoever could claim to be in possesion. The Singh Sabha movement (q.v.), from its foundation in 1873, had awakened Sikhs to the unsatisfactory nature of this situation, and, prompted by the growing strength of the Tat Khalsa (q.v.), many expressed misgivings. The British rulers, however, were anxious to uphold the validity of their settlement; Sanatan Sikhs (q.v.) who, through the Chief Khalsa Divan (q.v.) exercised administrative dominance within the Singh Sabha, were concerned about staying on good terms with them. In late 1920 radical Sikhs, irritated at the loyal obedience of the Chief Khalsa Divan, announced two decisions from Akal Takhat (q.v.) reached by the newly-formed Central Sikh League (q.v.). The first was the foundation of the Shiromani Gurdwara Parbandhak Committee (SGPC) (q.v.), a group to manage all major Sikh shrines. This was followed by the creation of the Akali Dal (Akali Army), a body based on a military model which would train men to confront the government and occupy gurdwaras. Until the splits of recent years, the Akali Dal was much the largest of the specifically Sikh political parties, and Akalis (q.v.) have been (and still are) a prominent feature of Sikh life.

AKALI DAL HISTORY. The Akali Dal was founded in 1920 as an explicitly Sikh organization and has remained so ever since. Throughout the Gurdwara Reform Movement (q.v.) it operated on military lines with small groups led by jathedars (q.v.). The Sikh Gurdwaras Act of 1925 (q.v.) signalled victory, and since then the Akali Dal (or Shiromani Akali Dal) has functioned as a Sikh political party. Within the Panth (q.v.) its power has always been contested by members of the Indian National Congress. Its authority has remained unchallenged within the highly influential Shiromani Gurdwara Parbandhak Committee (q.v.) which has an exclusively Sikh electorate, but in state politics (where voting is shared with Hindus) it has been less successful. In national politics its influence is negligible except for the period when it stood against Mrs. Gandhi during the Emergency of 1975–77. For much of its career the Akali Dal was dominated by Tara Singh (q.v.). In 1961, following an abortive fast, he was challenged for the leadership by Fateh Singh (q.v.), and the party split. It has remained split ever since, the dominant faction for many years associated with Fateh Singh, Parkash Singh Badal, and Harchand Singh Longowal (q.v.). Since the 1984 assault by Indian Government troops on the Golden Temple (q.v.), it has, however, divided into several factions, with no one faction able to claim controlling dominance. The Akali color is dark blue, and male Akalis often wear turbans of this color. *See also* POLITICAL PARTIES; POLITICS; RECENT HISTORY.

AKHAND KIRTANI JATHA. An organization headed by Amarjit Kaur, whose husband was killed in the Amritsar clash with the Sant Nirankaris (q.v.) in April 1978. For some years after, members of the Jatha lived near the Akal Takhat and organized kirtan in Harimandir Sahib (qq.v.). Its members also belong to the Bhai Randhir Singh da Jatha (q.v.), and the two titles are commonly used interchangeably. Amarjit Kaur was close to Harchand Singh Longowal and opposed to Jarnail Singh Bhindranvale (qq.v.). *See also* RECENT HISTORY.

AKHAND PATH. An 'unbroken reading' of the Guru Granth Sahib (q.v.). This is performed by a relay of readers who, reading in turn without intermission, complete the task in approximately forty-eight hours. It is held on all occasions of importance to Sikhs such as a marriage, the opening of a new business, or a funeral. Karah prasad (q.v.) should be brought into the presence of the Guru Granth Sahib before beginning an Akhand Path; the six appointed stanzas of *Anand Sāhib* (q.v.) should be read, Ardas (q.v.) should be recited, and a hukam (q.v.) should be taken. The reading concludes with a bhog ceremony (q.v.). Much the same procedure is followed with a Sadharan Path or a Saptahak Path (qq.v.). The practice of holding Akhand Paths appears to have developed during the late eighteenth or early nineteenth centuries. A practice rarely undertaken is that of the Ati Akhand Path which involves only one person. The task, which takes about twenty-seven hours, can be performed only by a person of uncommon stamina and reading skill.

AKHARA. 'Wrestling arena'; a center of either the Udasis or Nirmalas (qq.v.). The number of Udasi akharas was estimated at more than 250 in the mid-nineteenth century, some located in places well beyond the Punjab. There were fewer belonging to the Nirmalas, but their influence was equal to the Udasis. *See also* DHUAN; BAKHSHISH.

ALCOHOL. This is an ongoing issue within the Panth (q.v.). Consumption of alcohol and drugs are prohibited by *Sikh Rahit Maryādā* (q.v.), yet a substantial number of Sikhs (particularly in rural areas) partake of alcohol, frequently of a singularly fiery kind. Voting for the elections of the Shiromani Gurdwara Parbandhak Committee (q.v.) also requires the voter to certify that he/she does not consume alcohol, yet in fact, a large majority of the male voters are not abstainers. Passages from the Adi Granth (q.v.) can be interpreted in support of either side, though it seems clear that the Gurus were against the use of either alcohol or drugs. The controversy continues. *See also* VEGETARIANISM.

ALL-INDIA SIKH STUDENTS' FEDERATION (AISSF). Although the AISSF was founded almost sixty years ago, it was never prominent until the mid-seventies when it adopted an anti-communist stance. In the early 1980s, under its president Amrik Singh, it became a dedicated supporter of the militant Jarnail Singh Bhindranvale (q.v.), strongly critical of the moderate political policies of Harchand Singh Longowal (q.v.). Amrik Singh was killed with Bhindranvale when the Indian Army attacked the Golden Temple complex in June, 1984. *See also* RECENT HISTORY.

ALMAST (1553–1643). An Udasi and a disciple of Gurditta (qq.v.), he established a shrine dedicated to Nanak (q.v.) at Nanakmata (near Pilibhit in the Kumaon Hills). By tradition,

Nanak had visited the place and made sweet the bitter fruit of a soap-nut tree. Hargobind (q.v.) included Nanakmata on one of his tours.

AMAR DAS (1479–1574). Third Guru, born in Basarke (q.v.), the son of Tej Bhan Bhalla. According to tradition, he was a pious Vaishnava, prompted to search for a Guru by another devotee. On his way to the Ganga he happened to overhear the daughter of Guru Angad (q.v.), who had married his brother's son, singing one of the hymns of Nanak (q.v.). So captivated by it was he that he insisted on being taken to Khadur (q.v.) to pay his respects to Nanak's successor, Angad. There he became a Sikh. Amar Das greatly impressed Guru Angad by his devotion, and although well advanced in years he was appointed to succeed him as third Guru of the Panth (q.v.). When he became Guru in 1552 he was already seventy-three, remaining in the position until he died at the age of ninety-five. While Angad was still alive he was sent to the neighboring village of Goindval (q.v.), and when he succeeded as Guru this became the new center of the Panth. He continued the tradition of married Gurus, his wife being Mansa Devi, and his family numbering two sons and either one or two daughters.

AMAR DAS'S POLICY. Amar Das assumed responsibility for the Panth (q.v.) in 1552 at a time when it was settling down after the first flush of its early years. It was spreading geographically, and to preach the faith still further pious followers were appointed, each as a manji (q.v.). The anti-caste langar (q.v.) was apparently inaugurated in his time; at least three rituals were introduced for the Sikhs. A sacred well (**bāolī**) was dug as a pilgrimage center in Goindval, two festival days were designated, and a sacred scripture was recorded in four volumes (the so-called Goindval Pothis [q.v.] or Mohan Pothis). In instituting these changes Amar Das seemed to be directing his Sikhs back to the external customs which they had renounced under Nanak (q.v.). The **bāolī**, with its eighty-four steps corresponding to the eighty-four lakhs of existences in the transmigratory cycle, was to be a visible **tīrath** (q.v.) or center of pilgrimage; and the festivals were those celebrated by Hindus. They were, however, changes with a specifically Sikh content. The **tīrath** was in Goindval, and the festivals were celebrated by Sikhs. Under Nanak the Panth consisted of first-generation Sikhs who had been drawn to him by the attraction of his teachings. Now Sikhs were increasingly appearing who had been born into the faith, and for them the Panth needed exterior rituals and practices. *See also* MOHAN.

AMARO. The daughter of Guru Angad (q.v.) whose singing of a hymn by Nanak (q.v.) was overheard by Amar Das (q.v.) and led him to become a Sikh. She was married to a nephew of Amar Das and resided in Basarke (q.v.).

AMAVAS. The night of the new moon, the last night of the 'dark' fortnight when the moon is waning (**badī**), followed by a 'light' fortnight when the moon is waxing (**sudī**). The occasion, also called Masia, is an important festival for the Panth (q.v.). *See also* PANCHAMI; PURAN-MASHI; SAN-GRAND.

AMRIT. 'Deathless'; [the water of] eternal life; the nectar of immortality.

AMRIT-DHARI. A Sikh who has 'taken **amrit** (nectar),' i.e., been initiated into the Khalsa (q.v.). This is done by the ceremony of **amrit sanskār** (q.v.). There is no way of accurately estimating the proportion of Sikhs who are amrit-dhari, though 15% is sometimes hesitantly mentioned. Strictly speaking, only the amrit-dhari Sikhs constitute the Khalsa, though in practice kes-dhari Sikhs (q.v.) are usually included also. *See also* IDENTITY.

AMRIT SANSKAR. The order for Khalsa initiation is detailed in *Sikh Rahit Maryādā,* the contemporary rahit-nama (qq.v.). It is also called **amrit chhaknā**. An open copy of the Guru Granth Sahib (q.v.) is required at the place of initiation together with six baptized Sikhs, each bearing the five Khalsa symbols. One sits with the scripture, while the ceremony is conducted by the other five. Either men or women can officiate, though normally the participants are men. Those who administer initiation should be physically sound. Anyone who is old enough to understand the ceremony, who affirms belief in the Sikh faith, and who vows to live according to Khalsa principles can take initiation. *See also* AMRIT SANSKAR PROCEDURE; KHANDE DI PAHUL; NAMING CEREMONY.

AMRIT SANSKAR PROCEDURE. Candidates for Khalsa initiation, having bathed and washed their hair, present themselves for the rite wearing the Five Ks (q.v.). After the initiates have confessed their faith and a hukam (q.v.) has been read, the five officiants take their places beside the large iron bowl which is to be used for the initiation. Fresh water is poured into it and soluble sweets added. Having done this, the officiants adopt the 'heroic posture' (**bīr āsan**) in which the right knee is laid on the ground, and the left knee is held upright. One of the officiants then recites five passages from scripture (*Japjī, Jāp,* the *Ten Savayyās,* a portion of *Benatī Chaupaī,* and six stanzas from the *Anand* [qq.v.]), all the time stirring the water with a two-edged sword. This is done with the right hand, the left hand resting on the bowl. The other four keep both hands on the bowl, with their eyes fixed on the water. The recitation completed, all five stand up holding the bowl and one of them recites Ardas (q.v.). The initiates then adopt the 'heroic posture,' and each cups his/her hands with the right hand over the left. Five times the sanctified water (**amrit**) is poured into the cupped hands. As each portion is drunk the officiant who gives it cries, '**Vāhigurū jī kā khālsā, vāhigurū jī kī fateh,**' and after drinking it the recipient repeats the cry. The water is then sprinkled five times onto the initiate's eyes and five times over the hair. The remainder of the water is then drunk in turn by the initiates. Next the initiates are required to repeat the Mul Mantra (q.v.) five times in unison, and the Rahit (q.v.) is expounded to them by one of the officiants. This requires them to wear the Five Ks, and they are commanded ever after to avoid the four **kurahits** (q.v.). Certain people and practices are to be avoided, such as eating from the same dish as a patit (q.v.) or a person who has not received Khalsa initiation. Ardas is recited again, a hukam is taken, and if the initiate has not received a name from the Guru Granth Sahib, one should be conferred in the approved manner, each male adding 'Singh' to his name and each female adding 'Kaur' to hers (qq.v.). Finally karah prasad (q.v.) should be distributed, all taking it from the same iron dish.

AMRIT SANSKAR (UNORTHODOX FORMS). The orthodox form of Khalsa initiation (q.v.) is set out above. Certain groups or sects follow forms different in detail. For example the Damdami Taksal and the Sikh Dharma movement (qq.v.) insist on reciting the whole of *Benatī Chaupaī* and *Anand* (q.v.) instead of the portions specified in *Sikh Rahit Maryādā*. The Damdami Taksal also observes a different form of **bīr asaṇ,** laying the left knee on the ground with the right knee upright. A distinctive practice of the Bhai Randhir Singh ka Jatha (q.v.) involves the laying of hands on the initiate's head in order to transfer the spiritual power of the divine Name (q.v.). The form of the Rahit which they communicate requires total vegetarianism and amends the Five Ks, insisting on **keskī** instead of **kes** (qq.v.). The order followed by Nihang Sikhs (q.v.) is also different in detail.

AMRIT VELA. The last watch of the night (the period between three and six a.m.) which because of its stillness is particularly suitable for meditation. In a greatly loved passage from *Japjī* 4 (Adi Granth, p. 2) Nanak (qq.v.) says: "In **amrit velā** meditate on the grandeur of the one true Name (q.v.)." *Sikh Rahit Maryādā* (q.v.) states that Sikhs are expected to arise in the **amrit velā** and, after bathing, to meditate on the divine Name.

AMRITSAR. Founded by Guru Ram Das (q.v.) on instructions from Guru Amar Das (q.v.) in the late sixteenth century. The settlement was first known as Guru ka Chak or as Ramdaspur. Amritsar ('the waters of eternal life') was the name of the pool dug by Ram Das which surrounds Harimandir Sahib (q.v.). Guru Arjan (q.v.) completed both Harimandir Sahib and the town, making the latter his center. His successor, Hargobind (q.v.), was forced to leave the plains, and for much the century which followed Amritsar was in the hands of the Minas (q.v.). In the eighteenth century it eventually recovered its pre-eminence as the Sikhs battled for its possession, first with the Mughals and then with Afghans. It was finally secured late in the century, and although Ranjit Singh (q.v.) used neighboring Lahore (q.v.) as his capital, Amritsar was regarded as first among the religious centers of the Sikhs. It still retains that status, with central positions occupied by the Golden Temple and Akal Takhat (qq.v.).

ANAHAD SHABAD. The mystical 'sound' or 'unstruck music' which is 'heard' at the climax of hatha-yoga (q.v.). The term is also used by the Gurus to communicate the sense of the inexpressible condition of sahaj (q.v.).

ANAND GHAN. An Udasi (q.v.) scholar of the late eighteenth/early nineteenth century who, living in Banaras, wrote commentaries on the Adi Granth (q.v.) strongly influenced by Brahmanical thought. Santokh Singh (q.v.) worked under him for a time.

ANAND KARAJ. The Sikh marriage ceremony. Anand Karaj was not performed until the middle of the nineteenth century, although it is certain that at least the *Anand Sāhib* (q.v.) portion was well established for a long time prior to that. The marriage ceremony was, however, essentially a Hindu one performed around a sacred fire. The Nirankari sect (q.v.) claims that it devised or recovered Anand Karaj earlier in the nineteenth century and that its example was copied by the Singh Sabha for the wider Panth (qq.v.). The introduction of Anand Karaj as the only approved order for Sikh marriage was a major concern of the Singh Sabha, an emphatic demonstration that Sikhs were not Hindus. Eventually the Anand Marriage Act, which laid down a specific order for Sikhs, was passed in 1909. According to this order, the couple being wed sit before the Guru Granth Sahib (q.v.) and are instructed by an officiant concerning the duties of marriage. The hem of a scarf or other garment worn by the groom is then placed in the bride's hand, and she follows him around the sacred scripture in a clockwise direction four times (**lāvān** [q.v.]). Before they make each round a verse of Guru Ram Das's *Suhī*

Chhant 2 is sung by the scriptural reader or ragis (q.v.), and the verse is repeated by the congregation while they make the round. Six stanzas of *Anand Sāhib* are then sung, and the ceremony concludes with Ardas and the distribution of karah prasad (qq.v.).

ANAND SAHIB. The 'revered [song of] joy.' (Adi Granth [q.v.], pp. 917–22.) A portion of Guru Amar Das's Anand commands a particular prominence in Sikh ritual and liturgy. The section comprising the first five stanzas and the last is sung or chanted as a part of the evening order of Raharas; before commencing a reading of the complete Adi Granth and again at the conclusion (both **sādhāran pāth** and **akhaṇḍ pāṭh**); prior to the distribution of karah prasad; at the conclusion of orders of service for child-naming and marriage; during the brief post-cremation ritual; and as part of the Khalsa initiation ceremony (qq.v.).

ANANDPUR. Anandpur (or Anandpur Sahib) is situated on the edge of the Shivalik Hills (q.v.), near the Satluj river. Guru Tegh Bahadur (q.v.) moved his center from Kiratpur (q.v.) to neighboring Makhoval, and having rebuilt it renamed the new village Anandpur. It was there that the Khalsa (q.v.) was inaugurated. Kesgarh Gurdwara (q.v.), which commands the heights of Anandpur, is one of the five takhats (q.v.).

ANANDPUR SAHIB RESOLUTION. A charter of demands which was proposed by the Akali Dal (q.v.) in 1973 and confirmed in 1982. This lodged both economic demands (notably fair distribution of canal waters from Punjab rivers) and also religious ones. There are actually three different versions of it and, as it was originally written in English, translation into Punjabi created further problems. The author of much or all of it is reputed to have been Kapur Singh (q.v.). It acquired importance in the Sikhs' dispute with the Central Government in the 1980s. One interpretation holds that it demands an independent state of Khalistan (q.v.).

ANGAD, GURU (1504–52). Second Guru. Born as Lahina (q.v.), probably in the village of Harike in central Punjab, he married Khivi, the daughter of a Khatri of Khadur (q.v.), and had three children. Lahina was the religious teacher of Khadur, a follower of the goddess Durga. While leading a village group on pilgrimage to Jvalamukhi he encountered Guru Nanak in Kartarpur (qq.v.) and was converted to the Sikh way. Prior to Nanak's death in 1538 or 1539 he was chosen to succeed him, preferred to either of Nanak's sons, and was renamed Angad (**ang** means 'limb') to indicate his closeness to the first Guru. Angad appears in the janam-sakhis (q.v.), always as one noted for his unquestioning obedience to his master the first Guru. His few works recorded in the Adi Granth (q.v.) testify to his reputation for austerity and loyal obedience. All of his works are **shaloks** (q.v.), there being no **shabads** (q.v.) amongst them. Before his death Angad chose Amar Das as his successor (q.v.), also noted for his implicit obedience to the Guru's will.

ANGLO-SIKH WARS *see* ANNEXATION OF THE PUNJAB.

ANI RAI (b. 1619). A son of Guru Hargobind (q.v.).

ANJUMAN-I-PANJAB. Society for the Diffusion of Useful Knowledge. Founded in 1865 by Leitner, Principal of Government College in Lahore (q.v.), the society began a free public library in Lahore and vigorously encouraged education in the Punjab. Amongst those influenced by it in the second half of the nineteenth century were Khem Singh Bedi, Attar Singh of Bhadaur, and Gurmukh Singh (qq.v.).

ANNEXATION OF THE PUNJAB. War between the British and the Punjab broke out in 1845, six years after the death of Maharaja Ranjit Singh (q.v.). During these years the Lahore court was in increasingly serious disorder. The first Anglo-Sikh war, 1845–46, was fought because the British, fearing a disturbed Punjab on their borders, reached a secret agreement with the authorities in Lahore (q.v.). Because the army was beyond control, British assistance was needed to restore order. After stiff resistance from the troops and treachery on the part of their commanders, the Punjabi army succumbed. The British annexed the Jalandhar Doab, Gulab Singh was permitted to purchase Jammu and Kashmir, and the Punjabi army was reduced in strength. A British force was stationed in Lahore and the child Duleep Singh (q.v.) remained on the throne. Dalhousie, the Governor-General of India, then watched and encouraged the continuing crisis in the Punjab. An incident in Multan led to the second war (1848–49). This too was vigorously fought (including the British defeat at Chillianwala), but finally the Sikh forces were overcome. The remainder of the Punjab was then annexed to British India on 29 March 1849.

ANTIM SANSKAR *see* FUNERAL.

ANUP KAUR. A woman of Lahore (also called Rup Kaur) who unsuccessfully tried to seduce Guru Gobind Singh (q.v.). The *Triā Charitra* (q.v.) or tales of the wiles of women included in the Dasam Granth (q.v.) are sometimes said to be the Guru's warning against such temptations.

ARATI. A Hindu ceremony of adoration which consists of waving round the head of an idol a platter containing five burning wicks. Nanak (q.v.) reinterpreted this in the hymn *Dhanasari* 3 (Adi Granth, pp. 13, 663), declaring that the whole universe was the scene for the proper performance of Arati. The hymn is part of Kirtan Sohila and is also sung at Sikh funerals (qq.v.).

ARCHITECTURE. A distinctively Sikh architecture, which evolved during the late eighteenth and early nineteenth centuries, is exemplified by gurdwaras (q.v.) . Harimandir Sahib ([q.v.] the Golden Temple) in Amritsar (q.v.) is the primary example, having been finally rebuilt in the time of Ranjit Singh (q.v). The gurdwara is late Mughal, an origin at once evident in its domed pavilion and in the **chattrī** (a structure resembling a minaret) at each of the four corners. It differs from a mosque, however, having doors on all four sides and no miharab (q.v.). Normally the dominant color of a gurdwara exterior is white, but in the case of Harimandir Sahib the upper two storeys were gilded by Ranjit Singh, who was also responsible for much of the inlaid marble. Although most gurdwaras were built in the twentieth century, they generally still replicate the basic elements of style present in Harimandir Sahib.

ARDAS. A formal prayer recited at the conclusion of most Sikh rituals. Although it is called the Sikh Prayer, the title is perhaps misleading as the content is strongly Khalsa (q.v.) rather than that of the wider Panth (q.v.). When any ritual draws to its close a portion of *Anand Sāhib* (q.v.) is read. Ardas is then recited by a leader, with the congregation joining in at set points. A hymn from the Adi Granth (q.v.) is read, and the service concludes with the distribution of karah prasad (q.v.). Ardas is the Punjabi form of the Persian **'arz-dāsht,** 'a written petition.' Used in its ordinary sense, it meant a deferential request. In Sikh tradition it is commonly used to express the act of laying a petition before the Guru (q.v.), and the Gurus themselves used it as a form of address to Akal Purakh (q.v.). At some stage during the eighteenth century, however, **ardās** assumed a more specific meaning in Sikh usage. There developed the convention of prefacing requests for divine assistance with the invocation to *Chaṇḍī kī vār* (q.v.) which is recorded in the Dasam Granth (q.v.), an invocation which calls to mind the grace and virtues of the first nine Gurus. To this was added a similar reference to the tenth Guru, and the supplemented invocation came to be known as Ardas in a particular sense. *See also* ARDAS: CONTENTS.

ARDAS: CONTENTS. In the modern version of Ardas (q.v.) the invocation from *Chaṇḍī kī vār* (q.v.) remains mandatory and, together with the two concluding lines of Ardas, it is the only portion which is unalterable. A lengthy sequel then follows this standard invocation. There exists a generally agreed text for this sequel, most of it comprising a review of the past trials and triumphs of the Khalsa (q.v.) uttered in clusters by the leader. Each cluster concludes with the congregation responding in unison with a fervent **Vāhigurū** (q.v.). The text of this second section was largely composed early in the twentieth century by scholars of the Tat Khalsa (q.v.) and is printed in *Sikh Rahit Maryādā* (q.v.). Variant versions are used, however. A third section may follow in which personal or community intercessions are offered. These are usually brief and follow no set text. The prayer concludes with the mandatory two-line exhortation and the Khalsa salutation.

ARJAN, GURU (1563–1606). The fifth Guru, the youngest of the three sons of Guru Ram Das (q.v.). In 1581 he succeeded his father as Guru, the two older brothers having been passed over. The decision of Guru Ram Das to select Arjan as his successor was not welcomed by his eldest son, Prithi Chand (q.v.), who made at least one unsuccessful attempt to poison Arjan's only son Hargobind (q.v.). Prithi Chand managed to secure recognition amongst a portion of the Sikhs, branded by the followers of Arjan as Minas (q.v.) or 'scoundrels.' According to tradition, Prithi Chand's followers were circulating spurious hymns and this convinced Arjan that a definitive scripture was needed. Whatever the reason, a volume (subsequently finalized as the Adi Granth [q.v.]) was prepared in 1603–04, with Bhai Gurdas (q.v.) serving as the Guru's amanuensis. A substantial basis for the new scripture was provided by the Goindval Pothis (q.v.) which had been compiled under instructions from the third Guru, Amar Das (q.v.), and to this Arjan added the works of his father and his own extensive range of compositions. His wife was Ganga (q.v.) and Hargobind was their only child. When he died in 1606, Hargobind succeeded him as Guru.

ARJAN'S DEATH. During the period of Guru Arjan and his predecessors, the Sikh Panth (q.v.) was steadily extending its popularity in the Punjab, notably amongst the rural population and in particular with those who were Jat (q.v.) by caste. It was still, however, an exclusively religious Panth, preaching liberation through remembrance of the divine Name (q.v.). Arjan's death in 1606 marks the bridge between an exclusively religious Panth and one with political and military features. The Mughal rulers of the Punjab were evidently concerned with the growth of the Panth, and in 1605 the emperor Jahangir made an entry in his memoirs, the *Tuzuk-i-Jahāngīrī*, concerning Guru Arjan's support for his rebellious son Khusro. Too many people, he wrote, were being persuaded by his teachings, and if the Guru would not become a

Muslim the Panth had to be extinguished. Mughal authorities seem plainly to have been responsible for Arjan's death in custody in Lahore, and this may be accepted as an established fact. Whether death was by execution, the result of torture, or drowning in the Ravi river remains unresolved. For Sikhs, Arjan is the first martyr Guru. Tradition adds that prior to his death he gave instructions to his son and successor Hargobind (q.v.) that after his death the Guru should bear arms, the Panth should also be armed, and tyranny should be resisted. *See also* MUGHAL DYNASTY.

ARMY, ARMED FORCES. During the seventeenth and particularly the eighteenth centuries the Khalsa (q.v.) fought tenaciously for the Punjab, and such features as the sword and steel became symbols of power for them. Ranjit Singh (q.v.) created a strong army, showing a particular preference for Sikh troops, and in the 1840s the Khalsa army met the British in determined battles. This won British respect for the Khalsa, and they extensively recruited Sikhs for the Indian Army. The British also insisted on Sikh troops retaining the Khalsa symbols. Following independence opportunities have opened up in the navy and air force, but the Government of India has steadily cut back the number of Sikhs in the army, arguing that each region is entitled to a quota. Sikhs reply that quality is much more important for an army than regional quotas and that the Punjab is the region on the border with Pakistan (the potential or actual enemy). *See also* MARTIAL RACES; MILITANCY.

ARORA. A mercantile caste (q.v.) of northwest India, some of whom are Sikhs.

ARRANGED MARRIAGES. In India marriages are usually arranged by families, not by individuals, and most Sikhs still prefer the system whereby the spouse is chosen by the head of the family. An increasing number are following the western style of individual choice, but this still involves only a small fraction of the total population. In some cases arrangements are handled entirely by elders. Usually, however, prospective partners are given an opportunity to meet and to approve the choice. Families arranging marriages are expected to select partners who are well suited to each other in terms of age, education, economic status, and general suitability. Sikhs almost always observe caste rules when arranging marriages, choosing partners belonging to the same zat and of a different got (qq.v.). *See also* CASTE.

ART. Sikhs have been ambivalent towards art. On the one hand, it would be difficult to claim that any 'great' art has emerged within the Panth. Amrita Sher-gil (1911–41) was an artist of talent; her mother was Hungarian, however, and most of her work was scarcely Sikh. On the other hand, the 'popular' art of the Sikhs (expressed in such forms as embroidery and murals) is vigorous and rich. The ambivalence towards sophisticated art is encouraged by the suspicion of scholars, held by the Singh Sabha (q.v.), concerning paintings of the Gurus (a suspicion probably derived from Muslim example). The earliest extant paintings by Sikhs (predictably of Guru Nanak) go back to a janam-sakhi (q.v.) of the mid-seventeenth century. Janam-sakhi illustrations continue into the twentieth century, the form changing with the introduction of printing in the late nineteenth century. In the twentieth century bazaar posters assume primacy. Nanak and Gobind Singh (q.v.) are particularly popular subjects, Nanak dressed soberly and Gobind Singh in gorgeous apparel. Sikh martyrs are popular; the headless body of Dip Singh (q.v.) fighting with his head in his hand is prominently displayed, and the two children of Gobind Singh being bricked up alive are commonly portrayed.

ARTI *see* ARATI.

ARYA SAMAJ. A Hindu reformist movement, founded in 1875 by Swami Dayananda Saraswati, which secured a particularly strong following in the Punjab, particularly from Khatris (q.v.). Initially it had many Sikh members, but Dayananda's writings and an attack by several members on the Gurus in 1888 led to considerable Sikh opposition to the movement which has continued ever since.

ASA KI VAR. The most cherished of all the vars (q.v.) in the Adi Granth (q.v.), appearing on pages 462–75. The twenty-four **pauṛīs** (q.v.) which form the structure are by Guru Nanak (q.v.) and likewise forty-four of its fifty-nine **shaloks** (q.v.). The remaining fifteen **shaloks** are by Guru Angad (q.v.).*Āsā kī Vār* is regularly sung in gurdwaras (q.v.) early in the morning, daily in the case of large gurdwaras, and weekly or as occasion demands in the smaller ones.

ASCETICISM. This was not encouraged by the Gurus, their emphasis instead being upon moderation in all things. All the Gurus who were old enough were married men, and the life of a grahasti (q.v.) was enjoined. In spite of this, a preference for celibacy has remained amongst many Sikhs, particularly for sants (q.v.).

ASTROLOGY. Astrology, which is so influential across India, is also powerful in the Punjab, with extensive patronage bestowed on the Brahmans who practise it. The Tat Khalsa, as opposed to the Sanatan Sikhs (qq.v), took a hostile view of it as superstition and banned it in *Sikh Rahit Maryādā* (q.v.). It is impossible to estimate the effect of their ban on the Panth (q.v.). *See also* DIVINATION.

ATAL RAI (1619–28). The youngest of the five sons of Guru Hargobind (q.v.), Atal Rai died aged nine. According to tradition this was because of his father's rebuke for having raised a playmate from the dead. To atone for his mistake he entered a trance from which he did not awaken. *See also* BABA ATAL GURDWARA.

ATMA (Skt. **atman**). 'Breath'; spirit; soul. *See also* PARAMATMA.

ATTAR SINGH OF BHADAUR (1833–96). Related to the Phulkian princes (q.v.), he controlled a large estate near Barnala under the suzerainty of Patiala. He chose, however, to be member of the Lahore Singh Sabha (q.v.). A learned person, he possessed a copious library and excelled in historical research. He was involved in the founding of Khalsa College (q.v.) and educational issues generally.

ATTAR SINGH MASTUANA (1866–1927). A famous sant of Malwa (qq.v.), renowned for his austerities, preaching, and kirtan (q.v.). He was educated by the Nirmalas (q.v.) and adopted celibacy. Travelling around the Punjab he was received with the reverence accorded to great sants. To receive **pāhul** (q.v.) at his hands was considered a high honor. Attar Singh was for a time a patron of the Bhasaur Singh Sabha (q.v.), but abandoned it when Babu Teja Singh (q.v.) adopted views which were considered too extreme. He remained a supporter of the Tat Khalsa movement (q.v.).

AURANGZEB (reigned from 1658–1707). The Mughal emperor who was responsible for the execution of Guru Tegh Bahadur (q.v.) and for a generally hostile attitude to Guru Gobind Singh (q.v.) (who is said to have addressed the letter *Zafar-nāmā* (q.v.) to him).

AUSTERITY. In contrast to many branches of the Hindu tradition, rigorous austerity is forbidden by Sikhism. A moderate lifestyle is commended, one which falls between asceticism and gross materialism, and the way of the grahasti (q.v.) is upheld as ideal. *See also* NAM JAPO, KIRAT KARO, VAND CHAKO.

AVATAR. A 'descent'; the incarnation of a deity (usually Vishnu). The term is also used for the birth of Nanak (q.v.).

AVTAR SINGH VAHIRIA (b. 1848). The principal apologist for the Sanatan group in the controversy with the Tat Khalsa for control of the Singh Sabha (qq.v.). A follower of Khem Singh Bedi he wrote a rejoinder to Kahn Singh Nabha's *Ham Hindū Nahīn* ('We are not Hindus') (qq.v.). His principal work, *Khālsā Dharam Shāstra,* was first issued in 1894 and then in an expanded edition in 1914.

B

B40 JANAM-SAKHI. An unusually clear janam-sakhi (q.v.) in terms of period, place, and sources. It is dated S.1790 (1733 C.E.) and was evidently recorded near Nanak's village of

Kartarpur (qq.v.). The sources include those used by the *Purātan* tradition, the *Ādi Sākhīs,* small amounts from the *Miharbān* and *Bālā* traditions (qq.v.), and some from oral tradition. The janam-sakhi is called after its accession number in the India Office Library.

BABA. 'Old man,' a title of great respect applied to men (or even boys) of wisdom and piety. The janam-sakhis (q.v.) normally use this title for Nanak (q.v.) in preference to 'Guru.'

BABA ATAL GURDWARA. A nine-story gurdwara (q.v.) built close to the Golden Temple in Amritsar (qq.v.) to commemorate the early death of Atal Rai (q.v.). The octagonal building was erected during the late eighteenth century and remains the tallest in Amritsar. On the walls of the first floor are series of frescos, the most conspicuous of them being scenes with text from the janam-sakhis (q.v.) painted in the last decade of the nineteenth century.

BABA BAKALE. Tradition relates that the child Guru Har Krishan (q.v.), before he died, uttered the words '**Bābā Bakāle**' (The Baba [who is in] Bakala [will be the next Guru]). Claimants hastened to Bakala, a village in Amritsar District, thereby posing a problem as to who was the designated one. A merchant called Makhan Shah Labana, whose life had been in danger during a storm at sea, had promised to donate 500 gold mohurs to the Guru if he was saved. To fulfil his vow he travelled up to the Punjab and in Bakala was confronted by several claimants. (The number varies.) To test them he presented each with five mohurs. (This also varies.) When he laid the mohurs before Tegh Bahadur (q.v.), he was asked where the remainder were. At once he rushed up to the rooftop to proclaim that he had found the true Guru.

BABAR-VANI. "Utterances concerning Babur (q.v.)," four hymns composed by Nanak (q.v.) about the devastation caused by Babur's army. The four hymns are *Āsā* 39, *Āsā ashṭapadi* 11, *Asa ashṭapadī* 12, and *Tilaṅg* 5 (Adi Granth, pp. 360, 417, 417–18, and 722–3).

BABBAR AKALI. 'Lion Akali.' A revolutionary group which embraced violence in the fight for control of the gurdwaras (q.v.) in the early 1920s. The group was suppressed by the British. *See also* GURDWARA REFORM MOVEMENT.

BABBAR KHALSA. An extremist offshoot of the Akhand Kirtani Jatha (q.v.) which claimed responsibility for killing many Sant Nirankaris (q.v.) in the 1980s. *See also* RECENT HISTORY.

BABUR (1483–1530). The first Mughal emperor of India, who won a portion of North India by defeating Sultan Ibrahim Lodi at the battle of Panipat in 1526. Babur had first ruled in Farghana but was forced out of there and then harried in Kabul by the invading Uzbegs. This turned his attention to north India. Although the anecdotes of the meetings between Nanak (q.v.) and Babur recorded by the janam-sakhis (q.v.) are not believable, the naming of Saidpur (q.v.) as a town attacked by Babur is certainly credible. At some point Nanak evidently witnessed Babur's invasion of India. The four hymns known collectively as the *Bābar-vāṇī* (q.v.) point to this. *See also* MUGHAL DYNASTY.

BACHITAR NATAK. The term is sometimes used for the entire Dasam Granth (q.v.), but is normally confined to a poetic composition in it attributed to Guru Gobind Singh (q.v.). The form is autobiographical, describing the Guru's pre-birth meditation and early battles in his career. It concludes before the founding of the Khalsa (q.v.), which probably took place in 1699.

BAGARIAN. A distinguished lineage of Bhais (q.v.) dating back to the time of Hargobind (q.v.). By caste they were Tarkhans. Their ancestral village is in Ludhiana District where the lineage still flourishes today.

BAHAUDDIN. Shaikh Baha' al-Din Zakariyya, Pir of Multan, widely acclaimed in the Sufi hagiography of the Punjab. Although he died in 1266, he appears in several meetings with Guru Nanak in the janam-sakhis (q.v.) where he is known as Makhdum Bahauddin.

BAISAKHI. The New Year festival held on the first day of the month of Baisakh (March/April). Technically the new year begins a month earlier, but Sikhs regard Baisakhi as the appropriate date. It marks the ending of the previous agricultural cycle and the beginning of a new one. Guru Amar Das (q.v.) took over the existing Baisakhi festival and made it a day for visiting the Guru. The Panth (q.v.) believes that Guru Gobind Singh (q.v.) chose this day for the inauguration of the Khalsa (q.v.) in 1699, when large numbers would be visiting Anandpur Sahib (q.v.). The festival is marked by visits to gurdwaras (q.v.), where the nishan (q.v.) is replaced, and by singing and dancing of the bhangra and the giddha (qq.v). Baisakhi is also the occasion for many Sikhs to be initiated into the Khalsa. *See also* KHALSA INAUGURATION.

BAKALA *see* BABA BAKALE.

BAKHSHISH. 'Grant'; traditionally one of six foundations from which certain Udasi (q.v.) orders trace their origin. Other Udasi orders trace their origins to one of the four **dhūāns** (q.v.). *See also* AKHARA.

BAL GUNDAN. 'Plaiting the hair,' a ceremony which may be performed when a child is five. In the presence of the Guru Granth Sahib (q.v.) the hair is either tied in plaits or in a topknot.

BALA. Bhai Bala, or Bala Sandhu, is named by the janam-sakhis of the *Bālā* tradition (q.v.) as one of the two companions of Nanak (q.v.) in his early life and travels. There is no doubt that Mardana (q.v.) was a companion of the Guru. The existence of Bala is, however, doubtful, and if he did exist he occupied a very minor place in Nanak's life. Popular portraits of Nanak frequently depict him flanked by Mardana the minstrel and by Bhai Bala fanning him with a peacock feather.

BALA JANAM-SAKHI TRADITION. The most popular of the janam-sakhi (q.v.) traditions among ordinary Sikhs. For more than two centuries the janam-sakhis of the *Bālā* tradition have appealed to the popular imagination because of the extent to which they feature the grossly miraculous and the bizarre. They have enjoyed this reputation in spite of the fact that the tradition probably had its origins among a schismatic group, the Hindalis (q.v.). The tradition takes its name from Bhai Bala (q.v.) who figures very prominently in most of the anecdotes. There are two recensions of the tradition, one which includes the death of Nanak (q.v.) and the other ending before it.

BALAK SINGH (1799–1862). Founder of the Namdhari sect (q.v.).

BALDEV SINGH (1902–61). A Jat and an Akali politician (qq.v.) prominent in the negotiations for India's independence. After independence he joined Nehru's government and remained there until 1957.

BALVAND AND SATTA. Rai Balvand and Satta the Dum were two rabab players who, according to tradition, sang kirtan for Guru Angad (qq.v.). After some years they became increasingly insubordinate and left the Guru's service. When they found that they no longer enjoyed popularity, they were humbled. To signal their contrition they wrote the first five stanzas of *Tikke dī Vār* (q.v.), composing the remaining three stanzas in the time of Guru Arjan (q.v.).

BANA. The dress of the Khalsa (q.v.), at least for males. It comprises tight-fitting trousers and a long shirt worn outside the trousers. The Five Ks (q.v.) must be worn, with the kirpan (q.v.) on a baldric across the right shoulder.

BANDA (1670–1716). The early history of Banda Bahadur, or Banda the Brave, is known only by tradition. Probably born in Poonch, on the northern fringe of the Punjab, he was called Lachhman Dev but became a Vaishnava ascetic under the name of Madho Das. He was dwelling in the Deccan when Gobind Singh (q.v.) came south, and meeting him shortly before the latter's death in 1708, he was instantly converted to the Sikh faith. Renamed Banda ('Slave') he was commissioned to return to the Punjab and to wreak vengeance on

Vazir Khan (q.v.) who had executed the Guru's two sons. Banda journeyed up to the Punjab and gathered an army of peasants. From this point on his history can be established, at least in general outline, though there are numerous questions which remain unanswered. The towns of Samana and Sadhaura were sacked, and in 1710 he confronted Vazir Khan near Sirhind. Fighting with great determination he defeated and killed him. For five years Banda's fortunes ebbed and flowed as he led peasant armies fighting against the embattled Mughal rulers of the Punjab. Finally, he was trapped in the village of Gurdas Nangal in Gurdaspur District by Abdus Samad Khan (q.v.) and after a lengthy siege was captured. Escorted to Delhi in chains, he was barbarously executed in June 1716.

BANDAI SIKHS. During the years of warfare of the early eighteenth century, a dispute within the Panth (q.v.) opened up between the followers of Banda (the Bandai Sikhs) and those who identified with one of Gobind Singh's widows, Mata Sundari (the Tat Khalsa [qq.v]). This concerned Banda's decision to abandon the blue clothing of the Khalsa (q.v.) for red, his insistence that his followers be vegetarians, and the introduction of a new Khalsa slogan ("Fateh darshan"). The dispute, which probably indicates factionalism within the Khalsa, has tarnished Banda's reputation to a limited extent.

BANGLA SAHIB. A handsome gurdwara in central New Delhi which marks the spot of Raja Jai Singh's bungalow. Guru Har Krishan (q.v.) stayed here for some months prior to his death in 1661.

BANGLA SAHIB GURDWARA. A gurdwara (q.v.) near the center of New Delhi marking the spot where the child Guru Har Krishan (q.v.) stayed in the house of Raja Jai Singh and contracted smallpox from which he died. The gurdwara is large and wealthy and attracts numerous worshippers.

BANI. 'Sound'; 'speech.' In Sikh usage **bāṇī** designates the utterances (believed to be inspired) of the Gurus and bhagats recorded in the Adi Granth or Dasam Granth (qq.v.). *See also* GURBANI.

BANNO, BHAI. A Sikh of Guru Arjan (q.v.) who lived in the village of Mangat in Gujrat District. Unreliable tradition relates that he secured permission to take Arjan's newly-dictated scripture back to his village on loan. The reluctant Guru granted permission, provided he promised to keep it there for one night only. This condition Banno circumvented by travelling very slowly to and from Mangat, copying the entire scripture on the way. This is one tradition of the purported origin of the Banno Bir (q.v.). The other is that the new scripture was sent with Banno to Lahore for binding and that he made his copy while on this mission. *See also* ADI GRANTH RECENSIONS.

BANNO BIR. 'Banno volume'; the Banno recension of the Adi Granth (q.v.) which disagrees with the Kartarpur recension (q.v.). A manuscript is held in Kanpur which purports to be the original Banno version. This claim is still unproven. *See also* ADI GRANTH RECENSIONS.

BAPTISM *see* AMRIT SANSKAR.

BARAH-MAHA. 'Twelve months,' a poetic form in which the author reflects feelings through the changing aspects of nature as portrayed in the twelve month cycle. Nanak and Arjan (qq.v.) each composed a barah-maha (Adi Granth, pp. 1107–10, 133–36).

BASANT PANCHMI. The spring festival held on the fifth day of the light half of the month of Magh (January/February), observed by Hindus and Sikhs. Everyone should wear a yellow garment.

BASARKE. Guru Amar Das's (q.v.) native village, situated near Amritsar (q.v.).

BAVAN AKHARI. 'Fifty-two letters.' A poem based on the alphabet, each verse beginning with a letter in sequence. The form is named after the Deva-nagri alphabet of Sanskrit which has thirty-three consonants, sixteen vowels, and three conjuncts. There are two bavan akharis in the Adi Granth (q.v.).

Guru Arjan's (q.v.) has an introductory **pauṛī** and **shalok** (qq.v.) followed by fifty-five **pauṛī** and **shaloks** (*AG*, pp. 250–62). Kabir's has forty-five **pauṛīs** (*AG*, pp. 340–43).

BEAS SATSANG *see* RADHASOAMI.

BEDI. The Khatri (q.v.) sub-caste to which Guru Nanak (q.v.) belonged. Comparatively few Bedis became Sikhs, but those who did enjoyed considerable prestige as Guru-vans (q.v.). One distinguished lineage was that of the Bedis of Una descended from Sahib Singh Bedi (q.v.). Another was the lineage centered on Rawalpindi which included Khem Singh Bedi (q.v.).

BENATI CHAUPAI. 'Invocation in the **chaupai** metre.' The epilogue to the *Pakhyān Charitra* (q.v.) from the Dasam Granth (q.v.) which is a part of Sodar Raharas (q.v.).

BENI. A bhagat (q.v.), unknown apart from his three compositions in the Adi Granth (q.v.).

BHAGAT. A bhakta; an exponent of bhagti (q.v.). In Sikh usage a bhagat is one of the Sant poets, such as Kabir or Namdev (qq.v.), whose works appear in the Adi Granth (q.v.).

BHAGAT BANI. 'The utterances of the bhagats,' **shabads** or **shaloks** by bhagats (qq.v.) which are included in the Adi Granth (q.v.).

BHAGAT-RATANAVALI. A work unreliably attributed to Mani Singh on the bhagats listed in Var 11 of Gurdas (qq.v.). The work is also called *Sikkhān dī Bhagat-māl(ā)*. *See also* GYAN-RATANAVALI.

BHAGAT SINGH (1907–31). A young revolutionary, active against British rule during the late 1920s. He was captured in 1929 and executed in 1931. Although he came from a Sikh family, his beliefs were those of an atheist. Attempts to reclaim him are sometimes made by members of the contemporary Khalsa (q.v.).

BHAGAUTI. The goddess Durga (or Devi) who appears in three works in the Dasam Granth (q.v.). Her appearance created a problem for Tat Khalsa (q.v.) scholars who strongly affirmed monotheism. The question was settled by concluding that Bhagauti symbolizes God as the Divine Sword. As such she (or it) is addressed in the invocation to Ardas (q.v.). *See also* CHANDI KI VAR; DEVI WORSHIP.

BHAGO. Mai Bhago, a Sikh woman who was initiated Bhag Kaur when the Khalsa (q.v.) was first established. She fought for Guru Gobind Singh (q.v.) in the battle of Muktsar (q.v.) and remained with him thereafter.

BHAGTI (BHAKTI). Adoration of a personal God.

BHAI. 'Brother,' a title of reverence traditionally conferred on male Sikhs of acknowledged piety and learning. Amongst those who have received the title are Gurdas, Nand Lal, and Mani Singh (qq.v.). The title continues to be used today with its strong sense of respect still intact, two twentieth-century examples being Vir Singh and Jodh Singh (qq.v.). A second usage emerged, however, in the nineteenth century when bhai came to be applied to teachers in Gurmukhi schools. A third usage developed in modern times whereby ragis (q.v.) are also known by the same title. When applied to ragis it loses much of its traditional veneration and may even be used in a pejorative sense.

BHAI BALA *see* BALA.

BHAI RANDHIR SINGH DA JATHA. 'The followers of Bhai Randhir Singh' (q.v.) form a fundamentalist sect of Sikhs in the literal sense of the word, with members laying paramount emphasis on the the sacred text of scripture. Great importance is attached to kirtan (q.v.), and congregations frequently devote the whole night to it. They also attach particular significance to the word **Vāhigurū** (q.v.). Vegetarianism is strictly observed, and in place of the kes in the Five Ks (q.v.) they substitute the keski (q.v.) which women wear as well as men. References to caste differences are strictly forbidden. Although Randhir Singh was himself a Jat, the leadership of the sect is now in the hands of Khatris and Aroras (qq.v.). Ludhiana is the center of the group. *See also* AKHAND KIRTANI JATHA; ORTHODOXY; RAG-MALA; RAHIT BIBEK.

BHALLA. The Khatri (q.v.) sub-caste to which Guru Amar Das and Gurdas (qq.v.) belonged.

BHANGANI. In 1688 Guru Gobind Singh (q.v.) won the battle of Bhangani, the most important of those which he fought with his neighbors in the Shivalik Hills (q.v.) until the 1704 attack on Anandpur (q.v.). In this battle, which is vividly described in *Bachitar Nāṭak* (q.v.), he defeated Fateh Shah of Garhwal (q.v.).

BHANGI MISL. A large misl (q.v.) centered on a village in the Amritsar district. It was founded early in the eighteenth century by Hari Singh and acquired its name because of his fondness for bhang (cannabis). It grew in size and strength, dividing into several groups under individual sardars (q.v.) and forming a confederacy. For a time it controlled territory extending from Attock to Multan, briefly emerging as the paramount power of west Punjab. A succession of deaths in the late 1760s, however, deprived the federation of effective leadership. In the 1790s the Bhangis opposed the rising power of the Shukerchakia misl under Ranjit Singh (qq.v.) but collapsed following the confrontation at Bhasin in 1799 and soon after disappeared.

BHANGRA. A lively Punjabi folk dance performed by men or boys dressed in colorful garb.

BHANI, BIBI (1535–98). The daughter of Guru Amar Das, wife of Guru Ram Das, and mother of Guru Arjan (qq.v.). Renowned for her pious service, particularly towards her father Amar Das.

BHAPA. 'Brother' in the Pothohari dialect spoken around Rawalpindi, used of the Sikhs from that area by the Sikhs of central Punjab (Manjh, Doaba, and Malwa [qq.v.]). By caste, the Sikhs of the Rawalpindi area are predominantly Khatris and Aroras, and the term is typically used dismissively by Jats to express opprobrium towards Sikhs of these castes (qq.v.). Until recently it was never used in polite company or in print, but today the word is used quite openly.

BHASAUR SINGH SABHA. The branch of the Singh Sabha (q.v.) which was founded by Teja Singh Bhasaur (q.v.) of the village of Bhasaur in the princely state of Patiala. The actual foundation was in 1893. In 1907 it became the Panch Khalsa Divan (also known as the Khalsa Parliament), thus marking its divergence from the Chief Khalsa Divan (q.v.). Teja Singh Bhasaur was not its founding president, but he was the spirit behind it. For him, the Sanatan Sikhs (q.v.) were far too timid, and the Tat Khalsa (q.v.) was not much better. His ideal was strictly fundamentalist and offered an awkward challenge to the dominant views of the Singh Sabha and of the Chief Khalsa Divan. Brahmanical concepts which he detected in Sikhism were one of his targets and likewise caste. Both conversion of non-Sikhs and re-conversion of lapsed Sikhs were vigorously advocated, ideals which were prominently displayed at a famous gathering at the village of Bakapur in 1903. In the Bhasaur Singh Sabha beards flowed free, women were required to wear turbans, Sahaj-dharis (q.v.) were cast out, Ardas (q.v.) was changed, and the *Rāg-mālā* (q.v.) was dropped from the Adi Granth (q.v.). Eventually the actions of the Bhasaur Singh Sabha became altogether too radical for more orthodox Sikhs to accept, and in 1928 Teja Singh Bhasaur was banished from the Panth by Akal Takhat (qq.v.). The Panch Khalsa Divan then faded from view, losing the allegiance of some prominent Sikhs who had hitherto supported them. *See also* KHALSA RAHIT PRAKASH.

BHATRA. A tiny caste of peddlers and magicians, mainly from Sialkot and Hoshiarpur Districts. Some of the Bhatras were Sikhs, and the first identifiable Sikhs among the immigrants to England were from this caste. They went there in the early 1920s and earned a living peddling clothes from door to door.

BHATT. The Bhatts were a sub-caste of Brahmans from Malwa (q.v.) who by profession were bards. The allegiance of some of them to the Sikh Gurus evidently began when one of an extended family became a follower of Amar Das (q.v.). In the time of Arjan (q.v.) many of them composed panegyrics in praise of the various Gurus, and 123 of their compositions have been recorded in the Adi Granth (q.v.). Several of them also wrote Bhatt Vahis (q.v.). Like practically all Brahman Sikhs the various members of the sub-caste did not accept initiation into the Khalsa, and those who remained Sikhs adopted the style of Sahaj-dharis (q.v.).

BHATT VAHI. A genealogy ('account-book') of a Bhatt (q.v.). Because the Bhatts were bards by profession several of them recorded genealogies of the Gurus, supplementing these with extensive chroniclers' details. The information which they supply (particularly concerning the last two Gurus) can be useful if treated very cautiously.

BHIKHAN. Two works by Bhikhan appear in the Adi Granth (q.v.). Traditionally he is regarded as a Sufi (q.v.), from Kakori near Lucknow, who died in 1574. It is possible, however, that he was a Hindu sant (q.v.) of the same name.

BHOG. Lit. 'pleasure'; sexual intercourse; consummation. In Sikh usage the term also designates the ceremonial concluding of a complete reading of the Guru Granth Sahib (q.v.). The procedure is as follows. If guests are to be present they are invited to assemble immediately before the projected time of completion. The reading concludes with either the *Rāg-mālā* or (for those who dispute its authenticity) with Guru Arjan's *Mundāvaṇī* and attached **shalok** (qq.v.), the work which immediately precedes it on the last page of the Guru Granth Sahib. The six appointed stanzas of *Anand Sāhib* are then read; Ardas is recited; a hukam is taken; and karah prasad is distributed to all who are present (qq.v.). After it is over a mantle, whisk, or canopy for the Guru Granth Sahib is commonly donated, and langar (q.v.) may be served. *See also* AKHAND PATH.

BHOG MARK. The practice of inscribing an auspicious symbol (such as a swastika) on a blank folio of a manuscript of the

Adi Granth (q.v.) following the completion of an Akhand Path (q.v.).

BIDHI CHAND. He succeeded in recapturing two horses, Dilbagh and Gulbagh, which were being brought from Kabul for Guru Hargobind (q.v.) and had been seized by Mughal officials of Lahore (q.v.). This led to one of the skirmishes between Hargobind and Mughal forces.

BIKRAM SINGH (1842–98). Raja of Faridkot and the leading patron of the Singh Sabha (q.v.). A supporter of the Sanatan view (q.v.), he also favored modern education and persuaded the Singh Sabha to encourage it. In 1898 he played an important role in the controversy over the electrification of Harimandir Sahib (q.v.), leading to the success of the campaign. *See also* FARIDKOT TIKA.

BIKRAMA SINGH (1835–87). A younger brother of the Raja of Kapurthala and an important patron of the Singh Sabha (q.v.). A supporter of the Sanatan view (q.v.), he was a scholar of Sikh scriptures and a master of classical music.

BIKRAMI *see* SAMMAT DATING.

BIR. Volume; tome; recension.

BIR SINGH, BHAI (1768–1844). A prominent sant (q.v.) during the period immediately following the death of Maharaja Ranjit Singh (q.v.). Bir Singh commanded a large following during events leading to the collapse of the Punjab kingdom. He was killed in an attack on his center by Hira Singh Dogra.

BIRADARI. 'Brotherhood.' A patrilineal descent group, all of the members tracing their origins to a common ancestor. Most biradaris are limited to four or five generations and are confined to a compact area.

BIRTH CEREMONY. Water is poured into a steel or iron cup, sweets or honey added, and stirred with a kirpan (q.v.) while the first five stanzas of *Japjī Sāhib* (q.v.) are recited. A few drops are then given to the child to drink, the remainder being drunk by the mother. A prayer of thanksgiving is also offered. This ceremony is voluntary.

BLASPHEMY. This term, hitherto limited to Jewish, Christian, and Muslim usage, has recently begun appearing in Sikh publications. Literally meaning 'to damage a reputation,' it originally referred to speech, thought, or action which manifested contempt for God or denied his/her existence. In Sikh circles the term is loosely used for anything which contradicts the conventional teachings of the Panth (q.v.).

BOTA SINGH (d. 1739). A Sikh martyr. Tradition records that he went into hiding during attempts to exterminate the Sikhs but was shamed by a comment that the Khalsa (q.v.) never hid. With a companion Garja Singh (q.v.) he proclaimed his Khalsa allegiance and openly began collecting a toll on the highway near Tarn Taran. When this failed to attract notice he despatched a defiant letter to Zakariya Khan in Lahore (qq.v.). A large force was sent to capture them, and after resisting stoutly both were killed.

BRAHAM-GIANI. One who knows Braham (God); a model of piety and good works.

BRAHMAN. According to the varna hierarchy, the Brahman caste is at the apex. Sikhs, however, tend to regard Brahmans as pretentious (particularly in rural areas) and place them distinctly lower on the caste scale. This is partly due to the strictures which the Gurus laid upon Brahman pride and partly to the ordering of Punjabi rural society which normally confers dominance on the Jat caste (q.v.).

BRAJ. The vernacular spoken around Mathura and Brindaban, associated with the Krishna stories. Braj differs from Punjabi, though they have a certain amount in common. The greater part of the Dasam Granth (q.v.) is in Braj, recorded in the Gurmukhi script (q.v.).

BRAVERY. For the Khalsa (q.v.) unyielding bravery merits the highest praise. Such quotations as the following passage from the Dasam Granth (q.v.) are held up for emulation: "Strengthen me, O Lord, that I shrink not from righteous deeds, That freed from the fear of my enemies I may fight with faith and win. The wisdom which I crave is the grace to sing your praises. Grant that when life's span shall end I may meet my death in battle."

BUDDHA, BHAI (trad. 1506–1631). A Jat (q.v.) from Kathu Nangal who was originally called Bura Randhava. While still a child Nanak (q.v.) renamed him Buddha ('old man' or 'wise man') because of his youthful wisdom and piety. Bhai Buddha served as a faithful disciple of six of the Gurus, dying at the reputed age of 125. Traditionally he participated in the installation of all the Gurus after Nanak. Hargobind, Arjan's only child, is believed to have been conceived as a result of Bhai Buddha's blessing given to Arjan's wife Mata Ganga (qq.v.).

BUDDHA DAL *see* TARUNA DAL.

BUNGA. As the Sikhs gained control of Harimandir Sahib (q.v.) during the late eighteenth century, defensive buildings (bungā) were erected around its surrounding pool. Smaller clusters were built around other major Sikh shrines but nothing to equal those at Harimandir Sahib. These bungas were named for the people or groups responsible for their erection, whether misldars, important sardars, rich communities in the towns, or particular sects such as the Nirmalas or Udasis (qq.v.). One of them, Akal Bunga, houses Akal Takhat, the primary temporal center of the Panth (qq.v.). They remained in private hands until the Sikh Gurdwaras Act of 1925 (q.v.) recognized them as the property of Harimandir Sahib. The precise number is not known, but there would have been between seventy and ninety. During the nineteenth century the bungas provided accommodation for pilgrims, and some of them secured reputations as centers of learning. Santokh Singh (q.v.) was one poet who received his training in a bunga. Very few bungas now remain as the SGPC (q.v.) has demolished most of them to provide an uninterrupted parikarama (q.v.) around the pool.

C

CASTE. Sikhs explicitly reject caste in terms of status or privilege. Nanak (q.v.) denounced it, subsequent Gurus reinforced his message, and ritual observance confirms it. In gurdwaras (q.v.) all sit together, the only distinction being between men and women. All receive the same karah prasad and eat in the same langar (qq.v.), sitting in straight lines to do so. At Khalsa initiation (q.v.) all initiates must drink the same amrit (q.v.). Caste is, however, retained within the Panth (q.v.) as a social order. The Gurus, who were all Khatris (q.v.), married their children within the same caste. This convention has survived largely intact, with the result that virtually every Indian Sikh belongs to a particular caste (**jāt,** Punjabi **zāt** [q.v.]). Each zat is divided into a number of sub-castes (**gotra,** Punjabi **got** [q.v.]) and Sikhs (like most other Indians) are endogamous by zat and exogamous by got. In terms of zat an absolute majority are Jats (q.v.). Other important castes with both Hindu and Sikh sections are the Khatri and Arora (q.v.). Distinctive Sikh castes are the Ramgarhia, Ahluvalia, Mazhabi, and Ramdasia (qq.v.). *See also* ARRANGED MARRIAGES; DALIT.

CENTRAL SIKH LEAGUE. A political party formed by Sikh leaders in March 1919 for the following purposes: to rebuild the demolished wall of Rakab-ganj Gurdwara (q.v.); to bring Khalsa College (q.v.) under panthic control; to liberate gurdwaras (q.v.) from their existing control; and to inspire Sikhs to participate in India's freedom struggle. An existing newspaper, *Khālsā Akhbār,* was taken over as organ of the party and renamed the *Akālī.* In 1920 the more radical Akali Dal (q.v.) was formed. Under the leadership of Kharak Singh (q.v.) the Central Sikh League maintained a lively existence alongside the Akali Dal throughout the 1920s and early 1930s. In 1933 the two parties merged. *See also* GURDWARA REFORM MOVEMENT; POLITICAL PARTIES.

CHALI MUKTE. The 'Forty Liberated Ones.' Forty men from the Manjh region (q.v.) who deserted Guru Gobind Singh (q.v.) during the siege of Anandpur (q.v.) and returned to their homes. Shamed by Bhago (q.v.) and their other women they rejoined the Sikhs shortly before the battle of Muktsar (q.v.) in which all were killed. In recognition of their restored loyalty the Guru, responding to the pleas of Mahan Singh (the last to remain alive), tore up the disclaimer (**bedāvā**) which they had signed in Anandpur and declared them to be **mukte,** men who had attained deliverance.

CHAMKAUR. After vacating Anandpur (q.v.) in 1704, Gobind Singh (q.v.) withdrew to the village of Chamkaur where another battle was fought with the pursuing Mughals. The Guru's two eldest sons, Ajit Singh and Jujhar Singh, were killed in this battle, but he himself escaped. *See also* SAHIB-ZADE.

CHANANI. A canopy which is always over the Guru Granth Sahib in a gurdwara (qq.v.). It indicates great respect.

CHANDI CHARITRA. Two lengthy compositions in the Dasam Granth (q.v.), both in Gurmukhi Braj (qq.v.), relating the exploits of the goddess Chandi or Durga. One of the two is known as *Chaṇḍī charitra ukati bilās.*

CHANDI KI VAR. A work, correctly entitled *Vār Srī Bhagautī jī kī,* which is included the Dasam Granth (q.v.). It is attributed to Guru Gobind Singh (q.v.), but is probably by one of his entourage. The poem, which is in Punjabi (not Braj like most of the Dasam Granth), tells the story of the struggle between the goddess Chandi and demons. The source is the Markandeya Purana. Its invocation is used at the beginning of Ardas (q.v.). *See also* BHAGAUTI.

CHANDU SHAH. By tradition a Khatri of Lahore (qq.v.) who tried unsuccessfully to marry his daughter to Guru Arjan's son Hargobind (qq.v.). When this failed the humiliated Chandu Shah is said to have participated in the arrest and death of Arjan.

CHAR PADARATH. The four qualities: prosperity, observance of caste duties, success, and liberation.

CHARAN-AMRIT. 'Foot-initiation,' also called **charan-pāhul.** The pre-Khalsa method of initiation into the Panth (qq.v.). The Guru (q.v.) or designated deputy would touch water with the toe of his right foot, and the candidate would then drink it as a token of submission.

CHARHDI KALA. 'High spirits'; unwavering confidence in divine justice; absolute certainty which overrides all doubts; supreme bravery which rises above any thought of defeat; cheerfulness.

CHARITRO-PAKHYAN *see* PAKHYAN CHARITRA.

CHAUBIS AUTAR. Tales of twenty-four incarnations of the god Vishnu included in the Dasam Granth (q.v.). They comprise 4,371 verses, of which 864 concern the *Rām-avatār* and 2,492 the *Krishan-avatār*. The language is Braj (q.v.) and the script Gurmukhi (q.v.).

CHAUNKI. A period of kirtan (q.v.). All major gurdwaras (q.v.) have at least four chaunkis (or 'sittings') each day. Their names and starting times are: Asa di Var di chaunki (early morning); Bilaval di chaunki (four hours after sunrise); Raharasi di chaunki (immediately before the recitation of Raharas [q.v.]); and Kalyan di chaunki (immediately before Kirtan Sohila [q.v.]).

CHAUPA SINGH (d. 1723). A member of the Chhibbar Brahman family which was prominent in the retinue of Guru Gobind Singh (q.v.). Chaupa Singh achieved importance as an associate of the Guru from the latter's childhood onwards. *See also* CHAUPA SINGH RAHIT-NAMA.

CHAUPA SINGH RAHIT-NAMA. Chaupa Singh (q.v.) is said to have written the rahit-nama (q.v.) which bears his name. This work was written in the 1740s which is too late to be his, though it is possible that it has been influenced by an earlier work by him as it bears clear marks of his brahmanical background. In addition to setting out a version of the Rahit (q.v.) it also contains a narrative of the life of Gobind Singh (q.v.)

in which the date of the founding of the Khalsa (q.v.) is given as 1697.

CHAUPAI. A four-line stanza. In the Dasam Granth (q.v.) it designates a composition of twenty-five stanzas by Guru Gobind Singh (q.v.), correctly known as *Benatī chaupaī* (q.v.).

CHAURI. Chowrie; whisk used by a reader of the Guru Granth Sahib (q.v.) to protect the sacred volume from any impure object.

CHETO. A leader of the masands (q.v.) cast out by Guru Gobind Singh (q.v.) for misappropriation. *See also* PANJ MEL.

CHHIMBA. The depressed caste of calico-printers. During the twentieth century Sikh members of the caste have unsuccessfully tried to elevate their status by calling themselves Tank Kshatriyas.

CHHOTA GHALLUGHARA. The 'lesser holocaust.' An occasion in 1746 when the persecuting Lakhpat Rai (q.v.), chief minister of Lahore (q.v.), killed several thousand Sikhs in a single engagement.

CHHOTE MEL. The Sodhi (q.v.) lineage descending from Prithi Chand (q.v.) was known as the 'lesser relationship' as opposed to the 'greater relationship' of Suraj Mal's descendants (q.v.). This lineage formed the leadership of the schismatic Minas (q.v.), always mentioned as the first of the Panj Mel (q.v.).

CHIEF KHALSA DIVAN. The body created in 1902 to unite the divided Amritsar and Lahore Singh Sabhas with their respective satellite Singh Sabhas (q.v.). It acted as the principal voice of the Sikhs for the next eighteen years, amidst growing unease for its conservative and pro-British stance. The CKD was eventually overtaken by the more activist Akali movement (q.v.), but it contributed much to convincing at least literate Sikhs that the Singh Sabha interpretation of their past was the only correct one. The CKD still exists, but its activity is largely confined to organizing its annual Educational Conference. *See also* GURDWARA REFORM MOVEMENT; POLITICAL PARTIES.

CLERGY. One commonly reads references to Sikh 'clergy' or 'priests.' These are mistakes. The Sikh faith does not recognize ordination, nor is anyone set apart for religious functions. Within the Panth (q.v.) all duties may be performed by any amrit-dhari Sikh (q.v.) in good standing. *See also* GRANTHI; SACRAMENT.

CONTRACEPTION. There is no ruling nor convention for Sikhs concerning contraception. Each individual or couple should form their own attitude on the basis of the rules of morality which they accept. In practice this means that there is little objection to it.

CUNNINGHAM (1812–51). Joseph Cunningham's *A History of the Sikhs,* first published in 1849 and based upon actual observation, gives a sympathetic account of the Sikhs. Cunningham was at the time in the political service of the British and had witnessed the first of the Anglo-Sikh wars (q.v.). His book displeased his superiors, and he was returned to regimental duties. The book remains a classic.

CUSHION CONTROVERSY. The gadela (cushion) question created a deep rift between Sanatan Sikhs and the Tat Khalsa (qq.v.) in the 1880s. The Sanatan Sikhs said that descendants of the Gurus had the right to sit on cushions before the Guru Granth Sahib (q.v.), whereas the Tat Khalsa maintained that the egalitarian principles of the Sikh faith forbade it. The issue centered on Khem Singh Bedi (q.v.), a descendant of Guru Nanak (q.v.) and an important Sanatan leader, who insisted on using a cushion. As with all issues the Tat Khalsa won, but the victory was not complete. The deference shown by ordinary people to persons of acknowledged spiritual stature was too deeply held to be rooted out, and the extreme respect shown to sants (q.v.) still continues today. *See also* GURU-VANS.

D

DABISTAN-I-MAZAHIB. A Persian work about the religions of India by an unknown Zoroastrian visitor from Persia, previously attributed to Mohsin Fani but now thought to have been by Maubad Zulfiqar Ardastani. The author was personally known to both Guru Hargobind and Guru Har Rai (qq.v.). This work, completed in 1645, includes an important chapter on the Nanak-panthis (the Sikhs).

DAL KHALSA. (1) During the eighteenth century the fighting Khalsa was divided into jathas, most of which later formed misls (qq.v.). Sometimes they agreed to form a group of misls for a particular purpose (such as a campaign against the Afghan invader), and as such would constitute the Dal Khalsa or 'Army of the Khalsa.' Jassa Singh Ahluvalia (q.v.) was recognized as its commander. (2) In 1978 a Dal Khalsa was formed to fight for Khalistan (q.v.). The group briefly achieved prominence in 1981 at an Educational Conference organized by the Chief Khalsa Divan (q.v.) at which Ganga Singh Dhillon of California advocated the formation of Khalistan (q.v.). In this he was strongly supported by the Dal Khalsa. After the conference, however, the popularity of the Dal Khalsa rapidly declined. *See also* BUDDHA DAL; TARUNA DAL.

DALIP SINGH *see* DULEEP SINGH.

DALIT. From ḍalnā, to throw down. Dalit is the name preferred today by an increasing number of Outcastes. Whereas other terms (Untouchables, Harijans, Scheduled Castes, etc.) have been given by caste Hindus, they themselves have chosen Dalit (or 'Oppressed'). Mazhabis and Ramdasias (qq.v.) are Sikh Dalits.

DALLA. The land owner of Talvandi Sabo (Damdama Sahib [q.v.]) who welcomed Gobind Singh (q.v.) to his village in 1706 following the Guru's withdrawal from Anandpur (q.v.).

DALLEVALIA MISL. A misl (q.v.) of medium strength with territories in eastern Doaba (q.v.).

DAMDAMA. A small town twenty-eight kilometers southeast of Bathinda in southern Punjab, also known as Damdama Sahib or as Talvandi Sabo. Guru Gobind Singh (q.v.) stayed in the town for more than nine months in 1706 following his withdrawal from Anandpur (q.v.). In the early eighteenth century it acquired a reputation for learning associated with the Sikh scriptures, and it became the home of the Damdami Taksal (q.v.). In 1966 the SGPC (q.v.) raised it to the status of a takhat (q.v.). Takhat Sri Damdama Sahib was built in the 1970s. The town contains several other gurdwaras (q.v.) and Sikh shrines.

DAMDAMI BIR. According to tradition there once existed a third recension of the Adi Granth (q.v.) in addition to the Kartarpur and Banno versions. This version, known as the Damdami Bir, is said to have been dictated from memory by Guru Gobind Singh (q.v.) during his period in Damdama (q.v.) in 1706, adding to it the works of his father Guru Tegh Bahadur (q.v.). Afghan invaders are said to have carried off this version later in the century. This tradition is incorrect. In some unknown way an enlarged version, comprising the Kartarpur recension together with the works of Tegh Bahadur, had already been compiled in the late seventeenth century and had come to be regarded as standard. It is this enlarged version which today constitutes the Adi Granth. The tradition is, however, widely accepted, and printed copies of the Adi Granth are generally labelled Sri Damdami Bir. *See also* ADI GRANTH RECENSIONS; BANNO BIR; KARTARPUR BIR.

DAMDAMI TAKSAL. A 'school' of fundamentalist Sikh theology which today exists as a formal organization or sect. According to tradition Guru Gobind Singh (q.v.), while staying at Damdama (q.v.) in southern Punjab, founded a school for studying the Sikh scriptures. One of its first students was Dip Singh (q.v.) who subsequently converted the school into the Damdami Taksal ('Mint of Damdama'). Until the twentieth century it was unimportant. Under Sant Sunder Singh (d.

1930), however, it attracted some attention for its strictly traditionalist approach; it sprang to prominence under the militant leadership of Jarnail Singh Bhindranvale (q.v.) during the 1970s and early 1980s as a powerful fundamentalist force in Sikh politics. It still continues, with diminished strength, today.

DAMODARI (1597–1631). The first of Hargobind's three wives, the mother of Gurditta, and the grandmother of Dhir Mal and Har Rai (qq.v.)

DAN. Charity; a gift given to the poor. **Dān** is frequently enjoined in the Adi Granth (q.v.). *See also* DASVANDH; NAM DAN ISHNAN.

DARBAR. Royal court; a place where a guru or an important sant (qq.v.) gives audience; a grand mansion; the executive government of a princely state.

DARBAR SAHIB *see* HARIMANDIR SAHIB (AMRITSAR).

DARSHAN. 'Audience'; sight; [to be in] the presence of someone or something important; to meet someone or visit something.

DARSHAN SINGH PHERUMAN (1885–1969). Successively a member of the Akali Dal (q.v.), Congress, and the Swatantra Party. In 1969 he fasted to death as protest against the failure to have Chandigarh and other Punjabi-speaking areas incorporated in the Punjab.

DARSHANI DEORHI. The gateway to the causeway of Harimandir Sahib (q.v.).

DAS GRANTHI. A small book containing a selection from the Dasam Granth (q.v.). There is no prescribed content, but the selection usually includes (amongst other works) the *Jāp, Bachitar Nātak, Akāl Ustati* and *Giān Prabodh* (qq.v.). *See also* PANJ GRANTHI.

DAS SAVAYYE *see* TEN SAVAYYAS.

DASAM DUAR. The 'tenth door' of Nath (q.v.) physiological theory (in addition to the nine natural orifices of the human body); the portion of the skull corresponding to the fontanelle through which the liberated spirit passes at the climax of the hatha-yoga (q.v.) discipline. The Sikh Gurus use the term figuratively.

DASAM GRANTH. A second scripture which is recognized as canonical by the Sikhs, the primary scripture being the Adi Granth (q.v.). Its place in the canon is, however, a source of perplexity. During the eighteenth century it was treated (together with the Adi Granth) as the incarnate Guru (q.v.); over the last century doubts have surrounded it and the question has been largely shelved. Tat Khalsa reformers (q.v.) encouraged these doubts, for much of the Dasam Granth conflicted with their vision of the Sikh faith. For two decades after the death of Gobind Singh (q.v.), Mani Singh (q.v.) is believed to have collected the works which together constitute the Dasam Granth. This would have been a difficult task, as many such works were reputed to have been lost in the evacuation of Anandpur (q.v.) in 1704. An independent collection was gathered by Dip Singh (q.v.) and a third collection by Sukkha Singh of Patna. The greater part of the three collections is the same, but there were differences. In 1885 a committee was set up by the Sanatan Sikhs of the Amritsar Singh Sabha (qq.v.), and in 1902 it published an authorized version. The name 'Dasam Granth' was given to the collection when it was first printed in 1902. This title, 'the Book of the Tenth [Guru],' evidently served to distinguish it from the Adi ('Original') Granth. An alternative theory (much less likely) is that it means one tenth of a longer collection. The length of the modern printed version is 1,428 pages.

DASAM GRANTH AUTHORSHIP. Traditionally the whole of the Dasam Granth (q.v.) is regarded as the work of Guru Gobind Singh (q.v.). This view is rejected by most scholars who accept that the collection has come from Gobind Singh's entourage but believe that only a small part of it is actually by him. A third view holds that even this small part cannot be safely attributed to him, originating instead from the poets of his following. Although the specific origins are obscure, its association with Gobind Singh seems beyond doubt. Among the works attributed to him are the *Jāp*, an autobiographical work entitled *Bachitar Nātak*, the *Akāl Ustati*, and a defiant letter said to be by him entitled *Zafar-nāmā* addressed to the Emperor Aurangzeb (qq.v.). The last of these works was not definitively included in the collection until the end of the nineteenth century.

DASAM GRANTH CONTENTS. The Dasam Granth (q.v.) contains some works which are attributed to Guru Gobind Singh (q.v.) by most scholars. These include the *Jāp, Akāl Ustati,* and *Bachitar Nātak* (qq.v.). The great bulk, however, comprise a retelling of the Ram and Krishna legends and a lengthy series of diverting anecdotes, mainly tales of the ways of women (the *Trīā Charitra* [q.v.]). Most of the collection is written in the Braj language (q.v.), with little in Punjabi (q.v.). The script, however, is Gurmukhi (q.v.). *See also* BENATI CHAUPAI; CHANDI CHARITRA; CHANDI KI VAR; CHAUBIS AUTAR; GIAN PRABODH; HIKAYAT; PAKHYAN CHARITRA; SHASTAR NAM-MALA; TEN SAVAYYAS.

DASHMESH (DASMESH). The 'Tenth Lord,' Guru Gobind Singh (q.v.).

DASHMESH REGIMENT. An extremist anti-government Sikh organization which functioned for some years following the banning of the All-India Sikh Students' Federation (q.v.) in 1984. It claimed responsibility for several assassinations.

DASTAR BANDANA. The turban-tieing ceremony which may be performed when a boy is thirteen. In the presence of the Guru Granth Sahib (q.v.), the boy's father or a village elder ties on a first turban.

DASU (b. 1524). The elder of Guru Angad's (q.v.) two sons. He refused to accept his father's appointment of Amar Das (q.v.) as third Guru, but tradition relates that he was soon reconciled.

DASVANDH (DASAUNDH). A tithe, the portion of one's income that is given for community service. Gifts to a gurdwara (q.v.) are an example, frequently donated before the Guru Granth Sahib (q.v.) upon entry and thence into the Guru's **golak** (treasure-chest). Its distinction from **dān** (q.v.) (charity) is not clear, some saying that **dān** is included in **dasvandh** and some saying it is separate.

DATU (1537–1628). Guru Angad's (q.v.) younger son who, tradition relates, remained unreconciled to his father's successors until the time of Guru Arjan (q.v.).

DAULAT KHAN LODI (d. 1526). Nanak (q.v.), as a young man, worked in Sultanpur (q.v.) for a person called Daulat Khan. It seems likely that this was Daulat Khan Lodi, later governor of Lahore (q.v.) under Sultan Sikandar Lodi.

DAYA SINGH RAHIT-NAMA *see* RAHIT-NAMA DAYA SINGH.

DAYAL (1783–1855). Founder of the Nirankari sect (q.v.). Baba Dayal was born in Rawalpindi into a family of sahaj-dhari Khatris (qq.v.). During the later years of Maharaja Ranjit Singh (q.v.) and his successors he preached that contemporary Sikhs had strayed from the path of **nām simaraṇ** (q.v.) and instead had adopted Hindu practices.

DAYAL DAS (d.1675). An elder brother of Mani Singh (q.v.), one of three Sikhs executed in Delhi with Guru Tegh Bahadur (q.v.). *See also* MATI DAS; SATI DAS.

DEATH CEREMONY *see* FUNERAL.

DEGH TEGH FATEH. 'Victory by the grace of the Guru to the wielder of the sword,' a slogan of the eighteenth-century Khalsa (q.v.). In the eighteenth century the **degh** or **deg** (cooking-vessel) symbolized the langar (q.v.) which in turn symbolized the grace of the Guru to a casteless society. **Tegh** (or **teg**) meant the sword and **fateh** victory.

DELHI. Sikh history has frequently involved Delhi. Guru Har Krishan (q.v.) died there; Guru Tegh Bahadur (q.v.) was executed there; two of Guru Gobind Singh's widows remained there for several years; and during the late eighteenth century Sikh raids assailed the city. Several important gurdwaras (q.v.) are located in Delhi or its environs and are administered by the Delhi Sikh Gurdwara Management Committee, separate from the SGPC in Amritsar (qq.v.). The 1984 anti-Sikh disturbances which followed the assassination of Mrs. Gandhi were largely centered on the twin cities of Delhi and New Delhi, and many Sikhs were killed. *See also* BANGLA SAHIB GURDWARA; RAKAB-GANJ GURDWARA; SIS GANJ.

DELHI SIKH GURDWARA MANAGEMENT COMMITTEE. The body set up by the Delhi Sikh Gurdwaras Act of 1971 to manage gurdwaras (q.v.) and gurdwara property within the union territory of Delhi. The legislation was modelled on the 1925 Sikh Gurdwaras Act (q.v.), and the Committee it authorized is similar to the SGPC (q.v.). One difference is that only Amrit-dharis and Kes-dharis (qq.v.) are entitled to vote for the Delhi Committee, not Sahaj-dharis (q.v.).

DERA (DEHRA). Encampment. The dwelling place of a sant (q.v.).

DERA BABA NANAK. A small town previously called Pakhoke, located in Gurdaspur District on the left bank of the Ravi. It is immediately across the river from Nanak's village of Kartarpur (qq.v.), and much of the land belongs to his Bedi (q.v.) descendants. One of the gurdwaras (q.v.) has in its possession chola sahib, an old cotton cloak with Arabic inscriptions from the Qur'an on it. This is traditionally believed to have been worn by Nanak during his visit to Mecca and Medina. It is said that after having been held by his four successors, it passed to a descendant who kept it as a sacred relic. In 1895 attention was drawn to the chola by Ghulam Ahmad, founder of the Ahmadiyah movement, as evidence that Nanak was really a Muslim.

DERA SAHIB (GURU ARJAN). The gurdwara in Lahore (q.v.) which marks the death of Guru Arjan (q.v.) at the hands of the Mughals in 1606. *See also* MUGHAL DYNASTY.

DESA SINGH RAHIT-NAMA *see* RAHIT-NAMA DESA SINGH.

DEVI WORSHIP. For the Sikhs of the eighteenth century, the goddess Devi clearly had a considerable fascination, and much modern Singh Sabha (q.v.) scholarship has gone into disproving a tenacious tradition that Guru Gobind Singh, prior to inaugurating the Khalsa (qq.v.), made a sacrifice to her on the slopes of Naina Devi. Tales contained in the Dasam Granth (q.v.) and other sources also bear witness to this fascination. The explanation may be related to the Guru's conviction that physical force was necessary to restore a moral society and that he had been chosen for this purpose. As God had chosen her, so now had he been chosen to restore the balance of society. Devi worship was practiced by many rural Sikhs and Hindus in the eighteenth and nineteenth centuries. She also appears under various other names (Durga, Kali, Kalka, etc). *See also* BHAGAUTI.

DHADI. An itinerant singer of Sikh ballads and narrator of the heroic Sikh tradition. Usually working in pairs, dhadis accompanied their songs or narration with dhads (small hand-held drumlets).

DHANNA. A Jat bhagat (qq.v.), traditionally born in 1415 in Rajasthan and a disciple of Ramanand (q.v.). Four works by Dhanna are recorded in the Adi Granth.

DHARAM-RAJ. Yam (q.v.), the god of the dead, in his role of the divine arbiter of the fate of each individual.

DHARAM-SALA. The room or building which formed the center of the early Panth (q.v.). It was used for worship, congregational assembly, discourse, the singing of devotional songs, or any other religious purpose. The term was evidently used throughout the period of the Gurus, but during the eighteenth and nineteenth centuries it gradually gave way to **gurduārā** (anglicized as 'gurdwara' [q.v.]) which was previously used only for locations associated with one of the Gurus. As the term gurdwara was expanded to include dharam-sala, the meaning of the latter word came to be attached to a hospice attached to a gurdwara for travellers or visitors. The custodian of the early dharam-sala was called a dharam-salia.

DHARAM-YUDH. A 'war in defense of righteousness.' A major campaign of the Akali Dal (q.v.) may be termed a dharam-yudh.

DHARMA (DHARAM). The duties to be performed by any particular caste. In modern Punjabi **dharam** has been used as a translation for 'religion.'

DHIR MAL (b. 1627). Elder son of Gurditta (q.v.) and eldest grandson of Guru Hargobind (q.v.). Gurditta predeceased Hargobind, but although by this time the line of Gurus was firmly fixed in Hargobind's line, Dhir Mal was not considered suitable to be the seventh Guru. With his Sodhi family he resided in Kartarpur ([q.v.] located in Jalandhar District), and in 1643 he received a revenue-free grant from the Mughal emperor Shah Jahan who was evidently seeking to sow discord in the Panth (q.v.). His loyalties were diverging markedly from his grandfather Hargobind who was confined to Kiratpur in the Shivalik Hills (qq.v.) and, allied to the Mughals, he proved a growing menace to the followers of the orthodox line of Gurus. Hargobind, before he died, therefore chose as his successor Dhir Mal's younger brother, Har Rai (q.v.). *See also* DHIR MAL'S OPPOSITION; GURU-VANS.

DHIR MAL'S OPPOSITION. Dhir Mal was already hostile to orthodox Sikhs under his grandfather Guru Hargobind (q.v.), and this increased when he was passed over as Hargobind's successor. He was able to detach an indeterminate number of Sikhs from the orthodox line, particularly in the area around Kartarpur. From his father or grandfather he had secured possession of what purports to be the original copy of the Adi Granth (q.v.) and used it to buttress his claims to the office of Guru. The manuscript still resides in Kartarpur. After the accession of Tegh Bahadur (q.v.) in 1664, his opposition contributed to Tegh Bahadur having to leave the plains and withdraw to the Shivalik Hills (q.v.). His antagonism and that of his successor continued into the eighteenth century, and at the founding of the Khalsa (q.v.) the Dhirmalias were included in the Panj Mel (q.v.). Only in the second half of the eighteenth century was the exclusion of the Sodhi family of Kartarpur lifted. The successor who won this reprieve was probably Vadbhag Singh, famous as a banisher of evil spirits who initiated a cult which continues to the present day. *See also* KARTARPUR BIR.

DHUAN. 'Smoke'; hearth; a place where fire is always kept burning. The controlling centers of certain ascetic orders in India were referred to as dhuans, including several of the Udasi orders (q.v.). There were four Udasi dhuans, each controlling certain preaching areas. These were eastern India (with the main center at Nanakmata), western Punjab and Kashmir, Malwa, and Doaba (qq.v.). *See also* AKHARA; BAKHSHISH.

DHUR KI BANI. Original message; original text; revealed text.

DIASPORA *see* MIGRATION.

DIP SINGH (1682–1757). A celebrated Sikh martyr, killed in battle by the Afghans. He is believed to have been initiated into the Khalsa by Guru Gobind Singh (qq.v.) and to have assisted him in transcribing the scriptures during the period in Damdama (q.v.). Tradition records that while there he also founded the Damdami Taksal (q.v.). He fought for the Sikhs during the first half of the eighteenth century, latterly as a member of the Shahid misl (q.v.). In retirement at Damdama, he was roused by the sacrilege done to Harimandir Sahib (q.v.) by the Afghans in 1757 and with a small army marched on Amritsar (q.v.), vowing to cleanse the sacred gurdwara (q.v.) or die in the attempt. Several kilometers short of the city, his army was met by a much larger one, and in the battle which ensued his head was severed. At this point a divided tradition takes over. According to one version he held his head in his hand and fought on to Amritsar, dying when he reached the city. A second claims that he hurled his head over the intervening distance, landing it in the precincts of Harmandir Sahib. A third combines the first two. With severed head, Dip Singh fought as far as Ramsar on the outskirts of Amritsar and then threw his head the remaining distance to Harimandir Sahib. A hexagonal stone set in the parikarama (q.v.) marks the spot where it is believed to have fallen.

DITT SINGH (1853–1901). Like many Sikhs of the late nineteenth century he was a supporter of the Arya Samaj (q.v.), but renounced it in 1888 and turned instead to the Singh Sabha (q.v.). He became an influential leader of the Lahore group and thus of the Tat Khalsa (q.v.). As author, journalist, and preacher he did much to formulate and popularize Tat Khalsa ideals, writing more than forty books covering Sikh doctrine, history, martyrology, and social reform. He laid great stress on the difference between Sikhs and Hindus, endeavoring to persuade ordinary Sikhs to abandon folk religion in favour of what he regarded as pure Sikhism. Ditt Singh was a rare example of a Mazhabi Sikh (q.v.) who was an important leader of the Sikhs.

DIVALI. Festival of Light, held on the day of the new moon in the month of Kattak (October/November). The occasion has long been celebrated by Hindus with the theme of material wealth. Accounts are closed for the year, houses are cleaned, sweets are distributed, and countless lights are lit at night. Sikhs impart a distinctive meaning to it by commemorating the release of Guru Hargobind (q.v.) from Gwalior where he had been imprisoned by the Mughal emperor Jahangir. Celebrations center on Harimandir Sahib (q.v.) which is illuminated for the occasion.

DIVAN. A royal court; a Sikh congregation; Sikh worship; a collection of Persian poems by Nand Lal (q.v.).

DIVINATION. Divination has been widely practiced by the Panth (q.v.) and various methods are still used, commonly involving the Adi Granth (q.v.). Numerous usages are recorded in Sikh history and tradition, Ranjit Singh (q.v.) being a firm believer. It is difficult to draw a clear line between superstition (which met with Tat Khalsa [q.v.] disapproval) and faith, as for example with the practice of **hukam laiṇa** (q.v.). *See also* ASTROLOGY.

DIVINE NAME *see* NAM.

DIVINE WORD *see* SHABAD (SABAD).

DIVORCE. The contemporary Rahit (q.v.) frowns upon divorce, but marriage breakdown is tacitly acknowledged, and in such cases Sikhs are free to divorce. Sikhs have no personal Code, and when divorce is sought in India it must be by the Hindu Code.

DOABA. The plains territory bounded by the Beas and Satluj rivers, one of three areas into which central Punjab is divided. The inhabitants are known as Doabis. *See also* MALWA; MANJH.

DOGRA FAMILY. A family of Dogra Rajputs from Jammu who exercised substantial power under Maharaja Ranjit Singh (q.v.) and during the turbulent years immediately following his death in 1839. The most important members were Dhian Singh Dogra (chief minister of Ranjit Singh, assassinated in 1843), Gulab Singh Dogra (who, for aiding the British, received in 1846 the state of Kashmir), a third brother Suchet Singh Dogra, and Hira Singh Dogra (son of Dhian Singh and chief minister from 1843 until his assassination in 1844). All were murdered except Gulab Singh. Although they bore the name Singh the family were Hindus. *See also* SANDHAN-VALIA FAMILY.

DOLI. A litter used for women. A bride used to leave home in one. Today she commonly leaves in an automobile, but departure with the groom is still described as 'departure of the doli.'

DOWRY. There are variant views concerning dowries (**dāj**) in the Panth (q.v.), and the issue is a very complicated one. *Sikh Rahit Maryādā* (q.v.) opposes it, but the injunction (when obeyed) singles out only cash payments for condemnation. This allows expensive gifts in kind and consequently leaves the way open for a transfer of varying amounts of property at marriage from the bride's family to that of the groom. As such it continues to underline the importance attached to boys rather than girls. The Namdharis (q.v.) are explicit about banning all dowries, but their clear example is not always followed by orthodox Sikhs. During the period of Jarnail Singh Bhindranvale (q.v.) dowries were forcibly abolished for all Sikhs. With his death, however, they have shown clear signs of returning. For Sikhs they continue to present a problem, and it is impossible to generalize the orthodox response. *See also* ABORTION; GENDER.

DUBIDHA. 'The other'; that which is not eternal; **māyā** (q.v.).

DUKH NIVARAN. Patiala's leading gurdwara (q.v.), built in memory of a visit by Guru Tegh Bahadur (q.v.).

DULEEP SINGH (1837–93). The youngest of Maharaja Ranjit Singh's (q.v.) seven children. He was placed on the throne when his half-brother Sher Singh (q.v.) was assassinated in 1843 but deposed by the British when they annexed the Punjab in 1849. Placed in the care of an English couple, he became a Christian and was taken to England where he became a favorite of Queen Victoria. He received the estate of Elveden in Norfolk but found his expenses outrunning his capacity to pay, with little assistance forthcoming from his English patrons. In the Punjab the Kukas (q.v.) were astir with rumors of his return, and in this regard were greatly encouraged by Thakur Singh Sandhanvalia (q.v.). Thakur Singh corresponded with him, and in 1866 he set out for India, but the British intercepted him in Aden and sent him back to England. In Aden he underwent formal reconversion to the Sikh faith. In 1893 he died in a hotel room in Paris and was buried in Elveden. His grave now serves as a shrine for the Sikhs in England. His name is correctly spelled Dalip Singh.

DYAL SINGH MAJITHIA (1849–98). Founder of *The Tribune* newspaper and, although a Sikh, a member of the Brahma

Samaj. His death roused controversy when the Punjab Supreme Court, in opposition to his widow's claims regarding his will, declared him to have been a Hindu.

E

EIGHTEENTH CENTURY HISTORY. The eighteenth century was of critical importance for Sikhs in general and for the Khalsa (q.v.) in particular. It began with the foundation of the Khalsa, probably in 1699 and ended with the triumph of Ranjit Singh (q.v.) in 1800. Between these two dates the Sikhs went through a period of revolt under Banda (q.v.) followed by decades of suppression. This was succeeded by the invasions of Ahmad Shah Abdali (q.v.) which Sikhs opposed with increasing success, leading to the creation of the misls (q.v.) and the establishment of their authority over much of the Punjab. With the external enemy removed, the misldars began fighting amongst themselves. Eventually one of them, Ranjit Singh, rose above all the rest and in 1801 was installed as Maharaja. To this period the Khalsa owes many of its heroes, martyrs, and enemies. It also owes some distinctive features to it. During the century its Rahit (q.v.) was evolving, and major items in the Rahit can be traced to particular characteristics of the period. Some of these reflect the social background, others the political. The Sikhs, for example, were fighting against enemies who were Muslim, whether Mughals or Afghans, and items which derived from this conflict were clearly written into the early rahit-namas (q.v.) .

EK-OANKAR *see* IK-OANKAR.

EMINABAD *see* SAIDPUR.

EQUALITY. One of the prime virtues of the Sikh faith, particularly of the Khalsa (q.v.). As opposed to the emphasis on caste differences of traditional Hindu society, Sikhs maintain that within the Panth (q.v.) there is complete equality. Although most Sikhs continue to observe caste (q.v.) in terms of marriage arrangments, those who are true to the Khalsa ideal insist that this in no way obstructs their acceptance of equality. A few Sikhs do draw other distinctions on the basis of caste, but on sacred ground (which means in the gurdwaras [q.v.]) the ideal is certainly maintained. Anyone can attend a gurdwara or a langar (q.v.), and those who do must sit in status-free rows. Karah prasad (q.v.) and langar food are distributed indiscriminately; all recipients of Khalsa initiation are required to drink from the same vessel.

EXCOMMUNICATION. Since the Shiromani Gurdwara Prabandhak Committee (q.v.) was constituted in 1925 it (or its President) has on occasion formally ejected from the Panth (q.v.) some person who is held to have seriously violated its religious or political interests. Such decisions are routed through the Jathedar of Akal Takhat (qq.v.). An offender is an unrepentant tanakhahia (q.v.), and in English the action is called excommunication. An early example was Teja Singh Bhasaur of the Panch Khalsa Divan (qq.v.). Another was G.B. Singh who published a book on the manuscripts of the Adi Granth (q.v.). When an individual is excommunicated, the opportunity may be provided to confess errors and perform humiliating punishment. When this has been completed the offender is re-admitted to the Panth. *See also* BLASPHEMY; TANAKHAH.

F

FAIZULAPURIA MISL *see* SINGHPURIA MISL.

FAQIR. 'Poor man'; Muslim renunciant. The word is loosely used to designate a Sufi (q.v.) and also a non-Muslim renunciant.

FARID (1173–1266). A famous Sufi (q.v.) who lived in the Punjab and is buried in Pak Pattan where his tomb is still the object of reverent devotion. Hindus and Sikhs as well as Muslims have been greatly attached to the compositions attributed to Sheikh Farid for the sant spirit which they incorporate. Four of his **shabads** and 130 of his **shaloks** (qq.v.) have been included in the Adi Granth (q.v.). Nanak is said by the janam-sakhis (q.v.) to have discoursed with him. This is not possible, but it is quite credible that he met the incumbent pir (q.v.) in the line descending from Farid. *See also* SANT TRADITION.

FARIDKOT TIKA. The Faridkot Commentary on the Adi Granth (q.v.). When Trumpp (q.v.) published his translation of a part of the Adi Granth in 1877 Sikhs were deeply insulted by its introduction. In the same year Raja Bikram Singh of Faridkot (q.v.) commissioned Giani Badan Singh Sekhvan to produce an authoritative commentary. The task proved to be much more difficult than had been foreseen, but three volumes were finally published in 1905 and 1906, and later the fourth and final volume was produced. The collection was the first example of a published commentary, but the Faridkot Tika never attained authoritative status and was soon superseded by other exegetical works.

FATEH SHAH. The Raja of Garhwal against whom Gobind Singh (q.v.), in alliance with the Raja of Sirmur, fought the battle of Bhangani (q.v.) in 1688.

FATEH SINGH, SANT (1911–72). A Jat (q.v.) from Ganganagar District who was brought into the Akali Dal by Tara Singh (qq.v.). In 1960 he organized a massive campaign for Punjabi Suba (q.v.) against the Punjab government and in 1961 took the disgraced Tara Singh's place as leader of the Akalis. Punjabi Suba was eventually granted in 1966.

FATEHGARH SAHIB. Gurdwara Fatehgarh Sahib in Sirhind marks the spot where the two younger sons of Guru Gobind Singh (q.v.) were executed by being bricked up alive. *See also* SAHIB-ZADE.

FATEH-NAMA. The 'triumphant letter.' A Persian poem of twenty-four short stanzas attributed to Guru Gobind Singh (q.v.) said to have been written in Machhiwara shortly after the evacuation of Anandpur (q.v.) in December 1704 and addressed to the Mughal emperor Aurangzeb (q.v.). It was later followed by *Zafar-nāmā* (q.v.).

FEMALE INFANTICIDE. Practiced among certain sections of the Sikhs prior to its suppression by the British in the late 19th century. Explicit directions prohibiting it have been commonly written into the rahit-namas (q.v.), including *Sikh Rahit Maryādā* (q.v.). Boys were much preferred to girls, with the result that midwives were sometimes instructed to kill the child if it was female. This was done by turning the newborn baby's face into the placenta so that she suffocated in her mother's blood. Amongst Sikhs the practice was particularly prevalent with the Bedis (q.v.), a result of their high social and ritual status. It was essential to marry daughters to a higher sub-caste (**got** [q.v.]), but because they occupied the highest rank of their section of the **zāt** (q.v.) the Bedis had nowhere to go. Often they preferred infanticide as the solution. The custom was practiced throughout India as a whole, not just among Sikhs. There is little sound evidence for its continuation today. *See also* CASTE.

FEMINISM *see* GENDER and PATRIARCHY.

FIVE. In common with other traditions in India and beyond, the number five (**pāñch** or **pañj**) was of particular significance for the Sikhs. At the inauguration of the Khalsa (q.v.) Guru Gobind Singh (q.v.) chose five Sikhs to form the foundation of the new order; today members of the Khalsa must wear the Five Ks (q.v.). Many other important items are grouped in fives. *See terms beginning with* FIVE *and* PANJ.

FIVE ABLUTIONS. Washing of hands, feet, and mouth preceding **nam simaraṇ** (q.v.) or entry of a gurdwara (q.v.).

FIVE EVIL DEEDS. Lying, calumny, evil gossip, misappropriation, and ingratitude.

FIVE EVIL IMPULSES. Lust, anger, covetousness, attachment to worldly things, and pride. Also known as the **pañj dūt**.

FIVE Ks. The **pañj kakār** or **pañj kakke,** five external symbols which all amrit-dhari Sikhs (q.v.) must wear, so called because each begins with 'k.' The five are **kes** or **kesh** (uncut hair), **kaṅghā** (comb), **karā** (iron or steel ring round the wrist), **kirpān** (sword or dagger), and **kachh** or **kachhahirā** (shorts which must not come below the knee) (qq.v). The time of introduction of these five symbols is obscure. Tradition insists it was at the inauguration of the Khalsa (q.v.). At the inauguration, however, only three of the items were named (**kes, kirpān** and **kachh**). Although there are early references to 'five weapons' (q.v.) which the Khalsa Sikh is expected to bear, the **pañj kakke** are not mentioned at this stage. A reference in a later version of the *Chaupā Siṅgh Rahit-nāmā* lists five items, but in addition to the original three it names **bāṇī** and **sādh saṅgat** (qq.v.). Only in the nineteenth century does definite mention of five items beginning with 'k' occur, and only with the influence of the Tat Khalsa (q.v.) does the custom receive explicit inclusion in the Rahit (q.v.). The one piece of evidence which seems to deny this is a **hukam-nāmā** (q.v.) which Guru Gobind Singh is said to have directed to his Kabul Sikhs in S.1756 (1699 CE). This **hukam-nāmā** must be regarded as spurious, as it possesses neither the initials nor seal of the Guru and conflicts with other contemporary evidence which clearly indicates only three items.

FIVE Ks: PURPOSE. The purpose of the Five Ks (q.v.) is obscure, although reasons can be suggested for the earliest three. The **kes** (q.v.) may be a borrowing from the conventions of the Jats (q.v.) who by this time were strongly dominant in the Panth (q.v.), and the **kirpān** and **kachh** (qq.v.) were appropriate for a people preparing to fight. Their introduction into the rahit-namas (q.v.) seems not to have been linked to their initial 'k.' At this early stage they rank with other conventions of the Khalsa (q.v.), such as the ban on the hookah (q.v.). Reasons for the choice of the Five Ks are, of course, frequently suggested in modern apologetics. Today they are absolutely mandatory for all amrit-dhari Sikhs. The five (or some of them) are also commonly worn by kes-dhari Sikhs (q.v.).

FIVE LOVED ONES *see* PANJ PIARE.

FIVE SINS. Theft, fornication, gambling, drunkenness, and lying.

FIVE WEAPONS. The early Khalsa was commanded to pay particular respect to the following five weapons and when practicable to carry them: sword (**kirpān**), bow (**kamān**), musket (**bandūk**), a kind of dagger (**kaṭār**), and either lance (**nezā** or **barchhā**) or quoit (**chakkar**).

FOLKLORE. Throughout its history the Panth (q.v.) has included a large segment believing in elements from popular Punjabi culture. These include such things as benign and malevolent spirits, omens, and miracles wrought by long-dead saints. The Tat Khalsa segment of the Singh Sabha movement (qq.v.) regarded such beliefs as rank superstition. The Sanatan Sikhs (q.v.), however, were much more tolerant of them. In the struggle between the two groups the Tat Khalsa clearly emerged as victor, but the essentially intellectual view of the faith which they projected has not caused folk belief to die out. The Tat Khalsa view strongly dominates the presentation of Sikhism through literature. Folklore is, however, abundantly present in popular beliefs such as those mentioned above or in legends such as those of Hir Ranjha or Sohni Mahival.

FORTY SAVED ONES *see* CHALI MUKTE.

FUNDAMENTALISM. The question of whether there are fundamentalists among the Sikhs causes problems as the word actually has two different meanings. One means those who adhere to an inerrant view of scripture, and the other concerns those who are militants in a political sense. The latter meaning certainly applies to extremist supporters of Khalistan (q.v.), though their number has been considerably diminished in the recent past. The inerrancy of scripture, however, is not an issue amongst Sikhs. There are few historical facts in the Adi Granth (q.v.), and the multitude of hymns praising the **nām** (q.v.) do not present the kind of material which requires a listener or reader to decide whether it is factually right or wrong. The Adi Granth certainly has much to say about truth, but the meaning which should be attached to the words translated as 'truth' is distinctively different from what the term connotes in western thought. The question of fundamentalism is one which has arisen in a western context with specific application to Judaism and Christianity. It does not arise in connection with Sikhism. *See also* SAT.

FUNERAL. Where possible the deceased should be cremated. The corpse should be bathed and clad in clean garments. In the case of an Amrit-dhari (q.v.) all Five Ks (q.v.) are essential. At the cremation ground the funeral pyre should be lit by a son, a relative, or a close friend. When it is ablaze Kirtan Sohila (q.v.) should be sung, followed by a recitation of Ardas (q.v.). After the cremation a path (q.v.) should be commenced, preferably to be completed within ten days. When the pyre has cooled, the ashes are gathered and either deposited in running water or buried at the place of cremation. Depositing the ashes in the Ganga, Satluj, or Ravi rivers is not approved.

G

GADDI. 'Cushion'; seat; throne; position of authority.

GAMBLING. Gambling is prohibited by *Sikh Rahit Maryādā* (q.v.).

GANGA (d. 1628). Mata Ganga, the wife of Arjan and the mother of Hargobind (qq.v.).

GANGU-SHAHI. Gangu Das is said to have been a manji (q.v.) of Guru Amar Das (q.v.), preaching in the Shivalik Hills (q.v.). His great-grandson Javahar Singh banded his followers together as the Gangu-shahis and for a time commanded a sizeable force in the hills.

GARJA SINGH (d. 1739). The Ranghreta (q.v.) companion of Bota Singh (q.v.), killed by soldiers of Zakarya Khan in 1739.

GENDER. The Sikh faith does not recognize differences in gender. Women have the same religious obligations as men and receive the same rewards. They are entitled to read the Guru Granth Sahib (q.v.) in public, to be members of the Panj Piare (q.v.), and in general to discharge any of the roles which might be construed as male. Sikhism has, however, been located in a society which observes patriarchal control, with the result that in some important respects the operative observances of Sikhs differ from the normative prescriptions of their faith. Very few Sikh women appear in Sikh history, and today most major Sikh institutions are overwhelmingly male in membership and control. This gender difference is defended on the grounds that only men can provide their women with necessary protection. Signs of change are appearing, particularly among Sikhs living overseas. There is, however, a considerable distance to travel before gender equality is attained. This applies in particular to rural Sikhs, where gender ranking is determined in large part by the ownership of property. Jats (q.v.) customarily leave land only to their sons. *See also* DOWRY; PATRIARCHY.

GENDER OF GOD. Punjabi and Sant Bhasha (q.v.) are more suitable languages for referring to God than English, though they are not perfect. They lack the explicitly male and female pronouns; verb endings denote gender, and the agreement required by an adjective usually indicates the gender of the noun to which the adjective is attached. Similarly the use of terms which can be translated as 'Lord,' 'Master,' etc. will frequently imply that God is thought to be masculine. Referring to him/her by masculine verbs, pronouns, or titles may be merely held to demonstrate the weakness of any language which does not make provision for a common gender. It may also demonstrate patterns of dominance in the society which uses any particular language. Punjabi society certainly maintains concepts of male dominance, and references to God reflect this. Sikhs are, however, much better placed in this regard than (for example) Christians. In Christian usage God is traditionally masculine, and the English language renders this explicitly. In the Sant Bhasha of the Adi Granth (q.v.) God is normally left undefined in gender terms, and in some places he/she (or the mystical Guru [q.v.]) is identified with conglomerates which include feminine as well as masculine. In *Japjī* 5 the divine Guru is Shiva, Vishnu, and Brahma (who may arguably be regarded as masculine), but he/she is also Parvati (who is definitely feminine). Akal Purakh (q.v.) is, Sikhs maintain, far above all such distinctions, and the Adi Granth generally supports them.

GENDER OF GOD: TRANSLATIONS. The real difficulty concerning the gender of God occurs when the scripture is translated into a language such as English. Here the problem is inescapable, and partly because Christians had until recently always regarded God as male, he/she has almost always been rendered as masculine in Sikh translations. One solution is to insist that the scripture never be translated. Portions may be translated as aids to understanding, but the Adi Granth (q.v.) itself must remain inviolable. Others insist that this must necessarily rob those who do not comprehend the original Adi Granth language of the deeper meaning which the scripture conveys. This particularly applies to people raised outside India, and it is inevitably in the West that the rumbles of discontent may be heard. The problem is serious.

GHADR MOVEMENT. A revolutionary movement, partly Hindu but mainly Sikh in membership, which arose among immigrant laborers to the west coast of the United States and Canada shortly before the First World War. In 1913 a newspaper called *Ghadr* (Revolution) was begun in Stockton, California, and was soon circulating in many countries. Sympathies were with the Germans, and men volunteered to return to the Punjab to take up the cause. The Punjab, however, was scarcely ready for revolution, and by 1915 the movement there had collapsed. An effort to ship arms from the United States similarly failed. The United States government tolerated the movement only as long as it was neutral in the war. When it entered the war in 1917, the Ghadr movement ceased.

GHAHNAIYA RAM (BHAI GHAHNAIYA). A servant of Tegh Bahadur and Gobind Singh (qq.v.), who earned particular commendation from the latter for serving water during the battle of Anandpur to the Guru's wounded enemies as well as to those of his own troops. Followers of Bhai Ghahnaiya later formed the Seva Panth (q.v.). His name is also spelled Kahnaiya, Kanhaiya, Kanaiya, or Kanahiya.

GIAN PRABODH. A section of the Dasam Granth (q.v.) consisting mainly of stories from the *Mahābhārata*.

GIAN SINGH, GIANI (1822–1921). A Nirmala (q.v.) and disciple of Tara Singh Narotam (q.v.) who achieved considerable prominence as a traditional historian. Gian Singh combined Singh Sabha concerns with the gur-bilas tradition which preceded it (qq.v). His *Panth Prakāsh* (1880) and his lengthy *Tavarīkh Gurū Khālsā* (1891–1919) are still extensively consulted.

GIANI. A wise or learned man.

GIANI SCHOOL. The hereditary Gianis were those exegetes of the Adi Granth (q.v.) who did not follow the strongly Vedantic cast of Nirmala thought (q.v.). According to tradition, some Sikhs were appointed to interpret the scripture by Guru Gobind Singh (q.v.). It was in the nineteenth century, however, that certain families acquired reputations for teaching and interpretation, particularly in Amritsar. Their most influential pupil was Santokh Singh (q.v.).

GIDDHA. A Punjabi dance performed by women or girls.

GOBIND SINGH, GURU (1666–1708). Tenth and last personal Guru of the Sikhs. He was born in Patna (q.v.) as Gobind Rai, the only child of the ninth Guru, Tegh Bahadur (q.v.). At the age of five he was brought to his father's town of Anandpur (q.v.), situated on the northeastern edge of the Punjab where the Shivalik Hills (q.v.) meet the plains. There he was educated in Sanskrit and Persian, acquiring the arts of both poetry and warfare. In 1675 his father was executed in Delhi by the Mughal emperor Aurangzeb (q.v.), an event which must have made a considerable impression on the child. He succeeded to the title of Guru and for several more years continued his education in the Shivalik Hills. It was as the ruler of a small Shivalik state that he grew to manhood and participated in wars against the other chieftains of the hills. Hunting was a sport in which he delighted. Following the creation of the Khalsa (q.v.), the Guru was again attacked in Anandpur, this time by the other Shivalik chieftains assisted by troops sent by the Mughal governor of Sirhind. In 1704 he was compelled to evacuate his fort, losing two of his sons in the process, with the remaining two cruelly executed later in Sirhind by being bricked up alive. Gobind Singh escaped to southern Punjab where he inflicted a defeat on his pursuers at Muktsar (q.v.). He then stayed in nearby Damdama (q.v.) and is said by tradition to have been occupied with the preparation of the final version of the Adi Granth (q.v.). After the Mughal emperor Aurangzeb died in 1707, Gobind Singh agreed to accompany his successor, Bahadur Shah, to the south. There, in Nander (q.v.) on the banks of the Godavari river, he was assassinated in 1708, possibly by an agent of the Mughal administrator of Sirhind. Guru Gobind Singh ranks as the supreme exemplar of all that a Sikh of the Khalsa (a Gursikh [q.v.]) should be. His bravery is admired, his nobility esteemed, his goodness profoundly revered. The duty of every Khalsa member must be to strive to follow his path and in their lives perform works that would be worthy of him. *See also* BHANGANI; DASAM GRANTH; DASHMESH; JAITA; KALGIDHAR; KHALSA INAUGURATION; MUGHAL DYNASTY; TRADITION.

GOBIND SINGH'S DOCTRINE: Gobind Singh (q.v.) regarded himself as the legitimate Guru (q.v.), the only true successor of his nine predecessors; he accepted the emphasis on the divine Name (q.v.) which had descended from Nanak (q.v.). There was, however, a further development of his belief in God. From time to time the forces of good and evil veer out of balance as the strength of the latter increases alarmingly. God then intervenes in human history to set the balance right. Particular individuals are chosen to act as agents of God, combatting with physical strength the forces of evil which have acquired too much power. Gobind Singh believed that he was such an agent and that the Panth (q.v.) must be prepared to fight under him. Overcoming the dispersed nature of the Panth under the masands (q.v.) was evidently a reason for the creation of the Khalsa (q.v.).

GOBIND SINGH'S FAMILY. Guru Gobind Singh (q.v.) had three wives. The first was Jito (q.v.), married in 1677 and mother of Jujhar Singh, Zorawar Singh, and Fateh Singh. The second was Sundari (q.v.), married in 1684 and mother of his oldest son Ajit Singh. The third was Sahib Kaur (q.v.), married in 1700 and without issue. *See also* SAHIB-ZADE.

GOD *see* AKAL PURAKH and VAHIGURU.

GOINDVAL. A town on the right bank of the Beas river near its confluence with the Satluj, by tradition named for a man called Gobind who had begun building it in honor of Guru Angad (q.v.). Angad declined to live in the new village, sending instead his faithful disciple Amar Das (q.v.) to reside there. The town became Amar Das's center when he succeeded Angad as Guru.

GOINDVAL POTHIS. The earliest known recension of the Adi Granth (q.v.). According to tradition Guru Amar Das (q.v.) had the works of the first three Gurus, together with those of the bhagats (q.v.), copied out by his grandson Sahans Ram in a series of three or (more likely) four pothis (volumes). A pothi, which purports to be an original one, was in the possession of the late Baba Dalip Chand of Mandi Darapur in Hoshiarpur District and is now held by his family in Jalandhar. Another, also claiming originality, was with the family of the late Bhagat Singh of Patiala and is now in Pinjore. Both families are Bhallas, the sub-caste to which Guru Amar Das belonged. Guru Arjan (q.v.) evidently had access to the collection when preparing the later recension of the Adi Granth. The text of the Kartarpur version (q.v.) is very close to that of the *Goindval Pothis,* particularly the works of the three Gurus. Although the two extant volumes are certainly old, the question of their being original copies remains to be definitively proven. The collection owes its name to Goindval (q.v.) as it was compiled there. Because the manuscripts were subsequently held by Mohan, son of Amar Das, they are also commonly known as the Mohan Pothis.

GOLDEN TEMPLE *see* HARIMANDIR SAHIB (AMRITSAR).

GOLDEN TEMPLE ASSAULT *see* RECENT HISTORY.

GORAKHNATH. An historical figure who lived in India, probably between the ninth and twelfth centuries CE. Virtually everything that is related of him is legend, but it seems that he must have been a very important religious figure. Guru Gorakhnath is acknowledged as the principal figure in the Nath (q.v.) movement. He appears anachronistically in numerous janam-sakhi (q.v.) incidents as an interlocutor of Nanak (q.v.).

GOT (GOTRA). Exogamous group within an endogamous **zat** (q.v.); a sub-caste.

GRACE. 'Grace' is expressed by several terms, of which **nadar** or **nazar** is a key one. Akal Purakh (q.v.) imparts grace when his glance (**nazar**) falls upon the beneficiary. Other terms meaning grace are **prasād** (q.v.), **bakhashīsh, bhānā, daiā (dayā), kirpā (kripā), mihar,** and **taras**. Grace, according to Nanak (q.v.), is essential for spiritual liberation to be secured. The practice of **nām simaraṇ** (q.v.) is certainly necessary, and for this the choice rests with each person. Alone, however, it is not enough. Only by the grace of Akal Purakh through the mediation of the Guru, coupled with the freely-chosen practice of **nām simaraṇ,** can liberation be achieved. *See also* NANAK'S DOCTRINE.

GRAHASTI. A householder; a married person.

GRANTH. 'Book'; the Adi Granth or Guru Granth Sahib (qq.v.).

GRANTHI. The custodian of a gurdwara (q.v.) responsible for its religious services and for upkeep of the building. It is a mistake to call a granthi a 'priest.' A granthi does not normally command high status in Sikh society.

GUGGA PIR. The legendary healer of snake bites, worshipped in the villages of the Punjab by Muslims, Hindus, and Sikhs alike.

GUJARI. The wife of Tegh Bahadur and mother of Gobind Singh (qq.v.). From a Khatri family (q.v.) of Lakhnaur (near Ambala).

GULAB-DASI. A follower of Gulab Das (1809–73), a hymnist who taught Vedantist ideals learnt from the Nirmalas (q.v.). The group enjoyed limited prominence in the late nineteenth century, but appears to be extinct today. Both Jawahir Singh Kapur and Giani Ditt Singh (qq.v.) had Gulab-dasi phases early in their careers.

GULAB-RAIA. A follower of Gulab Rai, great-grandson of Guru Hargobind (q.v.). Gulab Rai accepted initiation into the Khalsa by Guru Gobind Singh but after Gobind Singh's death tried to set himself up as successor. His effort died out early in the eighteenth century.

GURBAKHSH SINGH (d. 1765). A martyr of the Panth (q.v.), killed when he led a tiny force against a large army of Ahmad Shah Abdali (q.v.) which was desecrating Harimandir Sahib (q.v.).

GURBANI. Strictly speaking, gurbani refers only to the Gurus' works recorded in the Adi Granth and Dasam Granth (qq.v.). It can also apply, however, to the bhagat bani (q.v.). *See also* BANI.

GUR-BILAS. Literally 'the Guru's pleasure'; a style of hagiography which focused attention on the heroic qualities of the Gurus (notably the sixth and tenth Gurus). In contrast with the janam-sakhis (q.v.), it stressed the destiny of the Gurus in fighting against the forces of evil (identified with Mughal authority) and their supreme courage in doing so. Gur-bilas works all attach great importance to the story of the goddess Devi as preparation for the founding of the Khalsa (q.v.). *See also* DEVI WORSHIP; GOBIND SINGH'S DOCTRINE.

GURDAS (c.1558-c.1637). Bhai Gurdas is the most famous of all Sikh poets and theologians. Born in Goindval, he was a Khatri of the Bhalla sub-caste (qq.v.) and was related to Guru Amar Das (q.v.). From his earliest days he appears to have been closely associated with the line of orthodox Gurus, serving successively Amar Das, Ram Das, Arjan, and Hargobind (qq.v.). During these years he was a missionary, steward, and personal messenger, his main task in the latter respect being to conduct negotiations with Prithi Chand (q.v.). He was also chosen to act as Arjan's amanuensis when preparing the Adi Granth (q.v.). His puzzled acceptance of the change of atmosphere in the Guru's entourage is spelled out in a famous verse, the fifth Guru having been a man of peace and the sixth Guru surrounding himself with the means of war (*Vār* 26:24). The enduring contribution of Gurdas is his poetry. This comprises 556 brief works in Braj known as kabitts and the much more popular 39 vars in Punjabi (qq.v.). It is upon the latter that his considerable reputation rests. *See also* VARAN BHAI GURDAS.

GURDAS II. There are actually forty vars attributed to Bhai Gurdas (q.v.), and some scholars regard them all as his work. Others treat the fortieth var as the work of a Sindhi poet of the same name who lived in the early eighteenth century. *See also* VARAN BHAI GURDAS.

GURDITTA (1613–38). Oldest son of Guru Hargobind (q.v.). He was being groomed to succeed his father, but predeceased him. Gurditta was apparently attracted by Udasi (q.v.) teachings.

GURDWARA. A place for Sikh worship and community gatherings. Any room or building is constituted a gurdwara by installation of the Guru Granth Sahib (the Adi Granth [qq.v.]) in it. In the Adi Granth the term **gurū duārā** refers to the grace of the Guru, understood as the 'voice' of Akal Purakh (q.v.).

Places associated with the Gurus acquired particular sanctity and as such imparted a special blessing. In this way the single word gurduara (anglicized as 'gurdwara') came to apply to Sikh places of pilgrimage visited in the manner that one visited a tirath (q.v.). During this early period the term used for an ordinary congregational center where a sangat (q.v.) met for such purposes as singing devotional songs was dharam-sala (q.v.). Gradually, during the eighteenth and nineteenth centuries, 'dharam-sala' was abandoned for this purpose and the meaning of 'gurduara' extended to take its place. Two developments produced this change. The first was the attribution of the Guru's authority to the Adi Granth. The second related development was the practice of installing copies of the scripture in dharam-salas. This meant that the means of grace and guidance was now located within the sangat's place of assembly. The place of assembly, formerly a dharam-sala, thus became known as a gurdwara. The gurdwara is a powerful institution in the Panth (q.v.), frequently providing Sikhs with a social center as well as a place of worship. This is particularly the case overseas. *See also* ARCHITECTURE.

GURDWARA CONTROL. Until the end of the nineteenth century the gurdwara (q.v.) served a broad section of the Punjabi community, being commonly controlled by non-Khalsa Sikhs and in some cases providing space for idols (qq.v.). Under the influence of the Tat Khalsa (q.v.) a campaign for cleansing them was initiated, leading to the Gurdwara Reform Movement (q.v.) and final victory in the Sikh Gurdwaras Act of 1925 (q.v.). Virtually all prominent gurdwaras in the Punjab were entrusted to the authority of the Shiromani Gurdwara Prabandhak Committee (q.v.), and with substantial funds flowing in from their estates, control of the SGPC is strongly contested. Within the area covered by the Sikh Gurdwaras Act the major gurdwaras are almost all controlled directly by the SGPC; those of Delhi are under the Delhi Sikh Gurdwara Management Committee. Lesser gurdwaras within these areas are, however, independent and so too are all gurdwaras elsewhere in India and the world. The organization of these gurdwaras is therefore strictly congregational, not dependent on control from above. *See also* AKALI DAL.

GURDWARA PROCEDURE. In a gurdwara (q.v.) worship is led by a reader and three ragis (q.v.). Every person who visits a gurdwara must remove footwear, and feet should be washed if unclean. The head must be covered. On entering the gurdwara he/she bows before the Guru Granth Sahib (q.v.), touching the floor with the forehead. Upon rising he/she may greet the sangat (q.v.) collectively with palms together, saying "Vāhigurū jī kā Khālsā, Vāhigurū jī kī fateh" (q.v.). He/she should then take a seat on the floor and listen to, or participate in, the singing of hymns. When walking around a gurdwara or the Adi Granth, each person should proceed in a clockwise direction. See also PARKASH KARNA; SUKHASAN.

GURDWARA REFORM MOVEMENT. An agitation, lasting from 1920 until 1925, for control of the major Sikh gurdwaras (q.v.) by the Panth (q.v.) rather than by the individual owners who had been granted possession by the British. Before World War I, Sikhs were restive about the control of their gurdwaras, and as soon as the war ended they took action. In 1919 the Central Sikh League (q.v.) was constituted, and it in turn formed the Akali Dal and the Shiromani Gurdwara Prabandhak Committee (qq.v.) in 1920. The purpose of these two organizations was to wrest control of the principal gurdwaras from the mahants (q.v.) and to make the government recognize that it had been transferred. The Akali Dal was to seize the gurdwaras, and the SGPC was to take over the management when they had yielded. Initially the Punjab government opposed the movement as ownership had been granted to the mahants who had title deeds to prove it. A series of incidents soon showed them that the Akali Sikhs were in deadly earnest, most notably the massacre at Nankana Sahib (q.v.). This persuaded the government that it would have to give way, but it delayed the drafting of appropriate legislation as it searched for a face-saving formula. Eventually it passed the Sikh Gurdwaras Act of 1925 (q.v.) which transferred ownership of a lengthy list of the more important gurdwaras in the Punjab to a committee to be elected by those people whom the Act defined as Sikhs. The title of the Shiromani Gurdwara Prabandhak Committee was then transferred by the Akalis to the committee which was to control the gurdwaras. *See also* GURU KA BAGH; JAITO; KEYS AFFAIR; POLITICAL PARTIES.

GURDWARA REFORM MOVEMENT: ORIGINS. By the beginning of the twentieth century many gurdwaras (q.v.) were actually owned by non-Khalsa mahants (q.v.) or hereditary supervisors, some of who claimed they were Udasis (q.v.). The accepted explanation was that in the eighteenth century, when Sikhs of the Khalsa (q.v.) were being hunted down, it was more convenient to leave Sikh shrines in the hands of people without the outward appearance of the Khalsa and that for this reason they were entrusted to Udasis. In the late nineteenth century the Singh Sabha (q.v.) had succeeded in arousing the awareness of many Sikhs, a process greatly hastened by the struggle between the Sanatan Sikhs and the Tat Khalsa (qq.v.). This struggle was in part resolved by the creation in 1902 of the Chief Khalsa Diwan (q.v.) as a means of drawing the two sides together. It soon became clear, however, that the Chief Khalsa Diwan was too politically conservative for many of the Tat Khalsa. Before World War I the Rakab-ganj Gurdwara affair (q.v.) indicated a growing sense of dissatisfaction on the part of many Sikhs and a feeling that their Khalsa rights were not adequately recognized. Soon after the war the Gurdwara Reform Movement (q.v.) began.

GUR-MANTRA. 'The Guru's mantra'; the Khalsa (q.v.) mantra or sanctified formula; an expression which is piously repeated as a form of **nām simaran**(q.v.). This may be **sat nām** (True Name) or **sat nām vāhigurū**. Trumpp (q.v.) believed it to be **sat akāl srī gurū**. Gian Singh (q.v.) claimed that it comprised the first five stanzas of *Japjī* (q.v.).

GURMAT. 'The teachings of the Guru'; Sikhism. Gurmat is a very important term and deserves to be in English usage.

GURMATA (GURUMATA). During the eighteenth century the dispersed forces of the Khalsa developed the practice of representatives of the various misls (q.v.) meeting together before Akal Takhat in Amritsar (qq.v.). When a decision was made by an assembly of the Sarbat Khalsa (q.v.) it was regarded as a gurmata, 'the will of the Guru,' and all were expected to accept it. The sanction of such decisions came from their being reached in the Guru's actual presence in the scriptural form of the Guru Granth Sahib (the Adi Granth and also the Dasam Granth [qq.v.]). Open copies were present at such assemblies.

GURMUKH. 'One whose face is turned towards the Guru'; a faithful follower of the Guru. *See also* MAN; MANMUKH.

GURMUKH SINGH (1849–98). Born into a family of poor Jats (q.v.), he began as a cook in the kitchen of the princely state of Kapurthala. Assisted by the raja he acquired western education and rose to be a professor of Punjabi at Oriental College in Lahore. He identified with the Lahore branch of the Singh Sabha and so with its Tat Khalsa (qq.v.) section. A case was brought against him by conservatives, and he was banished from the Panth (q.v.) in 1887 for his radical approach. Eventually, however, he was vindicated. His campaign against doctrinal conservatism and caste (q.v.) continued, and his Tat Khalsa interpretation did much to indicate the future direction of the Sikh faith.

GURMUKHI. 'From the mouth of the Guru,' the script of Punjabi. To devout Sikhs it possesses a sacred quality. The tradition that it was invented by Guru Angad (q.v.) is incorrect, though he may possibly have adapted it and introduced it to Sikh writings. Gurmukhi closely resembles the script of Khatri traders (q.v.), and it was from this source that the Gurus obviously derived it.

GURPURAB. Anniversaries of significant events associated with the Gurus, celebrated on lunar dates of the Indian calendar. Three are of particular importance: 1. Nanak's birthday, traditionally observed on a date in November. 2. Gobind Singh's birthday (December/January). 3. The martyrdom of Arjan (May/June) (qq.v.). Numerous other Gurpurabs are also celebrated. The practice was greatly encouraged by the Singh Sabha (q.v.).

GURSIKH. A 'Sikh of the Guru'; a devout Sikh; an amrit-dhari Sikh (q.v.).

GUR-SOBHA *see* SAINAPATI.

GURU. 'Guru' means 'preceptor' and for Hindus has normally indicated a human teacher. Within the Sant tradition (q.v.), however, 'Guru' came to be identified with the inner 'voice' of Akal Purakh (q.v.). This view was inherited and transmitted by Nanak (q.v.), for whom the Guru or Satguru (q.v.) represented the divine presence, mystically apprehended and inwardly guiding the truly devout along the path leading to mukti (q.v.). Because Nanak communicated this essential truth with unique clarity, he, as human vehicle of the divine Guru, eventually received the title of Guru. This role was transmitted in turn to each of his nine successors, the divine spirit successively inhabiting ten enlightened individuals. Guru Gobind Singh (q.v.) is traditionally believed to have announced that the personal transmission would end at his death, but that the mystical Guru would remain embodied in the scripture and the corporate Panth (q.v.). *See also* GURU GRANTH; GURU PANTH.

GURU DI CHARANI LAGNA. 'Entering the Guru's shelter'; the ceremony observed by some families when a child begins reading the Guru Granth Sahib (q.v.) for the first time.

GURU GRANTH. Sikhs recognize only one Guru (q.v.), pre-existent before Nanak (q.v.) as the mystical 'voice' of Akal Purakh (q.v.) and then successively incarnated in ten men. By tradition, before he died Guru Gobind Singh (q.v.) decreed that no personal Guru would follow him. Instead, the mystical Guru would be enshrined jointly in the sacred scripture (Guru Granth) and the corporate decisions of the Panth (Guru Panth [qq.v.]). During the eighteenth century Sikhs recognized the Dasam Granth (q.v.) as the Guru as well as the Adi Granth (q.v.). Since that time preferences have shifted increasingly to the Adi Granth, a process greatly encouraged by the Tat Khalsa (q.v.). Today the Adi Granth, together with a few works from the Dasam Granth, is tacitly recognized by many Sikhs as the only recorded voice of the Guru. Because of the status thus accorded to the Adi Granth it is usually called the Guru Granth Sahib (q.v.).

GURU GRANTH SAHIB. 'The sacred volume which is the Guru (q.v.).' Strictly speaking, this entry is covered by that of the Adi Granth (q.v.), as both refer to the same sacred scripture. A separate entry is justified on the grounds that Sikhs attach such enormous importance to this scripture as the eternal Guru, treating it as central to all their observances. By tradition, shortly before he died Guru Gobind Singh (q.v.) announced that there would be no more personal Gurus and that at his death the functions of the Guru would be eternally embodied in the scripture and the Panth (q.v.). The Adi Granth thus became the Guru Granth Sahib. This belief evidently arose after his death, perhaps several decades later. When the Dasam Granth (q.v.) was compiled, it too came to be treated as the Guru, and later in the eighteenth century both volumes were displayed together. During the nineteenth century, however, the Dasam Granth receded in comparison with the Adi Granth, and for most Sikhs it is now the Adi Granth which alone possesses the title of Guru. As such its importance is absolutely supreme. The two terms can now serve different functions. Whereas Guru Granth Sahib is the sacred scripture venerated by believers, Adi Granth is a neutral title usually employed by scholars.

GURU KA BAGH. A gurdwara near Amritsar (qq.v.). In 1921, during the Gurdwara Reform Movement (q.v.), the custodian accepted initiation into the Khalsa (q.v.) but then complained to the police when Akalis (q.v.) started cutting timber from gurdwara land. The police acted forcibly, and the Akalis responded by organizing a regular series of non-violent groups to march on the gurdwara. They were met by considerable police brutality, but the marches continued. After three weeks the Governor of the Punjab was persuaded to visit the scene, and the violence was then stopped. As a face-saving device the gurdwara land was privately purchased and then given to the gurdwara, by this time in Akali hands.

GURU PANTH. The Guru Panth was a doctrine particularly suited to the circumstances of the eighteenth century, providing an effective means of decision making for Sikhs who were divided into several misls (q.v.). When unification was achieved under Ranjit Singh (q.v.) the practice of eliciting corporate decisions from the Panth (q.v.) was discarded. The doctrine is still maintained today, and efforts are occasionally made to seek the Guru's will by this means. It is, however, seldom invoked. The voice of the Guru is much more commonly sought through the words of the Guru Granth (q.v.).

GURU-VANS. 'The descendants of the Gurus.' These were Sikhs of the Bedi, Trehan, Bhalla, and Sodhi sub-castes of the Khatri caste (qq.v.) who were descended from one of the Gurus. Nanak's sub-caste was Bedi, Angad's was Trehan, Amar Das's was Bhalla, and Ram Das's was Sodhi. All the subsequent Gurus were the descendants of Ram Das and in consequence were also Sodhis. Throughout most of subsequent Sikh history the descendants of the Gurus were regarded with great respect and accorded privileges greater than those of ordinary Sikhs. This changed, however, with the influence of the Tat Khalsa (q.v.) who insisted that all Sikhs should be regarded equally. *See also* CUSHION CONTROVERSY.

GUTKA. A small book containing the readings for Nit-nem (q.v.) and a short anthology of popular hymns. Also known as a Sundar Gutka.

GYAN-RATANAVALI. A janam-sakhi based on Bhai Gurdas's Var 1 (qq.v.), erroneously attributed to Mani Singh (q.v.). It is an early nineteenth-century product of the Udasi sect (q.v.). *See also* BHAGAT-RATANAVALI.

H

HAKIKAT RAH MUKAM RAJE SHIV-NABH KI. 'The truth [concerning] the way to Raja Shiv-nabh's (q.v.) [abode].' A brief work which purports to describe how to reach the land ruled by Shiv-nabh, appended at the end of all copies of the Banno recension of the Adi Granth (qq.v.).

HALAL. 'Lawful.' Flesh of an animal killed in accordance with the Muslim ritual whereby it is bled to death. *See also* JHATKA; KUTTHA.

HAM HINDU NAHIN. 'We Are Not Hindus,' the booklet by Kahn Singh Nabha (q.v.), first published in 1898, which summarizes in its title a key aspect of the message of the Tat Khalsa (q.v.). The booklet largely comprises proof-text quotations.

HAQIQAT RAI (1724–42). A Khatri Sahaj-dhari (qq.v.) of Sialkot who was executed in Lahore in spite of pleas for his piety. He thereby acquired the title of a Sikh martyr, his memory being particularly venerated by Maharaja Ranjit Singh (q.v.).

HAR KRISHAN (1656–64). Eighth Guru of the Sikhs who succeeded to the title of Guru when only five years old. The history of his short life is obscure. His elder brother Ram Rai (q.v.) is said to have offended his father Guru Har Rai (q.v.) through his sycophantic dealings with the Mughal emperor Aurangzeb and was accordingly passed over in 1661, the title going instead to Har Krishan. In 1664 Aurangzeb summoned him from the Shivalik Hills (q.v.) to Delhi where he resided in the village of Raisina just outside Delhi at the house of Raja Jai Singh, marked by Gurdwara Bangla Sahib (q.v.). While there he contracted smallpox, which proved fatal. Tradition records that before he died he uttered the words 'Baba Bakale.' This indicated to his retinue that the next Guru was 'the Baba [who is] in Bakala,' Tegh Bahadur (q.v.), son of Guru Hargobind (q.v.) and his grandfather's half brother. His name is also spelled Hari Krishan. *See also* MUGHAL DYNASTY.

HAR RAI, GURU (1630–61). Seventh Guru of the Sikhs, a younger grandson of the sixth Guru, Hargobind (q.v.). His father, Gurditta (q.v.), had predeceased Hargobind, and his elder brother Dhir Mal (q.v.) was held to be unsuitable as a successor. When Hargobind died in 1644 Guru Har Rai withdrew from Kiratpur (q.v.) further back into the Shivalik Hills (q.v.) to avoid conflict and settled with a small retinue in the territory of Sirmur. From there he sometimes emerged onto the plains to preach and to visit his Sikhs. On the Malwa (q.v.) portion of the plains his masands (q.v.) were able to maintain his authority against competing interests, and on one of his visits he converted Phul, progenitor of the leaders of the Phulkian misl (q.v.) and of the princely families of Malwa. He is said to have been well disposed towards Dara Shikoh, the eldest son of emperor Shah Jahan and rival of younger brother Aurangzeb (q.v.) for the Mughal throne. Aurangzeb, having won the throne, summoned Har Rai to Delhi in 1661 to explain his conduct. The Guru sent his elder son Ram Rai (q.v.) who, according to tradition, sought to ingratiate himself with Aurangzeb by claiming that a line from the Adi Granth (q.v.) to which the emperor took exception had been mistranscribed. This convinced Har Rai that his successor should be his younger son Har Krishan (q.v.), only five years old when his father died. Guru Har Rai left no works, and sources for his life are particularly scarce. His name is sometimes spelled Hari Rai. There is disagreement concerning his wife or wives, one source naming two (Kot Kalyani and Krishan Kaur, each mother of one of his two sons) and another only one (Sulakhani). *See also* MUGHAL DYNASTY.

HARCHAND SINGH LONGOWAL (1932–85). President of the Akali Dal (q.v.) when the Indian Army attacked the Golden Temple complex in June 1984 (q.v.). In 1985 he signed an accord with the new Prime Minister Rajiv Gandhi which, had it been carried out, would have settled most of the Sikh grievances. Later that year he was assassinated, evidently by a militant Sikh. He was a sant (q.v.), and although the complexities of the Punjab situation frequently eluded him, he was a genuinely humble person.

HARGOBIND, GURU (1595–1644). The sixth Guru of the Sikhs who succeeded his father Arjan (q.v.) in 1606 (following the latter's death at Mughal hands). Four skirmishes were fought with Mughal troops during his period. In 1634 Hargobind withdrew with his armed retinue to Kiratpur (q.v.) at the edge of the Shivalik Hills (q.v.). This was much safer for him as it lay within Hindur, the territory of a vassal of the Mughal emperor rather than the actual empire. The direction of the Panth (q.v.) was now firmly fixed, emphasis being laid on military defence in addition to remembrance of the divine Name (q.v.). His eldest son Gurditta (q.v.) had predeceased him, and Gurditta's elder son Dhir Mal (q.v.) was considered unsuitable. The succession was already firmly fixed in the male line of the Sodhi Khatris (qq.v.), and the actual candidate chosen to follow him as Guru was Gurditta's younger son Har Rai (q.v.). Hargobind had three wives (Damodari, Nanaki, and Mahadevi [qq.v.]). Damodari was the mother of Gurditta and Nanaki of the ninth Guru, Tegh Bahadur (q.v.). Three other sons and one daughter were also born to him. No works were left by Hargobind. *See also* ANI RAI; ATAL RAI; MUGHAL DYNASTY; SURAJ MAL.

HARGOBIND: CHANGES OF POLICY. The period of Guru Hargobind (q.v.) makes clear a change in the Sikh Panth (q.v.) which had already begun to appear under his father Arjan (q.v.). When he succeeded to the office of Guru in 1606 the hostility of the Mughal rulers of the Punjab was already evident, and Hargobind had to spend some time imprisoned in Gwalior Fort. His following by this time consisted overwhelmingly of rural folk (particularly people belonging to the Jat caste [q.v.]), and these people were not inclined to submit to the threats of Mughal control. Hargobind, by tradition, marked this change by three symbolic gestures. The first was the wearing of two swords at his consecration, one representing the spiritual authority which his predecessors had always possessed (**piri**) and the other the temporal power which he was now assuming (**miri**) (q.v.). A second was that he had Akal Takhat (q.v.) erected in Amritsar (q.v.), a high platform signifying the same temporal power. The third was that he surrounded himself with armed men and preferred hunting to the peaceful pastimes of the first five Gurus. Many of his Sikhs were disquieted by this, preferring to have a Guru who stressed **nām simaraṇ** (q.v.) rather than these martial quali-

ties. The poet Bhai Gurdas (q.v.), however, recorded a famous verse in which he declared that the Guru alone can
judge the circumstances of the time. *See also* MUGHAL DY-
NASTY.

HARI. One of the most common names for God in the Adi Granth
(q.v.) as in Hindu usage. The abbreviated form 'Har' is also
used. *See also* AKAL PURAKH; RAM; VAHIGURU.

HARIMANDIR SAHIB (AMRITSAR). 'The Divine Temple of
Hari (God),' the gurdwara (q.v.) which is the prime focus of
Sikh reverence and devotion. Sikhs also call it Darbar Sahib,
or 'the Divine Court,' though strictly speaking this term covers the whole temple complex. To English speakers (particularly to Europeans) it is known as the Golden Temple. The
latter name was attached to it as a result of gilding of the upper two stories by Maharaja Ranjit Singh (q.v.), whereby it
came to be known as the Suvaran Mandir or the 'Golden
Temple.' Harimandir Sahib is situated within Amritsar (q.v.)
and is regarded as the holiest place in the holiest city. Guru
Ram Das (1574–81) (q.v.), who founded Amritsar, excavated
the pool which surrounds it, and tradition associates an ancient ber tree on the bank opposite Harimandir's entrance
with the water's power to cleanse leprosy. The gurdwara was
completed by Guru Arjan (1581–1606) (q.v.) who installed in
it the newly-completed Adi Granth (q.v.). His son, Guru Hargobind (1606–44) (q.v.), was compelled to withdraw to the
Shivalik Hills (q.v.) from Amritsar, and for almost a century
Harimandir remained in hostile sectarian hands. In the eighteenth century, however, Khalsa Sikhs (q.v.) returned and
fought for it. By mid-century the gurdwara had become the
principal focus of Sikh loyalty, and by 1800 it was firmly in
their hands, never again to be surrendered. In 1984 its environs were badly damaged by the Indian Army in its attempt
to dislodge Khalistan supporters (q.v.), some bullets actually
lodging in the gurdwara itself. Harimandir Sahib sits in the
middle of the pool with a causeway connecting it to the bank.
The space occupied by the actual gurdwara is relatively
small, but the building has three stories. The body of the gurdwara is built of marble with semi-precious stones inlaid in

various patterns. *See also* ARCHITECTURE; RECENT HISTORY.

HARIMANDIR SAHIB (AMRITSAR): ENVIRONS. Several important buildings surround Harimandir Sahib (q.v.). These include Akal Takhat (q.v.), which stands a short distance opposite the entrance to the causeway on the western side. On the eastern side of the pool are the langar (q.v.), the headquarters of the SGPC (q.v.), and the Guru Ram Das Sarai which provides accommodation for pilgrims. The Sikh Reference Library (southern side) was destroyed by fire during the army action in 1984, but the Central Sikh Museum (northern side) still stands. At the entrance to the causeway is an impressive gateway, the Darashani Deorhi. In the upper story is housed the Tosh-khana (Treasury), its contents displayed once a year. *See also* PARIKARAMA.

HARIMANDIR SAHIB (AMRITSAR): PROCEDURE. The gates of Harimandir Sahib (q.v.) are opened at three a.m. each morning, and kirtan (q.v.) is conducted from four a.m. until twelve midnight, with the remaining hours for cleaning. At five a.m. the Guru Granth Sahib (q.v.) is placed on a palanquin, brought in procession from Akal Takhat (q.v.), and installed in Harimandir until it is returned to its resting place (also in procession) before the closure each night. Crowds come for darshan (q.v.), particularly on festival days, though since the army action in 1984 numbers are much smaller. Four akhand paths (q.v.) are always taking place on the upper story, the relays of readers being amongst the numerous sevadars (q.v.). *See also* GURDWARA PROCEDURE.

HARIMANDIR SAHIB (PATNA). The gurdwara (q.v.) in Patna (q.v.) which marks the spot where Guru Gobind Singh (q.v.) was born in 1666 while his father, Tegh Bahadur (q.v.), was travelling in the east of India. It is one of the five takhats (q.v.). The present building was erected in the mid-fifties.

HARI SINGH NALVA (d. 1837). The most famous of Ranjit Singh's (q.v.) generals, brave in combat and a ruthless administrator. He was killed at the battle of Jamrud near the Khyber Pass.

HARSHA SINGH ARORA. First teacher of Punjabi at Oriental College, Lahore and with Gurmukh Singh (q.v.) the founder of the Lahore Singh Sabha (q.v.) in 1879.

HATHA-YOGA. 'Yoga of force'; the kind of yoga practiced by Nath yogis (q.v.), requiring extremely difficult physical postures. According to its physiological theory, there are three principal channels which ascend through the human body. Two of these terminate in the left and right nostril and the third (the susumna) is held to run along the spinal column. Along the susumna are six or eight 'discs' (**chakra**); and at its base, behind the genitals, is the kundalini, a latent power symbolized by the figure of a sleeping serpent. By means of the hatha-yoga discipline the kundalini is awakened, and ascending the susumna it pierces each disc in turn, thereby releasing increasing supplies of psychic energy. At the climax of the ascent it pierces the 'lotus of a thousand petals' said to be located at the top of the cranium. The dasam duar (q.v.) or 'tenth door' then opens, and the human spirit passes into the ineffable condition of sahaj (q.v.), the state of ultimate union with Brahman. This theory was a powerful contender in the days of the early Gurus, and Nanak in particular devoted many hymns to negating it. Some of the Nath terminology (notably **sahaj**) did, however, pass into his usage.

HAUMAI. Literally 'I-I' (the first person singular pronoun repeated). The self-centeredness of an unregenerate person which can only be overcome by meditation on the divine Name (q.v.).

HAWK. In popular art Gobind Singh (q.v.) is frequently depicted with a white hawk on his wrist. A hawk is identified as the bearer of the Guru's spirit, exhorting the Sikhs to hold fast during times of oppression. One was observed at Guru ka Bagh (q.v.) in 1921, and another was seen during the massacre of Sikhs following Mrs. Gandhi's assassination in 1984.

HAZARA SINGH (d. 1908). Member of a distinguished family of Amritsar gianis (q.v.) and a renowned scholar of Sikh literature. He supported the Singh Sabha (q.v.) at its inauguration in 1873 and contributed learned works to its program. Amongst these, his edition of the vars of Bhai Gurdas (q.v.) is still extensively used today. He was the maternal grandfather of Vir Singh (q.v.).

HAZUR SAHIB. The chief gurdwara in Nander (q.v.), recognized as one of the five takhats (q.v.). It is also known as Sach Khand Hazur Sahib.

HEAVEN *see* SVARAG.

HELL *see* NARAK.

HEMKUNT SAHIB. In the Himalayas of the Garhwal region, at a height of 4,636 meters, is Hemkunt. This spot is said to be the place where Guru Gobind Singh (q.v.), prior to his human birth, engaged in austerities. These austerities are described in *Bachitar Nāṭak* (q.v.) which traditionally was written by the Guru. A claim to have identified the place by its topographical resemblances was made in the early 1930s by Tara Singh Narotam (q.v.). A gurdwara in the modern style has recently been erected there, accessible only in the warmer months.

HIKAYAT. Eleven stories from the Dasam Granth (q.v.) in Gurmukhi Persian, principally about the ways of women.

HINDALI. Hindal (or Handal) was a Jat (q.v.) from Batala. Under his son Bidhi Chand the followers of Hindal (the Hindalis) formed a schismatic group which disputed the leadership of the Panth with Hargobind (qq.v.). The Hindalis have no importance, except that they are credited with originating the *Bālā* tradition of janam-sakhis (qq.v.). The group is also known as the Niranjani Panth. The Hindali center was Jandiala in Amritsar District.

HINDU ORIGINS. The question of whether Sikhs are Hindus surfaced explicitly during the Singh Sabha (q.v.) period, clearly dividing the Sanatan Sikhs from the Tat Khalsa (qq.v.). The Sanatan Sikhs had no difficulty in affirming that Sikhs are

Hindus, but the Tat Khalsa were adamantly opposed. The most famous publication to emerge during the Singh Sabha period was entitled *Ham Hindū Nahīn* ('We are not Hindus'), by the Tat Khalsa writer Kahn Singh Nabha (q.v.). As the Tat Khalsa view permeated the Khalsa (q.v.), this exclusivist view came to be accepted as orthodox, though sahaj-dhari Sikhs (q.v.) still maintained that it was incorrect. Nanak (q.v.) was certainly born a Hindu. Today, however, most orthodox Sikhs (which means Sikhs of the Khalsa) hold that they are definitely not Hindus. *See also* IDENTITY; SIKH.

HOLA MAHALLA. A Sikh festival which takes place on the 1st of Chet (March/April), the day following the Hindu festival of Holi. The instituting of the festival is attributed to Guru Gobind Singh (q.v.), the specific purpose being to provide for his Sikhs a day of military exercises. This, however, is most unlikely as Sikh sources indicate that Holi was celebrated by Sikhs into the nineteenth century. It is much more likely that Hola Mahalla was elevated to its present status by the reforming Tat Khalsa (q.v.). The festival is still celebrated at Anandpur (q.v.) with martial competitions and a mock battle in which the Nihangs (q.v.) participate prominently.

HOOKAH (HUQQAH). A smoking apparatus. The tobacco burns in a small bowl, from which smoke is drawn by inhaling it down through a receptacle containing water and thence up a lengthy (often flexible) stem. Hookahs were strictly forbidden to the early Khalsa (q.v.), probably because their use was identified as a distinctively Muslim custom. The prohibition now extends to tobacco in any form. Smoking is regarded with particular aversion by Sikhs and is treated as one of the kurahits (q.v.). *See also* TOBACCO.

HUKAM. 'Order.' The divine Order to which each person must submit in order that he/she may find liberation. In the teachings of Nanak (q.v.), the divine Order is the constant principle governing the entire universe, manifested in the perfect consistency and regularity of God's physical and moral creation. Each person must, through constant practice, strive to bring his/her life into accord with this principle. When the accord is perfect, liberation has been attained.

HUKAM LAINA. 'To take an order.' For 'taking a hukam' (or taking a vak) the procedure is to open the Guru Granth Sahib (q.v.) at random and read the first hymn which appears at the top of the left-hand page (if necessary going back to the preceding page for the beginning of the hymn). This hymn is the hukam (or vak). If the portion happens to be a part of a **vār** (q.v.), the complete stanza together with its associated **shaloks** (q.v.) should be read. A hukam is always taken at the conclusion of a worship service and as a part of the **bhog** ceremony (q.v.) following a complete reading of the Guru Granth Sahib. It may also be taken as a daily routine by devout Sikhs in the early morning.

HUKAM-NAMA. 'Letter of command.' From the time of Guru Hargobind (q.v.) such documents were sent to sangats (q.v.) or individuals, giving instructions or requesting assistance. Several examples are extant. Today hukam-namas are very rarely issued and always come from a takhat, normally Akal Takhat (qq.v.). The modern procedure is for the Dharmik Salahakar Committee of the SGPC (q.v.) to be summoned by the Jathedar (q.v.) of Akal Takhat, and if it decides that one should be issued it recommends doing so to him. In 1978 one was promulgated against the Sant Nirankari Darbar (q.v.). Hukam-namas are believed to carry the full authority of the Panth (q.v.) and disobeying them is held to be a very serious offense for Sikhs.

I

IDENTITY. There are five varieties of Sikh identity. Amrit-dhari Sikhs (q.v.) are initiated members of the Khalsa (q.v.), having received **amrit** or the sanctified water of initiation. Kes-dhari Sikhs (q.v.) are those who observe some or all of the Khalsa Rahit (q.v.), always including the uncut hair, but do not take initiation. All amrit-dhari Sikhs are also Kes-dhari, but only a minority of Kes-dharis are Amrit-dharis. Kes-dharis are usually regarded as members of the Khalsa, although a strict definition excludes all except the Amrit-dharis. The third group, the sahaj-dhari Sikhs (q.v.), cut their hair and do not observe the Rahit. The fourth group consists of those who belong to Khalsa families (bearing the name Singh for men or Kaur for women) but cut their hair. This group has no satisfactory name. The term Mona (shaven) Sikhs is sometimes used, but has pejorative overtones. Finally there are Patit (fallen) Sikhs (q.v.), a term which strictly designates Amrit-dharis who have committed one of the four kurahits (q.v.). It is, however, loosely used to mean all Kes-dharis who cut their hair. *See also* SIKH.

IDOL WORSHIP. For Sikhs today idol worship is strictly banned. Until the development of the Singh Sabha movement (q.v.) the practice was tolerated, and the Sanatan Sikhs (q.v.) could see no harm in keeping idols in the precincts of gurdwaras (q.v.). The Tat Khalsa (q.v.), however, was strenuously opposed to the practice, and in 1905 idols were removed from the precincts of Harimandir Sahib (q.v.). Tat Khalsa opposition was based on an insistence that God could never be thus represented and also on their conviction that Sikhs were not Hindus. Its view is now accepted as orthodox.

IK-OANKAR. A popular emblem used by Sikhs, a combination of the Gurmukhi figure 1 and the letter O, taken from the Adi Granth (q.v.) where it is employed as the first part of various invocations. It represents the unity of God ('One Oankar' or One Being). The emblem is a common feature of Sikh logos and frequently appears on buildings, clothing, books, letter-heads, etc. 'Oankar' is actually a cognate of 'Om' and can carry the same mystical meaning. Many Sikhs, however, object to any suggestion that they are the same word. For them 'Om' is Hindu whereas 'Oankar' is Sikh. *See also* HINDU ORIGINS.

IMMANENCE. In Sikh doctrine Akal Purakh (q.v.) is both immanent and transcendent. In his fullness, he is far beyond the understanding of mankind, yet he is known to them through the created world. One needs but open one's eyes, and the divine Name (q.v.) is everywhere to be seen. This message is repeatedly expressed in the hymns of the Adi Granth (q.v.).

INITIATION TO KHALSA *see* AMRIT SANSKAR.

ISHNAN. 'Bathing,' enjoined by the Adi Granth (q.v.) before meditation on the divine Name (q.v.). Sikhs are expected to bathe immediately after arising before commencing Nit-nem (q.v.). Where complete bathing is not practicable, **pañj ishnān** (q.v.) are permissible.

IZZAT. 'Prestige'; honor associated with the social status of a family. The sense of izzat is particularly strong among the Jats (q.v.).

J

JAI RAM. The husband of Nanak's sister Nanaki (qq.v.), employed as the steward of Daulat Khan Lodi in Sultanpur (qq.v.). He was certainly a Khatri (q.v.). His sub-caste is variously said to have been Uppal or Palta.

JAIDEV. A Bengali poet of the twelfth century. Traditionally he is regarded as the same Jaidev as wrote the *Gīt Govind*. There are two works by him in the Adi Granth (q.v.).

JAITA. Bhai Jaita was a Ranghreta Sikh (q.v.) who was present at the execution of Tegh Bahadur (q.v.) and who secretly carried the severed head up to Anandpur (q.v.) to lay it before Gobind Singh (q.v.). Tradition also relates that upon taking initiation into the Khalsa (q.v.), he assumed the name Jivan Singh and became a leading soldier under Guru Gobind Singh; he was killed at Chamkaur (q.v.) during the withdrawal from Anandpur (q.v.) in 1704.

JAITO. In 1923 the British Government of the Punjab forced the abdication of Ripudaman Singh, the Maharaja of Nabha. He

was reputed to be sympathetic to the Akalis (q.v.) who organized a number of akhand paths (q.v.) throughout the state in
sympathy. One of these, in the village of Jaito, was inter-
rupted by the police and led to a major episode in the Gurdwara Reform Movement (q.v.). The Akalis conducted a determined campaign, eventually establishing the right to
worship freely. Jaito also attracted much attention from
Gandhi and the Congress Party, though Gandhi stressed that
the religious issue should be detached from the political question of abdication.

JALAU. The public display of jewels and other precious articles
held by Harimandir Sahib, Akal Takhat, and Gurdwara Baba
Atal Rai (qq.v.). They are shown on the gurpurabs of Nanak,
Ram Das, and Gobind Singh (qq.v.) and on the anniversary
of the installation of the Guru Granth Sahib (q.v.).

JANAM-ASTHAN. The gurdwara (q.v.) in Nankana Sahib (q.v.)
which marks the birthplace of Nanak (q.v.). *See also*
NANKANA MASSACRE.

JANAM-SAKHI. A hagiographic work on the life of Nanak
(q.v.). The earliest dated janam-sakhi was recorded in 1658,
but clearly their origins go much further back, probably to the
actual lifetime of the Guru. Janam-sakhis first circulated
orally as individual anecdotes about Nanak. After some time
recorded versions began to appear, with the anecdotes loosely
grouped in various chronologies corresponding to birth,
childhood, manhood, and death. Later still some versions ordered the anecdotes about Nanak's adult life into a more
structured sequence. Beginning with stories of his childhood,
they take him through early manhood in the town of Sultanpur (q.v.), extensive travels within and beyond India, and a final period of teaching back in the Punjab at Kartarpur (q.v.).
Banaras, Sri Lanka, Mecca, and the legendary Mount Sumeru
are among the many places he visits on his travels. The
janam-sakhis derive from earlier Sufi models (q.v.), and
many of the anecdotes are taken from Hindu or Muslim
sources. Practically all of them are in simple Punjabi prose.
All quote extensively from the Adi Granth (q.v.), though their

versions are seldom correct copies. Very few facts can be ascertained from them, most of the anecdotes being tales of wisdom or marvellous deeds of a kind which so easily attach themselves to a great religious teacher. They have, however, been extensively used for writing 'biographies' of Nanak, with popular accounts favoring the *Bālā* tradition (q.v.) and more respectable accounts depending on the *Purātan* (q.v.). This misunderstands the nature of hagiographic writing, for no reliable account of Nanak's life can be derived from any of the janam-sakhis.

JANAM-SAKHI TRADITIONS. Several janam-sakhi (q.v.) versions or traditions have survived. The most important are the *Bālā* and *Purātan* traditions (qq.v.). Others are the *Ādi Sākhīs*, the *Gyān-ratanāvalī*, and the two versions of the *Mahimā Prakāsh* tradition (qq.v.), one of which is in verse. A significant version which did not give rise to a tradition was the *B40 Janam-sākhī* (q.v.). A rather different style is followed by the *Miharbān Janam-sākhī* (q.v.), a work which is traced to the Minas (q.v.). This uses the anecdotal framework to form the basis for a lengthy series of exegetical commentaries on the works of Nanak (q.v.).

JANG-NAMAH. A Persian work written by Nur Muhammad in 1764–65 while accompanying Ahmad Shah Abdali (q.v.) on his seventh invasion. It contains information about eighteenth-century Sikhs.

JAP. A work of 199 short verses attributed to Gobind Singh (q.v.) and included in the Dasam Granth (q.v.). It contains numerous terse descriptions of God, many only a single word. The *Jāp* (or *Jāp Sahib*) should not be confused with Nanak's *Japjī* (qq.v.).

JAPJI. 'Repeat [God's Name],' the best-known and most loved of all the scriptural works of the Panth (q.v.). *Japjī* (or *Japjī Sāhib*) is a composition by Guru Nanak (q.v.) which occurs at the beginning of the Adi Granth (q.v.) on pages one through eight, immediately after the Mul Mantra (q.v.). Unlike the remainder of the Adi Granth, it is recited or chanted, not sung. It is included in the early morning portion of Nit-nem (q.v.), to be said after waking and bathing. Many Sikhs observe only this part of the daily liturgy, murmuring *Japjī* while performing other duties such as preparing breakfast or proceeding to work. *Japjī* consists of thirty-eight stanzas with an epilogue by Guru Angad (q.v.), expressing in words of singular beauty a long hymn of praise to God. It concludes with a description of the five **khaṇḍs** (q.v.), the levels through which the soul ascends to perfect union with the divine. *Japjī* should be distinguished from Gobind Singh's *Jāp* (q.v.) which is also specified as a part of Nit-nem.

JARNAIL SINGH BHINDRANVALE (1947–84). A sant (q.v.), born in a poor family and sent by his father to the Damdami Taksal (q.v.) at the age of seven. The Taksal gave him an education in the Guru Granth Sahib (q.v.), and he became a fervent preacher of fundamentalist Khalsa traditions (q.v.). He also became leader of the Damdami Taksal at a young age. Punjab politics at this time were divided by hostility between the Akali Dal (q.v.) and the Central Government over the claim that the state should have greater autonomy in managing its affairs. The Congress Party (which controlled the Central Government) was seeking some sant to cause disruption within the Akali Dal and, unaware, Bhindranvale was selected for this purpose. In this he succeeded, going well beyond the intentions of the Congress and attracting an increasing number of Sikhs to his radical cause. As conditions in the Punjab deteriorated still further he took up residence in the Golden Temple complex (q.v.), ever exhorting the Sikhs to be true to their traditions and never to bow before the devious and cunning Hindus. Conditions became even worse, and the Central Government eventually mounted an attack by the Army on the Golden Temple complex in early June, 1984. In this attack Bhindranvale was killed. A considerable mythology gathered around him during his lifetime, and there is every indication that he will always be regarded as a great hero and martyr of the Panth (q.v.). *See also* POLITICAL PARTIES; RECENT HISTORY.

JASSA SINGH AHLUVALIA (1718–83). Prominent Sikh military leader during the turbulent middle years of the eighteenth century. He was born in the village of Ahlu near Lahore (q.v.) and became leader of the Ahluvalia misl (q.v.) with Kapurthala as its center. Together with other misl leaders he fought the Mughals and Afghans for control of the Punjab. On the occasions when the misls joined to form the Dal Khalsa (q.v.), Jassa Singh Ahluvalia was recognized as supreme leader. His only son had died young, but the territory which he controlled in Doaba (q.v.) survived under his successor Bhag Singh. Even within the united Punjab of Maharaja Ranjit Singh (q.v.), the next successor, Fateh Singh, was allowed considerable independence. Jassa Singh Ahluvalia was a Kalal (q.v.) by caste, a fact which acquired much importance when the Kalals were consciously elevating their status in the caste hierarchy of the Punjab.

JAT. A rural caste of Punjab and Haryana. In Pakistani Punjab the Jats are Muslims; in Indian Punjab, adjacent Haryana, and northern Rajasthan they are Sikhs; and in the remainder of Haryana most of them are Hindus. In rural Punjab the Sikh Jats are strongly dominant, owning most of the valuable land and controlling the administration. This control extends into the state politics of the Punjab, where all but one of the chief ministers since independence in 1947 have been Jats. In the Panth they are particularly prominent, comprising more than sixty percent of all Sikhs. There they are frequently in competition with the Bhapa Sikhs (q.v.) who, although much smaller in actual numbers, possess considerable skill in leadership and resources.

JATHA. A 'military detachment,' commanded by a jathedar (q.v.). During the eighteenth century the Sikhs fought in jathas. Today the Akali Dal (q.v.) is organized into jathas.

JATHEDAR. The commander of a jatha (q.v.); the chief officiant of a Sikh institution.

JAWAHIR SINGH KAPUR (1859–1910). A Khatri Sikh (q.v.) who joined the Lahore Singh Sabha (q.v.) in 1885 and became one of its most prominent members. Previously, he had belonged to the Arya Samaj (q.v.), but left it when its hostility to the Sikh faith became apparent. Education was for him a compelling interest.

JHATKA. The flesh of an animal killed with a single blow, approved for consumption by members of the Khalsa (q.v.). *See also* HALAL; KUTTHA.

JHINVAR. A depressed caste of porters, water carriers and basket makers.

JINDAN. The youngest of Maharaja Ranjit Singh's (q.v.) three wives and the mother of his seventh son, Duleep Singh (q.v.).

JITO. The first of Guru Gobind Singh's (q.v.) three wives, married in 1677; mother of Jujhar Singh, Zorawar Singh, and Fateh Singh.

JIVAN-MUKAT. 'One who has found liberation while yet physically living'; a person who, by reason of great piety, achieves the goal of liberation and union with the divine before death.

JODH SINGH (1882–1981). A Khatri Sikh (q.v.), member of the Singh Sabha (q.v.) and a leading educationalist.

JOINT FAMILY. Most Sikhs used to live in joint families, and many still do. The convention is weakening, however, as some Sikhs are now required to live as nuclear families or prefer to do so. The gradual passing of the custom is regarded with regret, at least by older Sikhs, as its weakening is accompanied by diminishing obedience traditionally shown to elders.

JOTI JOT. The expression "**jotī jot samāuṇā**" means 'to merge light into light' and is used for the death of a pious person (including the Gurus). It refers to the belief that each individual is a fragment of light from the Supreme Light or Paramatma (q.v.), and at the death of a pious person that fragment merges back into the Light from which it came without having to continue the rigors of transmigration.

JUGAVALI. An apocryphal work attributed to Nanak (q.v.) by the Colebrooke version of the *Purātan* janam-sakhi tradition (q.v.). *See also* KACHCHI BANI.

JURA (JOORA). The top-knot into which a male Sikh ties his hair.

K

KABIR (c.1440–1518). The most celebrated exponent of the Sant tradition of Northern India (q.v.) apart from the Sikh Gurus. Kabir's name is a Muslim one, but the beliefs which can be extracted from his many hymns seem much more Hindu. In view of the Nath (q.v.) terminology and concepts in them, he probably came from a family with Nath connections which had recently superficially converted to Islam. Kabir spent most of his life in Banaras where he followed his lowly caste occupation as a Julaha (weaver). Probably he was illiterate. Three collections of his works exist: the eastern (the *Bījak*), the western (the *Kabīr-granthāvalī* and the Punjabi (the Adi Granth [q.v.]). The Adi Granth collection appears to be the oldest. Each differs from the other two, but the degree of overlap and other similarities mean that they essentially have a common origin, significantly modified by their differing oral traditions. The Adi Granth contains 534 **shabads** and **shaloks** (qq.v.), making the Kabir collection the largest of the bhagat bani (q.v.). Through his works, Kabir emerges as a thorough sant (q.v.), at once blunt and mystical. All externals of religion are scathingly rejected, the way of true belief being wholly within.

KACHCHI BANI. A spurious composition falsely attributed to one of the Gurus. *See also* JUGAVALI; PRAN SANGALI.

KACHH, KACHHAHIRA. Shorts which must not reach below the knee. One of the Five Ks (q.v.) and as such mandatory for both male and female amrit-dhari Sikhs (q.v.). They may be worn as an undergarment.

KAHN SINGH NABHA (1861–1938). A learned Sikh, author of the detailed and generally accurate encyclopaedia of Sikhism entitled *Gurushabad Ratanākar Mahān Kosh* (first published in 1931). Born a Jat (q.v.), he took his name from the town of Nabha and was for a time chief minister of the small princely state of Nabha. It was as an apologist for the Tat Khalsa group within the Singh Sabha (qq.v) that he attained particular fame. One work of his, a small booklet entitled *Ham Hindū Nahīn* ([q.v.] 'We are not Hindus') first issued in 1898, became the standard-bearer in asserting that Sikhs are fundamentally different from Hindus. In spite of his work for the Tat Khalsa he was for some time regarded with caution because of his ties with the Panch Khalsa Diwan (q.v.) and his interest in the Namdharis (q.v.). His first name is also spelled Kahan and sometimes misspelled Kanh.

KAHNAIYA, BHAI *see* GHAHNAIYA RAM.

KAHNAIYA MISL. A misl (q.v.) of medium strength with territory northeast of Amritsar. The chieftain's son Gurbakhsh Singh was killed in fratricidal strife between misls in 1782. His widow Sada Kaur (q.v.), emerging as the effective leader of the misl, married her daughter to Ranjit Singh (q.v.) and was able for some time to protect it against absorption within the Kingdom of the Punjab. In 1821, however, Ranjit Singh annexed her territories.

KALGIDHAR. 'Wearer of the aigrette,' Guru Gobind Singh (q.v.).

KALIYUG (KALIYUGA). The fourth of the four eras in the cosmic cycle; the age of ultimate degeneracy which precedes the Satiyug or the Age of Truth. At present the world is passing through the Kaliyug, often likened to a stormy ocean. According to Gurmat (q.v.) only the **nām** (q.v.) can ensure that the ocean is crossed.

KALU. Known as Mahita Kalu, he was a Bedi Khatri (qq.v.), keeper of the land records in the village of Rai Bhoi di Talvandi (q.v.) and father of Guru Nanak (qq.v.). He was married to Tripta (q.v.) and had a daughter, Nanaki (q.v.), in addition to Nanak.

KAMRUP. In Kamrup the janam-sakhis (q.v.) set their story of the legendary **strī-desh** or 'Land of Women.' When Nanak and Mardana (qq.v.) arrive at its border, Mardana offers to go ahead to beg for food. There he is turned into a sheep by the women of Kamrup. Nanak follows, and they try to enchant him also, but to no effect. Eventually the women acknowledge his superior power and make their submission. Kamrup has been identified with the area of that name in Assam. This is not possible, partly because the janam-sakhis clearly have no idea of its actual location and partly because of the nature of the story. The actual origin is found instead in tantric mythology where Kamrup figures as a symbol of eroticism and dark magic.

KANA. Having only one eye and therefore an unsuitable person for administering initiation into the Khalsa (q.v.). The term is also used to mean a Muslim.

KANGHA. The small wooden comb worn in the top-knot by Sikhs of the Khalsa (q.v.). One of the Five Ks (q.v.).

KANPHAT see NATH TRADITION.

KAPUR SINGH (1909–84). An important intellectual in the campaign for Punjabi Suba and in the Khalistan agitation (qq.v.).

KAPUR SINGH, NAWAB (1697–1753). Prominent Sikh military leader during the eighteenth-century struggle for supremacy against Muslim power in the Punjab. He first attained prominence in 1733 when Zakariya Khan (q.v.), trying peaceful means of controlling the Khalsa (q.v.), offered the rank of Nawab to anyone chosen by the Sikhs. Kapur Singh was selected, and for a few years the Punjab remained relatively quiet. Later the forces of the Khalsa divided into misls (q.v.), Kapur Singh leading the Faizulapurias (q.v.). For a time he was recognized as the leader of the Dal Khalsa (q.v.), but later stood aside in favour of Jassa Singh Ahluvalia (q.v.). Kapur Singh was a Jat (q.v.).

KARA. The iron or steel ring which is worn round the right wrist by Sikhs of the Khalsa (q.v.). One of the Five Ks (q.v.).

KARAH PRASAD. '[Sacramental] food prepared in a karah.' A karah is a large shallow iron dish used for boiling confections and other food. Karah prasad is distributed to every partici- pant in a gurdwara (q.v.) at the conclusion of ordinary wor- ship or of any special ritual such as an akhand path, amrit san- skar, or anand karaj (qq.v.). It may be offered by an individual worshipper who then retains a portion, the remainder being distributed to others. The actual origins of the practice are un- certain, though it has presumably been taken over from the Hindu custom of offering prasad (q.v.) in temple worship. The connection with an iron utensil suggests that the Sikh karah variety of prasad must have developed as a Khalsa (q.v.) ritual and that it should be traced no further back than the beginning of the eighteenth century. There is, however, a reference in the first var of Bhai Gurdas (q.v.) which may in- dicate that it dates from the sixteenth century. Karah prasad is prepared with equal parts of coarsely refined wheat flour (āṭā), clarified butter (ghī), and raw sugar (guṛ), with water added. While it is being prepared bani (q.v.) is sung or re- cited. It is then brought into the presence of the Guru Granth Sahib (q.v.), and the six appointed verses of *Anand Sāhib* (q.v.) are read. Ardas (q.v.) is recited, and finally the karah prasad is touched with a kirpan (q.v.) to signify that it is duly sanctified. It may then be distributed. Other portions which are brought to the gurdwara during the day may be added to it.

KARAM (KARMA). The destiny or fate of an individual gener- ated in accordance with the deeds performed in present and past lives. The Gurus affirmed karam but taught that it could be overcome by regular meditation on the divine Name (q.v.).

KARORSINGHIA MISL. A misl (q.v.) with territory around Hoshiarpur. Also known as the Karoria misl.

KAR-SEVA. 'Work-service.' Work which is undertaken without pay for some large task in the service of the Panth (q.v.). The construction of a gurdwara (q.v.) would be an example. A special karseva is the de-silting of the pool surrounding Harimandir in Amritsar (qq.v.) every fifty years. Sikhs from all walks of life consider it an honor to participate in cleaning the pool.

KARTAR (KARTA, KARTA PURUKH). 'Creator.' A term commonly applied to God.

KARTARPUR. There are two towns of this name. One is on the right bank of the Ravi river, directly opposite Dehra Baba Nanak (q.v.), and was founded by Guru Nanak (q.v.). The other is in Jalandhar District, the town settled by Dhir Mal (q.v.) (the location of the Kartarpur volume of the Adi Granth [q.v.]).

KARTARPUR BIR. 'Kartarpur volume'; recension of the Adi Granth (q.v.) held in Kartarpur (q.v.). It is believed to be the copy dictated by Guru Arjan (q.v.) in 1603 and 1604 to his amanuensis Bhai Gurdas (q.v.).

KATHA. 'Homily.' A discourse, normally strongly hortatory, on a passage from Sikh scripture, an anecdote from the janam-sakhis (q.v.) or from traditional Sikh history.

KAUR. All female Amrit-dharis (q.v.) must add Kaur to their first name. As the custom is also followed by Kes-dharis (q.v.) and those of Khalsa (q.v.) background, the name is thus borne by a large majority of female Sikhs. The etymology of the word is uncertain. Most regard it as a female form of **kumār,** 'prince,' translating it as 'princess.' *See also* AMRIT SANSKAR; IDENTITY; NAMING CEREMONY.

KAURA MAL (d. 1752). A sahaj-dhari Sikh (q.v.) who served under Mir Mannu (q.v.), remembered by the Sikhs as Mittha ('sweet') Mal instead of Kaura ('bitter') Mal because of favors towards them.

KES (KESH). Uncut hair. One of the Five Ks (q.v.).

KESAR SINGH CHHIBBAR. A member of the Chhibbar Brahman family which enjoyed power in the retinue of Guru Gobind Singh (q.v.). Author of *Bansāvalī-nāmā dasān pātshāhīān dā*, completed in 1769. This is an account of the Gurus from the author's point of view, biased by the family's loss of influence to the militant Khalsa (q.v.). He gives the date of the founding of the Khalsa as 1696.

KES-DHARI (KESH-DHARI). 'One who wears hair [uncut].' Sikhs are generally identified by uncut hair (**kes** or **kesh**). Not all Sikhs can be recognized in this way, however, for the Khalsa (q.v.) rule forbidding the cutting of hair is not accepted by every Sikh. Kes-dhari Sikhs are those who do keep their hair uncut, forming a large but indeterminate majority of the Panth (q.v.). The men are easily recognized by their distinctive turbans. Kes-dharis are generally (if loosely) regarded as the Khalsa, but only a small minority of them actually take initiation into the Khalsa. The remainder do not necessarily observe all of the Rahit (q.v.), though they do retain their hair. All Amrit-dhari Sikhs ([q.v.] those who have taken initiation) are also Kes-dhari, but only some Kes-dhari are also Amrit-dhari. *See also* IDENTITY.

KESGARH SAHIB. The most famous gurdwara (q.v.) in Anandpur Sahib (q.v.), overlooking the place where Guru Gobind Singh (q.v.) inaugurated the Khalsa (q.v.). One of the five takhats (q.v.) is located at Kesgarh Sahib.

KESKI. A small under-turban, approximately one quarter the length of a normal turban, worn by a kes-dhari male (q.v.) when he is not appearing in public. The keski may also be worn when sleeping. When a Kes-dhari is fully dressed it is commonly retained under his turban with a small portion showing where the two sides of the turban meet on the upper forehead. In such cases it is normally of a different color.

Amrit-dharis (q.v.) are permitted to wear keskis. A few Sikhs, principally those of the Bhai Randhir Singh da Jatha (q.v.), hold that the **kes** is not one of the Five Ks (q.v.) which all amrit-dhari Sikhs must wear, substituting instead the keski for women as well as men.

KEYS AFFAIR. An incident in the Gurdwara Reform Movement (q.v.). which took place in 1921. The District Commissioner of Amritsar decided that he would demand the keys of the Golden Temple treasury from the Shiromani Gurdwara Parbandhak Committee (qq.v.) and entrust them to his own nominee. The seizure created a considerable disturbance, with the result that the Governor of the Punjab backed down and returned the keys.

KHADUR. The home village of Angad (q.v.) and the Sikh center during his period as Guru. It is in Amritsar District, near the right bank of the Beas river.

KHALASA SIKH. A term used for Sahaj-dharis (q.v.) in the eighteenth and early nineteenth centuries.

KHALISTAN. The name adopted in the 1980s for a sovereign Sikh state, independent of India.

KHALISTAN COMMANDO FORCE (KCF). A guerrilla organization formed during the disturbances following the storming of the Golden Temple in 1984 (q.v.). It had connections with the Damdami Taksal and AISSF (qq.v.). In 1988 it was seriously weakened by betrayal and by the consequent killing of its commander Labh Singh.

KHALSA. The order instituted by Guru Gobind Singh (q.v.), certainly on Baisakhi Day (the first day of the Indian year) and probably in 1699. The traditional reason given for its founding was the Guru's decision to provide his followers with a militant and highly visible identity, essential if they were to withstand imminent trials. Evil men had arisen, with the result that God was about to intervene. The Khalsa was to be the means of intervention. To this a supplementary reason needs to be added. The Guru was determined to have a united following, an objective which was being frustrated by the masands (q.v.). The masands were to be disestablished, and all Sikhs would be required to pay their fealty direct to the Guru. Although the word **khālsā** derives from the Arabic/Persian **khālisā** ('pure'), a secondary meaning which had come to apply within the Mughal empire was 'lands under the emperor's direct control.' Some Sikhs were already under the immediate control of the Guru and remitted their offerings directly to him. All were now commanded to come under his direct control, renouncing their obedience to the masands. They were, in other words, to join his Khalsa. In doing so they were to join a militant order with a rigorous discipline, their loyalty to its Master to be without question. The Khalsa still continues, its membership being the mark of a truly orthodox Sikh. Entry into it is by a ceremony of initiation known as amrit sanskar (q.v.). Only a small minority of Sikhs actually undergo initiation, but those who do (the Amrit-dharis or the Gursikhs [qq.v.]) are generally regarded as full-fledged Sikhs. The word is also used to designate any individual member of the Khalsa. *See also* KHALSA DATE; KHANDE DI PAHUL.

KHALSA COLLEGE. Khalsa College in Amritsar was the leading Sikh educational institution until the founding of Punjabi University in 1962. The decision to establish it was made in 1883. After tussles for control between the Sanatan Sikhs and the Tat Khalsa, (qq.v.) both agreed that they needed the other, and a Khalsa School was opened in 1893. In 1897 Khalsa College was begun with an English principal and, although in the first years it was very unstable, by 1905 its future was assured. For its foundation it depended on donations from some wealthy supporters of the Sanatan cause. As it stabilized, however, it became clear that Khalsa College was very much a Tat Khalsa institution. It expressed the conviction, born of the British example, that every community in India needed premiere educational institutions to symbolize its strength and to prepare its young men for the future. In 1920 it refused a grant from the government, thus freeing itself from government control. It is now a college of Guru Nanak Dev University.

KHALSA DATE. The date of the inauguration of the Khalsa (q.v.) has been the cause of much perplexity. Kuir Singh gives a date which corresponds to 1689; Sainapati and Ratan Singh Bhangu give 1695; Kesar Singh Chhibbar gives 1696; and Chaupa Singh gives 1697 (qq.v.). This evidence is contested by the historian Bute Shah who, writing in the middle of the nineteenth century, claimed that a newswriter, sent by the emperor Aurangzeb to observe the event, names Baisakhi Day 1756 (1699 CE). Bute Shah is, however, much too late to be acceptable. Baisakhi Day 1756 (1699 CE) is first mentioned in an extant source by Sukkha Singh (q.v.) almost one hundred years later in 1797. The date is strongly supported, however, by the modern historian Ganda Singh in articles and by his interpretation of certain hukam-namas (q.v.). The academic issue has not been definitively settled, but there can be no doubt concerning the corporate view of the Panth (q.v.). Baisakhi Day 1699 is definitely the approved date.

KHALSA INAUGURATION. Probably on Baisakhi Day 1699 (the first day of the new year corresponding to March 30th) Guru Gobind Singh (q.v.) summoned his Sikhs to his center at Anandpur (q.v.) for what turned out to be the most important event in Sikh history. This was the inauguration of the Khalsa (q.v.), the militant order which Sikhs have ever since been encouraged to join. Much that happened on that Baisakhi Day is still subject to research. Two things, however, can be positively affirmed. These are that Sikhs who joined the Khalsa were thereafter required to keep their hair uncut and that they were to carry arms. According to tradition, the Guru appeared with drawn sword before his followers, gathered for the Baisakhi festival, and demanded the head of a loyal Sikh. A Sikh called Daya Singh eventually volunteered and was conducted behind a screen to be despatched. Four more volunteers were then required, and they too were taken behind the screen. With five victims apparently despatched, the Guru revealed that none of them had in fact been slain. One version claims that five goats had been killed instead. The Guru was merely testing their loyalty in order to form the nucleus of his new order. These five (the Panj Piare [q.v.] or 'Cherished Five') had thereby proven themselves.

The Guru then held an initiation ceremony for the Panj Piare, following this by the same ceremony for all Sikhs who were prepared to undertake the discipline of the Khalsa. *See also* AMRIT-DHARI; AMRIT SANSKAR; BAISAKHI; KHALSA DATE.

KHALSA JI KA BOL-BALA. The welfare, prosperity, of the Khalsa (q.v.). Given as the Panth's (q.v.) highest aspiration in the Anandpur Resolution (q.v.).

KHALSA PARLIAMENT *see* BHASAUR SINGH SABHA.

KHALSA RAHIT PRAKASH. A rahit-nama produced by Babu Teja Singh (q.v.) of the Bhasaur Singh Sabha (q.v.) which gave expression to his fundamentalist views of the Khalsa Rahit (qq.v.).

KHALSA TRACT SOCIETY. Founded by Vir Singh (q.v.) in 1894, it published pamphlets on themes of interest to the Tat Khalsa (q.v.). Simply written and cheaply produced, they secured a wide distribution. Most of the pamphlets were actually written by Vir Singh. Christian publications provided the model.

KHAND *see* PANJ KHAND.

KHANDA. (1) A two-edged sword. To Guru Gobind Singh (q.v.) the khanda represented God and is held in great reverence by the Khalsa (q.v.). (2) The modern insignia of the Khalsa which comprises a vertical two-edged sword over a quoit (**chakkar**), with two crossed sabres (**kirpān**) below the quoit. During the late nineteenth century the emblem appears to have consisted of a cooking vessel, a **kaṭār** dagger, and a sabre, corresponding to the Khalsa slogan "deg tegh fateh" (q.v.). It seems that this evolved into the modern insignia in the early twentieth century, the round cooking vessel becoming a quoit. Today the emblem is displayed on the Khalsa flag, turbans, building decorations, publications, car windows, etc.

KHANDE DI PAHUL. 'Initiation by the sword'; baptism into the Khalsa (q.v.). When administering initiation to a candidate, water (**pāhul** or **pad-jal,** lit. 'foot-water') must be stirred with a two-edged sword (**khaṇḍā** [q.v.]). *See also* AMRIT SANSKAR; CHARAN-AMRIT.

KHARAK SINGH, BABA (1867–1963). Prominent leader of the Sikhs during the 1920s in the Central Sikh League (q.v.) and later in the Congress. In the early 1920s he was active in the Gurdwara Reform Movement (q.v.). During the 1930s he formed his own group, the Central Akali Dal, in opposition to the Shiromani Akali Dal (q.v.). In the latter period he commanded little influence. Kharak Singh was an Ahluvalia (q.v.).

KHARAK SINGH, MAHARAJA (1803–40). The eldest son of Ranjit Singh (q.v.), he was poorly trained to succeed his father. In 1839 he became Maharaja but left administration to his son Nau Nihal Singh (q.v.). He died as a result of opium consumption in 1840.

KHATRI CASTE. A high-ranking caste (**zāt** [q.v.]) in the Punjab, occupying a position at or near the very top of the Punjab's urban hierarchy. The name is the Punjabi form of Kshatriya, the Khatris claiming that they were warriors who took to trade. In their traditional occupation they command the better positions and are commonly found in large industry, banks, and insurance companies. Many Khatris travelled to distant places in pursuit of trade, and early Sikh sangats (q.v.) in widely scattered locations were really Khatri foundations. They have also been very prominent in culture and education. The vast majority of Khatris have remained Hindus, only a little more than two percent of all Sikhs belonging to the caste. They have, however, had an influence on the life of the Panth (q.v.) far greater than their numbers would suggest (particularly on education and the professions). When contracting marriages, Khatri almost always marries Khatri. Most Khatri Sikh families have no inhibitions about marrying their children to Hindus of the same caste. All the Gurus were Khatris by caste. *See also* CASTE; GURU-VANS.

KHEM SINGH BEDI (1832–1905). A direct descendant of Guru Nanak (q.v.) and one of the founders of the Singh Sabha (q.v.)

in 1873. As a Sanatan Sikh (q.v.) who maintained that there were no essential differences between Sikhs and Hindus, he was opposed by reformers of the Tat Khalsa persuasion (q.v.). He had, however, a considerable following in north-west Punjab where his descent and considerable charisma brought him many devotees.

KHIDRANA *see* MUKTSAR.

KHIVI (d. 1582). A Khatri of Khadur, wife of Guru Angad (qq.v.).

KHWAJA KHIZAR. A legendary Muslim saint worshipped as the river god in the Punjab. According to the *Puratan* janam-sakhis (q.v.), Guru Nanak (q.v.) discoursed with Khwaja Khizar.

KINSHIP. Broad kinship relationships are very important to Sikhs (as to other Indians). Every individual is, in theory, a member of a joint family, a biradari, a got, and a zat (qq.v.). The number of familial words (much larger than in English) tes-tifies to this importance. Descent is patrilineal, and marriages link two groups of kin rather than two individuals.

KIRATPUR. A village in the Shivalik Hills (q.v.), situated by the Satluj river overlooking the plains. Guru Hargobind (q.v.) ac-quired it in some manner, perhaps from the Raja of Bilaspur, and retired there when conflict with the Mughal authorities made the plains too dangerous. His successor, Guru Har Rai (q.v.), was compelled to abandon it and move further into the safety of the Shivaliks. Guru Tegh Bahadur (q.v.) returned to it, but left it soon after and moved five miles northeast along the Shivaliks to the village of Makhoval which he rebuilt and renamed Anandpur (q.v.). *See also* MUGHAL DYNASTY.

KIRPAL CHAND. The brother of Mata Gujari (q.v.). He achieved prominence as a member of the retinue of Guru Gobind Singh (q.v.).

KIRPAN. The sword or poniard which is carried by members of the Khalsa (q.v.). One of the Five Ks (q.v.). Fierce controversy has erupted from time to time over the right to wear the kirpan and the size required. In general six to nine inches in total length is regarded as satisfactory, though many Sikhs wear miniatures less than one inch in length attached to the kangha (q.v.). The terms 'dagger' and 'knife' are commonly regarded as demeaning translations.

KIRTAN. The corporate singing of devotional songs. For Sikhs, these are usually compositions from the Adi Granth (q.v.).

KIRTAN SOHILA *see* SOHILA.

KOER SINGH *see* KUIR SINGH.

KOMAGATA MARU. Early in the twentieth century, the Canadian government, concerned at the increasing flow of immigration from India, decreed that all prospective entrants must come from their own country by means of a 'continuous journey.' The Canadian parliament was still subject to limitation by the British government, and as India was a part of the British Empire no overt discrimination could be allowed. Covertly, however, this was possible, and as no shipping line sailed direct from India to Canada without trans-shipping, the 'continuous journey' provision was acceptable. Gurdit Singh, a Singapore businessman, thwarted this by chartering a ship (the *Komagata Maru*) and sailing it from Calcutta to Vancouver where it arrived on May 23, 1914. On board it carried 376 Indians, all but 30 of them Sikhs. Permission to land was refused (except for 22 who were able to prove Canadian domicile), and a two-month legal battle ensued. The government of British Columbia was clearly in the wrong, but it held to its view. In the end, threatened by a cruiser and with provisions exhausted, Gurdit Singh had to weigh anchor and sail back to Calcutta. When the *Komagata Maru* berthed there the British ordered all its passengers to board a train for the Punjab. Gurdit Singh and his followers refused to obey and left the ship, carrying the Guru Granth Sahib (q.v.) in procession. The police opened fire, killing 18. Gurdit Singh and 28 others escaped and went into hiding. The remainder were captured and sent up to the Punjab, most of them to be interned

there. In Canada the *Komagata Maru* incident is still well remembered by the Sikhs.

KOTHA SAHIB. The room in Akal Takhat where the Guru
Granth Sahib, installed in the Golden Temple (qq.v.) by day,
is laid to rest at night.

KUIR SINGH. Alleged author of *Gur-bilās Pātshāhī 10,* the
heroic story of Guru Gobind Singh (q.v.). Although the work
claims an eighteenth-century origin it was actually written in
the early or mid-nineteenth century. *See also* DEVI WOR-
SHIP; GUR-BILAS.

KUKA SIKHS *see* NAMDHARI.

KULLA PATH. A complete reading of the Guru Granth Sahib
(q.v.) in an indefinite period with no preordained date for the
bhog ceremony (q.v.). *See also* SADHARAN PATH.

KURAHIT. Violation of the Rahit (q.v.) or 'Serious Sin.' The
modern Rahit, as set out in *Sikh Rahit Maryādā* (q.v.), specifies four prohibitions or **kurahits** which are particularly serious for amrit-dhari Sikhs (q.v.). These are cutting one's
hair, eating meat which is **kuṭṭhā** (q.v.), having sexual intercourse with anyone other than one's spouse, and using tobacco (q.v.). Anyone who commits any of these cardinal sins
must confess and then be re-initiated. Three of the prohibitions were included in the eighteenth-century Rahit. The sexual intercourse item, however, is evidently a modern development from the eighteenth-century prohibition of
intercourse with Muslim women.

KURI-MAR *see* FEMALE INFANTICIDE.

KUTTHA. Animals killed according to Muslim law (**halāl** meat
[q.v.]). One of the four kurahits (q.v.) which Sikhs of the
Khalsa (q.v.) must swear at initiation to avoid. The purpose
of making this a kurahit was clearly to distinguish Sikhs from
their enemies, the Muslims. Meat is **halāl** when the animal
has been allowed to bleed to death while the Muslim confes-

sion of faith is recited. Sikhs of the Khalsa may consume meat only from an animal which has been killed with a single blow (**jhaṭkā** [q.v.]).

L

LAHINA (1504–52). A Trehan Khatri of Khadur (qq.v.) who became a disciple of Nanak (q.v.). He was later renamed Angad (q.v.) and succeeded Nanak as the second Guru of the Sikhs in 1538 or 1539.

LAHORE. The chief city of undivided Punjab and the capital city of Ranjit Singh (q.v.) and his successors. Lahore has many shrines sacred to the Sikhs, among them Dera Sahib (q.v.) and Shahidganj.

LAKHI JUNGLE. A wasteland south of Firozpur where the Khalsa (q.v.) sheltered during periods of persecution in the eighteenth century.

LAKHMI DAS (trad. 1497–1555). One of the two sons of Guru Nanak (q.v.), traditionally believed to have opposed his father's appointment of Angad (q.v.) as second Guru. His descendants continue to this day. *See also* GURU-VANS; SIRI CHAND.

LAKHPAT RAI. A chief minister of Lahore under the Mughal governor Zakariya Khan (q.v.), noted for persecuting the Khalsa. In 1738 he had the custodian of Harimandir Sahib (q.v.), Mani Singh (q.v), executed. Under Zakariya Khan's successor Yahya Khan he continued his vigorous persecution, and in 1746 he killed several thousand Sikhs near Gurdaspur in the Chhota Ghallughara (q.v.).

LAKSHMAN SINGH, BHAGAT (1863–1944). A prominent if uncritical writer in the time of the Singh Sabha (q.v.). Author of *Guru Govind Singh, Sikh Martyrs* and a useful *Autobiography*.

LALO. According to later janam-sakhi tradition (q.v.), Nanak (q.v.) once stayed in Saidpur (q.v.) with a low-caste carpenter named Lalo. A rich Khatri (q.v.), Malik Bhago, wished to know why the Guru had not stayed with him. In reply Nanak took a portion of Lalo's coarse food in one hand and some of Bhago's rich fare in the other. When he squeezed them milk issued from Lalo's food and blood from that of Bhago. The amazed Bhago at once fell at his feet and, giving away his ill-gotten gains, became his faithful Sikh.

LANGAR. The free kitchen and dining hall, or other provision for serving meals, which must be attached to all gurdwaras (q.v.). The purpose was clearly to eliminate caste on the territory of the gurdwara and so to eliminate it as either a means or a hindrance to liberation. Everyone had to sit in the same status-free lines (**pangat** [q.v.]), and everyone had to take the food without knowing who had prepared it. The convention was borrowed from Sufi (q.v.) establishments (khanqahs). It is not known for certain which Guru introduced the practice, but it was evidently present in the time of Amar Das (q.v.). In smaller gurdwaras the langar may be operating only once a week; in the larger ones every day. Gifts of produce and fuel are **sevā** (q.v.) to the Guru, as is unpaid time spent serving in the langar.

LANGUAGES. Sikhs attach a deeply affectionate importance to the Punjabi language and its Gurmukhi script (q.v.). Although most of the janam-sakhis are recorded in Punjabi, the language of the Adi Granth (q.v.) is best described as Sant Bhasha ('Sant language') or as the Sacred Language of the Sikhs. The Dasam Granth (q.v.) is in the Gurmukhi script, but the language is predominantly Braj ([q.v.] the language of the Mathura region and the Krishna cycle). In the nineteenth century Sikh literary usage swung strongly back to Punjabi. *See also* ADI GRANTH LANGUAGE.

LAVAN. The act of circumambulating a sacred fire (Hindu rite) or the scripture (Sikh rite) during a marriage ceremony. In

Anand Karaj (q.v.) the couple make four **lāvān** round the Adi Granth (q.v.) while the four stanzas of Guru Ram Das's *Sūhī Chhant* 2 (*AG,* pp. 773–4) are sung.

LITURGY. By the time the Adi Granth (q.v.) was compiled in 1603 and 1604, a daily liturgy had clearly emerged within the Panth (q.v.) and is recorded on the opening thirteen pages of the scripture. This liturgy comprises Nanak's *Japjī* (early morning); Raharas (sunset); and Kirtan Sohila (before retiring at night) (qq.v.). *See also* NIT-NEM.

LOHARI. A festival marking the end of the short winter, held at night on the last day of the month of Poh (January).

LONGOWAL *or* LANGAVAL *see* HARCHAND SINGH LONGOWAL.

M

MACAULIFFE (1837–1913). A name deeply revered in the Panth (q.v.). Max Arthur Macauliffe was an ICS officer assigned to the Punjab. He rose to be a Deputy Commissioner in 1882 and a Divisional Judge in 1884. Meanwhile, he had been studying the literature of the Sikhs, and in 1893 he resigned from the ICS to devote his time exclusively to it. Trumpp's (q.v.) translation of the Adi Granth (q.v.) had caused deep offence to the Sikhs, and Macauliffe's intention was to produce a translation of his own that would repair the damage. Also, he argued, the government would be wise to understand a people who were potentially of great assistance to it. Working closely with Kahn Singh Nabha (q.v.) and various gianis in Amritsar (qq.v), he circulated his drafts widely among the Sikhs. Eventually the work was completed and was published as *The Sikh Religion* (six volumes in three) in 1909. It contains accounts of the lives of the ten Gurus and the bhagats (q.v.) of the Adi Granth, together with extensive translations of their works. Unfortunately the work received no patronage from the Punjab Government, and as a result the publication cost Macauliffe a large sum. *The Sikh Religion* has had an immense and continuing success. It is important to remember, however, that the author consistently reflects the Singh Sabha (q.v.) attitudes of his close Sikh associates. Highly sympathetic to the Tat Khalsa (q.v.), his work is generally uncritical in treatment of it.

MAHADEVI. The third of the three wives of Guru Hargobind (q.v.).

MAHALA. The word employed in the Adi Granth (q.v.) to indicate authorship by one of the Gurus. Mahala 1 (or M1) designates Guru Nanak (q.v.); Mahala 2 (or M2) Guru Angad (q.v.); and so on. The formula is used at the beginning of each work. The origin of the word is obscure. It may have been borrowed from Mughal usage which referred to a principality as a mahala. Alternatively **mahal** means 'abode'; and **mahalā,** deriving from **mahal,** may mean 'the place [where Akal Purakh (q.v.) resides].'

MAHANT. 'Superior'; the head of an establishment such as those of the Naths or Udasis (qq.v.). Its reputation for modern Sikhs has been tarnished beyond redemption, for this was the title applied to the hereditary proprietors of gurdwaras (q.v.), some of whom became a scandal to the Panth (q.v.) during the early years of the twentieth century. *See also* GURDWARA REFORM MOVEMENT.

MAHARAJ SINGH, BHAI (d. 1856). The successor of Bir Singh (q.v.), he attracted many thousands of Sikhs by his preaching and his reputation as a miracle worker. He fought against the British in the second Sikh War of 1848 and 1849 and after eluding capture was finally taken and transported to Burma.

MAHIMA PRAKASH. There are two different janam-sakhis (q.v.) of this name: the *Mahīmā Prakāsh Vāratak* (prose) and the *Mahīmā Prakāsh Kavitā* (verse). Apart from the fact that both originated in Khadur (q.v.) there is little to connect them.

Both appear to have been composed in the middle of the eighteenth century.

MAHTAB SINGH *see* MASSA RANGHAR.

MAKHAN SHAH. Makhan Shah Labana is traditionally said to have been a trader of the mid-seventeenth century who during a storm at sea vowed to give the Sikh Guru 501 gold mohurs if he should be spared. After the storm had abated he travelled up to the Punjab and was informed that the Guru was to be found in the village of Bakala. Upon proceeding there he found that many were claiming the title vacated by the recent death of Guru Har Krishan (q.v.). He decided to test them all, laying before each of the claimants two mohurs. When he reached Tegh Bahadur (q.v.) he was asked for the remainder which he had promised. Immediately he rushed up to the rooftop, proclaiming that he had found the true Guru.

MALA. A garland; a necklace; a rosary for aiding meditation.

MALCOLM (1769–1833). Following a visit to the Punjab with Lord Lake in 1805, John Malcolm published his *Sketch of the Sikhs* in 1810. The work, which was the result of extensive enquiries, mixes error with some very perceptive observations.

MALWA. The territory southeast of the Satluj river, one of the three areas into which central Punjab is divided. The eastern and southern boundaries are where the Punjabi language gives way to Hindi. The inhabitants are known as Malwais. *See also* DOABA; MANJH.

MAN. This word (a cognate of **manas** and pronounced 'mun' as in 'mundane') is of key importance in Gurmat (q.v.). It denotes the inner human faculty which combines the heart, mind, and soul of conventional western usage. When led astray by his/her own wayward notions, a person is following his/her **man** and is said to be **manmukh** (one who follows his/her own self-centered impulses). The opposite is **gurmukh** (q.v.). The way to truth involves the conquest of the

man. "Mani jītai jagu jītu," 'To conquer the **man** is to conquer the world' (*AG*, p. 6).

MANI SINGH (1673–1738). A Jat Sikh (q.v.), born in a village near Patiala. He became a devoted follower of Guru Gobind Singh (q.v.) and after the evacuation of Anandpur in 1704 escorted two of the Guru's wives to Delhi. Returning to join the Guru in Damdama Sahib, (q.v.) he inscribed a copy of the Adi Granth (q.v.) at the Guru's dictation. He is also said to have gathered together the various works which now form the Dasam Granth (q.v.). In the controversy over changes introduced into the Panth (q.v.) by Banda (q.v.), he evidently sided with the Tat Khalsa (q.v.). When the Punjab eventually quieted down following the execution of Banda, he was placed in charge of Harimandir Sahib (q.v.) by Mata Sundari (q.v.). In 1738 he was executed by the Mughal governor of Lahore (q.v.) on a spurious charge of failing to pay tribute. Since then he has been remembered by the Panth as a great martyr.

MANI SINGH JANAM-SAKHI *see* GYAN-RATANAVALI.

MANJH (MAJH, MAJHA, MANJHA). The Bari interfluvial tract; the territory between the Beas/Satluj and Ravi rivers, one of three areas into which central Punjab is divided. The inhabitants are known as Majhails. *See also* DOABA; MALWA.

MANJI. Considerable uncertainty surrounds the title of manji, granted to a small number of faithful Sikhs during the early years of the Panth (q.v.). Literally meaning 'string-bed' the word designated the person who, possessing authority or esteem, sat on the bed while everyone else sat on the ground. In this sense, the word is used today to designate the stool or lectern on which the Guru Granth Sahib (q.v.) rests. Guru Amar Das (q.v.) is usually credited with having appointed the first manjis and to have awarded the title to those empowered to preach in his name. The honor did not imply any geographical authority, and there is no justification for the parallel with the Emperor Akbar's twenty-two provinces (**bāī** sūbā). The order did not last very long and was replaced under Guru Ram Das (q.v.) by the masands (q.v.), men with a significantly larger and more formal authority than the manjis had possessed.

MANJI SAHIB. 1. The lectern on which the Guru Granth Sahib (q.v.) is placed in a gurdwara (q.v.). 2. Several shrines or gurdwaras bear the name of Manji Sahib, a prominent one being on the southeastern side of the pool of Harimandir Sahib in Amritsar (qq.v.) where Guru Arjan (q.v.) is said to have held regular audience. It has since been frequently used for Sikh gatherings and is now covered in by the Divan Hall.

MANMUKH. 'One whose face is turned to [his/her own] **man'** (q.v.); a self-willed, wayward person. *See also* GURMUKH.

MARDANA (1459–1634). A Muslim by religion and a Mirasi by caste, Mardana was born in Rai Bhoi di Talvandi (q.v.) and presumably earned his early living by his caste profession of minstrel, playing the rabab (q.v.). The janam-sakhis (q.v.) are unanimous in naming him as Nanak's (q.v.) regular companion and rababi, and this can be accepted. In the janam-sakhis he regularly appears as a foil to Nanak's wise sayings or miracles. Three compositions by him appear in the Adi Granth (q.v.).

MARRIAGE *see* ANAND KARAJ and ARRANGED MARRIAGES.

MARTIAL RACES. When the British developed their theory of the 'martial races' of India during the latter part of the nineteenth century, the Sikhs were one of the main beneficiaries. The British needed soldiers for the Indian Army who possessed both fighting skills and loyalty to their commanders. In response, they developed the theory of the martial races. The Sikhs were prime candidates for inclusion, partly because they had fought the British so vigorously in the Anglo-Sikh wars (q.v.) and partly because most of them proved to be hostile to the Indians responsible for the 1857 uprising. As a result they were strongly favored in recruitment, taking their place with other 'martial races' such as the Punjabi Muslims and the Gurkhas. Not all Sikhs were so favored, however, and recruitment officers had manuals which specified castes and regions which were regarded as sound or otherwise. Whereas in general the Jats (q.v.) were greatly esteemed, the Aroras (q.v.) were largely ignored. During World War II remittances to Punjab villages caused the Akali Dal (q.v.) to favor continued recruitment in spite of the fact that it had been aligned with the Congress Party which opposed it. After independence in 1947 the proportion of Sikhs in the armed forces was seriously cut back, places being filled by regional quotas. Sikhs, protesting this, claim that places ought rather to be filled by reputations for fighting ability. *See also* ARMY, ARMED FORCES; MILITANCY.

MARTYR *see* SHAHID.

MARYADA. Ritual; order of service; religious practice.

MASAND. Evidently a corrupted version of the Arabic **masnad,** 'throne' or 'one who sits on a throne.' The masands were first instituted as surrogates of the Guru, evidently by Ram Das (q.v.). It appears that they replaced the manjis (q.v.) appointed by Amar Das (q.v.), creating a regular order and significantly enlarging the responsibilities of the manjis. In addition to preaching, they were also commissioned to oversee individual sangats or groups of sangats and to collect offerings made to the Guru (the **dasvandh** [q.v.]). These would be passed on to the Guru whenever the masands made contact with him, perhaps at one of the annual festivals. During their early years, the masands apparently performed their duties faithfully, but by the time of Gobind Singh (q.v.) many of them had become largely independent and corrupt. The Guru therefore abolished them when he founded the Khalsa (q.v.), probably in 1699. A follower of a masand is called a masandia. *See also* PANJ MEL.

MASIA *see* AMAVAS.

MASSA RANGHAR. A Hindu Rajput appointed commandant of Amritsar (q.v.) by the Mughal governor of Lahore, Zakariya

Khan (q.v.). He used the precincts of Harimandir Sahib (q.v.) for amusement with dancing girls and in 1740 was daringly assassinated for his sacrilege by Mahtab Singh and Sukkhar Singh.

MATA. 'Mother'; a title of respect given to older women. The wives of the Gurus, for example, are always called Mata.

MATHA TEKANA. 'To place the forehead [on the ground],' the action performed before the Adi Granth (q.v.) by anyone entering a gurdwara (q.v.).

MATI DAS (d.1675). One of three Sikhs executed with Guru Tegh Bahadur (q.v.). *See also* DAYAL DAS; SATI DAS.

MAYA. In the Adi Granth (q.v.) **māyā** signifies the corrupt and corrupting world with all its snares, seductively presented to people as permanent and incorruptible and thus masquerading as ultimate truth. In some Sikh contexts it means filthy lucre.

MAYA SINGH. A prominent member of the early Lahore Singh Sabha (q.v.) and editor of the Urdu *Khalsa Gazette*. Formerly a member of the Arya Samaj (q.v.).

MAZHABI. A Sikh from the Chuhra (sweeper) caste; an Outcaste Sikh. *See also* CASTE; DALIT; RAMDASIA; RANGH-RETA.

MEHTAB SINGH (1879–1938). An Arora Sikh (q.v.). A prominent political leader in the early 1920s.

MEWA SINGH. A granthi (q.v.) in Vancouver who in 1914 killed an Anglo-Indian policeman called Hopkinson who was employed by the government of British Columbia to break up the Ghadr movement (q.v.). Mewa Singh is regarded as a martyr, and the anniversary of his execution is celebrated by the Sikhs of North America.

MIAN MIR (1550–1635). A Sufi (q.v.) with whom Guru Arjan (q.v.) is traditionally believed to have been friendly. The belief that he laid the foundation stone of Harmandir Sahib (q.v.) is unsubstantiated.

MIGRATION. Until the late nineteenth century migrant Sikhs were chiefly traders who settled elsewhere in India or in neighboring lands to the west. This range was substantially enlarged by the Indian Army of the British. Sikh soldiers stationed in Singapore and Hong Kong began the Punjabi migration to both territories, a small flow which soon extended down to Australia, New Zealand, and Fiji. Most were male Jats (q.v.), virtually all of them seeking temporary unskilled employment. Others had discovered opportunities along the west coast of North America, the first migrants arriving in 1903. Semi-skilled artisans (mainly Ramgarhias [q.v.]) were also taken across to East Africa to lay railways. Early in the twentieth century these doors were closed. When the Punjabi flow recommenced after World War II it issued from both India and Pakistan, with most migrating to England but significant numbers again going to North America. As before, a substantial majority of those from India were Sikhs from districts bordering the upper Satluj. By 1987 there were an estimated 269,600 Sikhs in Britain. There are also communities of roughly 175,000 each in the United States and Canada.

MIHARAB. The niche in a mosque which indicates the qibla (i.e. the direction of the Ka'bah in Mecca).

MIHARBAN (1581–1640). The son of Prithi Chand (q.v.) and his successor as leader of the Mina sect (q.v.).

MIHARBAN JANAM-SAKHI. A six-volume janam-sakhi (q.v.) attributed to Miharban (q.v.) and his successors. As they were Minas (q.v.), the janam-sakhi is generally thought to be heretical. This is not so, as the Minas, though schismatic, were generally orthodox. The work uses the janam-sakhi pattern as a framework, but adds extensive exegesis of the works of Nanak (q.v.) to each janam-sakhi incident. Only the first three volumes have survived.

MILITANCY. The Sikhs have won fame as a warrior race. This reputation has certainly been earned by many of them, but it needs to be qualified. It is the Jats (q.v.) who have been largely responsible for this reputation, other castes being less conspicuous. The Punjab has always been an area crossed by invaders, and open warfare is a useful means both of protection and offence. The Jats were notably successful in this respect, gradually establishing for themselves the position of the dominant caste in rural Punjab. A Jat normally went armed, at least with a stave, and the men had long since discovered that the force of their arms was the best method of securing their objectives. This attitude has been widely believed to be characteristic of the Panth (q.v.) as a whole. It should be noted that more than sixty percent of Sikhs are Jats, so the mistake is an understandable one. Moreover, other Punjabi castes such as the Khatris could also produce their warriors, including of course Guru Hargobind and Guru Gobind Singh (qq.v.). Sikhs sometimes show their sympathy for militancy in the personal names they choose. ('Karnail' and 'Jarnail' are the Punjabi forms of 'Colonel' and 'General.') It was also conspicuously displayed by the actions of many members of the Panth in opposing the Government of India in the troubles which affected the state between 1984 and 1992. *See also* ARMY, ARMED FORCES; MARTIAL RACES.

MILNI. The meeting of the relatives of both sides prior to the celebration of a wedding. At the place of marriage the father of the groom steps forward and is embraced by the father of the bride. Brothers and uncles then follow. Gifts are given to the groom's relatives by the relatives of the bride.

MINA ('dissembler,' unscrupulous scoundrel). The term applied to any follower of Prithi Chand (q.v.), eldest brother of Arjan (q.v.) and disappointed contender for the title of Guru. Ram Das (q.v.) had three sons, and although he had decided that the office should remain in his family, his choice of a successor went to his youngest son Arjan. Prithi Chand vigorously disputed this decision and on one occasion is said to have tried to poison the young Hargobind (q.v.), Arjan's only child. Prithi Chand was succeeded in his claim to be the rightful Guru by his son Miharban (q.v.). The group controlled

Amritsar (q.v.) for much of the seventeenth century, and under the second successor Hariji was able to keep Guru Tegh Bahadur (q.v.) from entering it. The Minas were included in the Panj Mel (q.v.). During the eighteenth century the group faded away and is now extinct.

MIR MANNU (d. 1753). Son of the Vazir of Delhi, his correct name was Muin ul-Mulk. He was appointed Governor of Lahore and Multan (qq.v.) in 1748 during the period when Mughal power was rapidly declining in the Punjab and made determined efforts to suppress Sikhs who were disrupting the province. He had to confront the Afghan invader Ahmad Shah Abdali (q.v.), however, which necessitated enrolling Sikhs in his army. With this danger past he returned to a policy of vigorous suppression. In 1753 he was killed when his horse fatally threw him.

MIRASI. A depressed caste of Muslim genealogists and musicians; the caste to which Mardana (q.v.) belonged. Also called Dum.

MIRI/PIRI. Hargobind (q.v.) is traditionally believed to have symbolically donned two swords when succeeding as sixth Guru. One sword was called **pīrī**, marking a continuation of the spiritual mission of his five predecessors. The other was new. This represented **mīrī**, the right of the Guru to wear arms and to fight against tyranny. Both terms are of Muslim derivation, **pīrī** signifying the spiritual role of a Sufi pir (q.v.) and **mīrī** the rank of a mir or chieftain. The term **mīrī/pīrī** seems not to have been used for some time, but it later attained popularity as a result of its rhyme and is frequently cited as justification for the duty of the Panth (q.v.) to fight against oppression.

MIRTAK SANSKAR *see* FUNERAL.

MISL. An armed group of Sikh horsemen during the middle and later decades of the eighteenth century. Under their misldars (q.v.) they acquired regional authority over areas of varying size. The misls (or misals) began as warrior bands providing protection for the Khalsa (q.v.) as order progressively broke down in the Punjab and taking advantage of conditions of growing lawlessness. Jats (q.v.) were particularly prominent in the misls, though other rural castes also participated. In the early years rudimentary misls fought against the declining authority of the Mughals. Later, as they became firmer in their organization, the chief enemy was the Afghan army under Ahmad Shah Abdali (q.v.). As the Afghan threat receded, the misls marked out their individual territories more distinctly and at times engaged in internecine warfare. Operations were based on **rākhī** or protection money, normally one-fifth of a village's produce. Two of them (the Bhangi and the Phulkian misls [qq.v.]) had meanwhile grown into confederacies. Finally one of their number, Ranjit Singh (q.v.) of the Shukerchakia misl (q.v.), defeated or absorbed all the misls north and west of the Satluj river and emerged as ruler of an undivided Punjab around 1800. Misls to the south of the Satluj were obliterated or protected by the advancing British. Those that were protected (all parts of the Phulkian federation) were retained as princely states, the chief amongst them Patiala. Twelve misls are recognized. These are the Bhangi, Shukerchakia, Kahnaiya, Ramgarhia, Nakkai, Faizulpuria (or Singhpuria), Ahluvalia, Dallevalia, Karorsinghia, Nishanvalia, Shahid, and Phulkian (qq.v.). In addition to these twelve there were other bands of Khalsa horsemen, each under its sardar (q.v.), which evidently lacked the distinction of a misl. The precise nature of the Sikh misls as fighting bands and as political authorities is still imperfectly understood. So too is the etymology of the word 'misl' which may perhaps derive from the Arabic **mishal,** 'equal.' *See also* EIGHTEENTH CENTURY HISTORY.

MISLDAR. The sardar (q.v.) in command of a misl (q.v.).

MOHAN. The elder of the sons of Amar Das (q.v.), he opposed his father's choice of Ram Das (q.v.) as fourth Guru. He retained custody of the Goindval Pothis (q.v.), recorded on his father's instructions by his son Sahans Ram.

MOHAN POTHIS *see* GOINDVAL POTHIS.

MOHAN SINGH VAID (1881–1936). An Ayurvedic doctor from Tarn Taran who worked enthusiastically for the Singh Sabha (q.v.). His principal contribution lay in his Punjabi writings (journalism, pamphlets, books, and novels) in which social issues were prominent. His large library was left to Punjabi University, Patiala.

MOHARI. The younger son of Amar Das (q.v.). He opposed his father's choice of Ram Das (q.v.) as fourth Guru.

MOKSHA *see* MUKTI.

MONA. Strictly, any person who has undergone ritual shaving of the head. Singh Sabha (q.v.) usage designated those who cut their hair after Khalsa initiation. In modern usage it refers loosely and somewhat pejoratively to any Sikh who cuts his/her hair.

MONOGAMY. *Sikh Rahit Maryādā* (q.v.) states that 'normally a Sikh should have only one wife.' The 'normally' is evidently added because Guru Hargobind and Guru Gobind Singh (qq.v.) both had three wives simultaneously. In the Punjab, strongly influenced by Muslim example, an important person would commonly be expected to marry more than once for such reasons as signifying alliances or providing protection to women needing it. Maharaja Ranjit Singh (q.v.) also had several wives.

MORCHA. 'Facing the enemy'; a campaign against the government waged by the Akali Dal (q.v.).

MOUNT SUMERU. The legendary Puranic mountain at the center of the earth. The janam-sakhis (q.v.) all relate a discourse which Guru Nanak (q.v.) held there with the eighty-four immortal Siddhs (q.v.).

MUGHAL DYNASTY. Babur, the first of the Mughals, invaded north India from Afghanistan and with the Battle of Panipat in 1526 established the Mughal dynasty. This falls within the lifetime of Nanak (q.v.). Aurangzeb (q.v.), the last of the six so-called Great Mughals, died in 1707, the year before the death of Gobind Singh (q.v.). The height of Mughal rule thus coincided with the ten Gurus. The line of Gurus first became the object of hostile notice by the Mughals when the fourth emperor, Jahangir, observed in his memoirs that it was attracting too many followers and that the incumbent Guru, Arjan (q.v.), had evidently offered support to the rebel Prince Khusrau. The action which was taken against Arjan is obscure, but it seems that he received a heavy fine which he was unable to pay and that he died in prison. Jahangir's enmity was carried over to the sixth Guru, Hargobind (q.v.), who after some brushes with Mughal troops found it expedient to withdraw in 1634 to Kiratpur in the Shivalik Hills (qq.v.). While they remained in the Shivaliks the Gurus were not seriously troubled by the Mughals, apart from a summons to Guru Har Rai (q.v.) in 1661 and the execution of Guru Tegh Bahadur (q.v.) at Aurangzeb's command in 1675. It was in the time of Guru Gobind Singh that relations became critical. Mughal troops joined hill chiefs in an assault on his center of Anandpur (q.v.) and in 1704, while the Sikhs were withdrawing from it, treacherously attacked them. The Guru managed to escape but lost all four sons. He withdrew to south Punjab where Aurangzeb evidently decided to conciliate him, suggesting that they should meet in the Deccan. Before they could do so Aurangzeb died. Gobind Singh went to the Deccan to meet his successor Bahadur Shah but was assassinated in Nander (q.v.) in 1708. *See also* SAHIB-ZADE.

MUKTI. Liberation of the human spirit from the bonds of transmigration. The term moksha is also commonly used.

MUKTSAR. In 1705 at Khidrana, south of Faridkot, Vazir Khan (q.v.) caught up with the army of Guru Gobind Singh (q.v.) but was repulsed. The site was renamed Muktsar, 'the Pool of the Liberated Ones,' in remembrance of the Chali Mukte (q.v.) who were all killed in the battle. *See also* BHAGO.

MUL MANTRA. The 'root mantra,' the Basic Credal Statement which begins the Adi Granth (q.v.). In translation it reads: "There is one Supreme Being, the Eternal Reality. He is the

Creator, without fear and devoid of enmity. He is immortal, never incarnated, self-existent, known by grace through the Guru." *See also* GENDER OF GOD.

MULA. A Chona Khatri of Batala, father-in-law of Nanak (qq.v.).

MULTAN. A city southwest of the Punjab proper and the capital of a suba (province) under the Mughals. Bhai Gurdas (q.v.) relates a story of how Nanak (q.v.), while approaching Multan, was sent a cup brimful of milk by the pirs (q.v.) of the city, signifying that it already had all the holy men it could contain. Nanak's answer was to lay a jasmine petal on the milk and return it without spilling a drop, thereby proclaiming that there was room for one more. This illustrates the kind of story which gains common currency in hagiography. The anecdote, applied to pirs, already had wide popularity among the Sufis (q.v.)

MUNDAVANI. A composition by Guru Arjan (q.v.) which, with its attached **shalok** (q.v.), concludes the text of the Adi Granth (q.v.) on page 1429. Only the *Rāg-mālā* (q.v.) remains.

MUSLIM RELATIONS. In the time of the Gurus the Mughal emperors, who were also Muslims, sometimes showed enmity towards them. During this period there is little evidence of strong hostility towards the Muslims on the part of the Sikhs. In the eighteenth century, however, this hostility grew markedly in response to attacks by Mughals and later by Afghans (also Muslims). So powerful did the feeling become that several anti-Muslim injunctions are specifically written into the early Rahit (q.v.) as it evolved during the eighteenth century. Under Ranjit Singh (q.v.) the feeling subsided to some extent, but it has always remained in at least a subdued form within the Panth (q.v.). In the events leading up to the partition of India in 1947 (q.v.), the Sikhs, faced by the choice between the Hindus and the Muslims, chose to confront the Muslims. The bloody events which followed partition produced the deepest bitterness. The Muslims of the Punjab felt the same with regard to both Sikhs and Hindus. During the struggle for Khalistan (q.v.) in the later 1980s, some efforts were made to reach agreement with the Muslims of Pakistan. It seems, however, that Pakistan's principal concern was embarrassment for India and no lasting friendship resulted. *See also* MUGHAL DYNASTY.

MUSLIM WOMEN. Eighteenth-century sources indicate that sexual contact with Muslim women was polluting, and Guru Gobind Singh (q.v.) is said to have commanded that during warfare they should not be seized for this purpose. This feature evidently perplexed the Singh Sabha (q.v.) reformers. Kahn Singh Nabha (q.v.) claimed that at the time most prostitutes were Muslim women and that the Guru's command can therefore be construed as a prohibition against sexual intercourse with any woman other than one's wife. This interpretation has been written into the contemporary Rahit (q.v.) where it appears in *Sikh Rahit Maryādā* (q.v.) as the third of the kurahit (q.v.).

N

NAGAR KIRTAN. 'Singing in town'; taking the Guru Granth Sahib (q.v.) on procession through a town on a day of religious celebration such as a Gurpurab (q.v.). Following ceremonies at a gurdwara (q.v.), the scripture is mounted above the cabin of a suitably decorated truck or other float. Preceded by Panj Piare (q.v.), normally with unsheathed swords, it leads a procession through the streets to the accompaniment of kirtan (q.v.).

NAGARA. A large drum. Every gurdwara (q.v.) should possess one, to be beaten on appropriate occasions. The origins are obscure, though it can be assumed to have played an important part in the martial activities of Guru Gobind Singh (q.v.).

NAI. The barber caste. A few Nais became Sikh, forming with members of the Tarkhan (carpenter) and Raj (blacksmith) castes the exclusively Sikh caste known as Ramgarhia (q.v.).

NAKKAI MISL. A small misl (q.v.) with territory bordering on Multan (q.v.). Ranjit Singh (q.v.), whose second wife was from the Nakkai misl, annexed its territories early in the nineteenth century.

NAM. The doctrine of the **nām** lies at the heart of Nanak's teaching, and in subsequent Gurmat (q.v.) it retains its primacy. The word means literally 'name,' sometimes used in combinations such as **hari-nām** or **rām-nām** (the 'Name of God') but normally standing alone. It is a convenient shorthand, designating in summary terms the nature and being of Akal Purakh (q.v.). Anything which may be affirmed concerning Akal Purakh is an aspect of the **nām**. This means that it embraces such concepts as love, power, omniscience, infinity, and other qualities of the divine. Ultimately the **nām** is beyond human grasp, but to each person is given the means for a sufficient understanding of it. Akal Purakh resides immanently in this world. By opening one's eyes, inward as well as outward, one can perceive the **nām** in all its wonder and all its glory. *See also* NAM JAPAN; NAM SIMARAN; SHABAD.

NAM DAN ISHNAN. 'The divine Name, charity, and bathing.' A popular formula for spiritual liberation spelled out frequently in the janam-sakhis (q.v.). The formula had been used by both Nanak and Arjan (qq.v.), but in their case 'bathing' probably meant inner purity.

NAM JAPAN. 'Repeating the Name.' **Nām japaṇ** is a less sophisticated form of meditation than **nām simaraṇ** (q.v.). It consists of uttering a word, syllable, or mantra of particular religious import (e.g. **satnām, vāhigurū**) either as a pious ejaculation or repeatedly. For the latter procedure a simarani (rosary) is commonly used. A more varied form, which may be characterized as either **nām simaraṇ** or **nām japaṇ,** is singing or chanting gurbani (q.v.). Gurdwara worship or daily nit-nem (qq.v.) is thus legitimate meditation.

NAM JAPO, KIRAT KARO, VAND CHHAKO. "Repeat the divine Name, work, and give a share [of your earnings to others less fortunate]." A popular proverb which sums up the duty laid upon all Sikhs. It does not appear in the Adi Granth (q.v.).

NAM SIMARAN. The Sikh meditation technique. Gurmat (q.v.) affirms that liberation is attained primarily through the discipline of **nām simaraṇ,** 'remembering' the divine Name (q.v.). By meditating regularly, one will progressively shed the bonds of haumai (q.v.). The spirit is gradually liberated from the afflictions of transmigration, and finally the faithful disciple enters the condition of sahaj (q.v.), or perfect peace. *See also* NAM JAPAN.

NAMDEV (1270–1350). A poet of the Varkari bhakti sect of Pandharpur in Maharashtra. Sixty-one works (possibly sixty-two) by Namdev appear in the Adi Granth (q.v.), a number which is second only to Kabir (q.v.) in the bhagat bani (q.v.). There is still some doubt whether the Adi Granth works are by the Pandharpur poet, and if so whether Namdev ever paid an extended visit to the Punjab. The first of these is a strong likelihood, and the second is at least possible. In the village of Ghuman near Batala there exists a tradition of a lengthy visit and a very old samadhi (cenotaph).

NAMDHARI. A Sikh sect, also known as the Kuka ('crier') movement, owing to ecstatic practices during religious services. Originally developed in northwest Punjab through the preaching of Balak Singh (1799–1862) the movement shifted its center to Bhaini Sahib in Ludhiana District under its second leader Ram Singh (q.v.). The orthodox belief that the line of personal Gurus ended with the death of Gobind Singh (q.v.) is denied by the Namdharis. They maintain that the tenth Guru lived for many years after 1708, eventually bestowing the succession on Balak Singh. They accordingly differ from the orthodox in claiming that the personal line of Gurus still continues. The Namdhari Sikhs are strict vegetarians and vigorous protectors of the cow. They attach equal importance to the Adi Granth and the Dasam Granth (qq.v.), and they include the Dasam Granth composition *Chaṇḍī Kī Vār* (q.v.) in their daily Nit-nem (q.v.). All Namdharis are at least Kes-dharis (q.v.). They wear only white homespun clothing, and the men are easily recognized by their method of tying turbans horizontally across the forehead. Their distinctive rituals include the fire ceremony (**havan**) and the practice of circumambulating a fire during the course of their wedding ceremony (normally conducted with many couples being married at the same time). *See also* NIL-DHARI; ORTHODOXY.

NAME. For the divine Name *see* NAM.

NAMING CEREMONY. As soon as convenient after birth, the family should take the baby to their gurdwara (q.v.), together with karah prasad (q.v.), and there give thanks. If a complete path (q.v.) has been arranged, this visit should coincide with the bhog (q.v.). The Guru Granth Sahib (q.v.) is then opened at random, and a name is chosen beginning with the same letter as the first composition on the left-hand page. When a hymn begins on the preceding page (as is usually the case) the person selecting a letter turns back to its actual beginning. No distinction marks boys' and girls' names (either can, for example, have the name Prem), but to a boy's name 'Singh' (q.v.) should be added (Prem Singh) and to a girl's name 'Kaur' (Prem Kaur) (q.v.).

NANAK, GURU (1469–1538 or 1539). The first Guru of the Sikhs. Sikhs date the foundation of the Panth (q.v.) from his life of teaching and example. Although there exist extensive hagiographic accounts of his life known as janam-sakhis (q.v.), little of the information which they provide can be accepted as proven or indeed as possible. His teachings are secure, however, as a large number of his authentic works are recorded in the Adi Granth (q.v.). Nanak shares a particular place in Sikh sentiments with Gobind Singh (q.v.). The life of simple piety which he lived, together with the beauty of his hymns, produce firm loyalty and a deeply-held affection. *See also* NANAK: DOCTRINE; NANAK: LIFE.

NANAK: DOCTRINE. Nanak taught a doctrine of liberation which was closely modelled on that of the Sant Tradition of

Northern India (q.v.), and his numerous hymns are contained in the Adi Granth (q.v.). In these hymns he holds up the **nām** (q.v.) (the divine Name) as the sole and sufficient means of liberation. All people are subject to transmigration (q.v.) in accordance with their past deeds, but by devoutly meditating on the divine Name they can overcome their evil impulses and attain liberation from the transmigratory round. The divine Name comprises all that is around one and all that is within, functioning in accordance with the **hukam** [(q.v.) order] of Akal Purakh (q.v.) (God). Akal Purakh utters the **shabad** [(q.v.) the divine Word] and the divine Word, if heard, illumines all that constitutes the divine Name. For this, grace (q.v.) is essential. Having received the divine Word by grace, it is each person's choice to accept or reject it. Accept it and you will perceive the signs of the divine Name in the world around and within you. Meditate on it and you shall find the means of liberation progressively revealed. Ascending to higher and yet higher levels of mystical experience the devout practitioner of **nām simaraṇ** [(q.v.) remembrance of the Name] experiences a mounting sense of peace and joy. Eventually **sach khaṇḍ** (q.v.) is reached, the 'abode of truth' in which the believer passes into a condition of perfect and absolute union with Akal Purakh. This condition is beyond description, known only to those who have experienced its transcending wonders. They are the sants (q.v.), the ones who know the truth, and they alone have found freedom from the transmigratory round. This Word is uttered within the believer by the mystical 'voice' of Akal Purakh which is the Guru (q.v.). Nanak, in communicating the Word, was performing this function, and so he came to be known as Guru Nanak. In appointing a successor Nanak was passing on the role of Guru as one torch is lit from its predecessor. The one Guru passed along the line of ten chosen men, that which illuminated the words and actions of Gobind Singh (q.v.) being the same Guru as had found expression in Nanak. *See also* PANJ KHAND.

NANAK: LIFE. Ample knowledge of the teachings of Nanak contrasts with the scarcity of detail concerning his life. Although the janam-sakhis (q.v.) are strictly hagiographic, they have been widely accepted within the Panth (q.v.), and the traditional account which they offer can be collectively summarized as follows. In 1469 Nanak, son of Kalu Bedi and Tripata, was born in the Punjab village of Talvandi Rai Bhoi (qq.v.). He had one sister, Nanaki (q.v.); his wife's name was Sulakhani (q.v.); and two sons (Lakhmi Das and Siri Chand [qq.v.]) were born to them. Many stories are recounted in the janam-sakhis concerning the marvels associated with the child Nanak. As a young man Nanak was despatched to Sultanpur (q.v.) where he received a mystical call from Akal Purakh ([q.v.] God) to surrender himself to a life of preaching the one means of liberation, the divine Name (**nām,** [q.v.]). The janam-sakhis diverge at this point, and many modern Sikhs accept the pattern of the *Purātan* janam-sakhis (q.v.). These take Nanak on a series of travels, dividing them into four major, and one minor, missionary journeys. On the major journeys (known as udasis [q.v.]) he visited respectively east India, Sri Lanka, the legendary Mount Sumeru, and Mecca. After they were over, he founded the village of Kartarpur (q.v.) on the right bank of the Ravi river, northeast of Lahore. Having attracted a following which was the nucleus of the Panth and appointed Angad (q.v.) as his successor, he died there in 1538 or 1539. This is the traditional account which is found in the janam-sakhis. Certain facts can be affirmed. Details concerning his family relationships are generally accurate; he travelled extensively to places unknown; he spent his latter years in Kartarpur; and Angad succeeded him. Of the remainder, however, very little stands up to historical analysis. *See also* TRADITION.

NANAKI. 1. The sister of Guru Nanak. 2. The second of Guru Hargobind's three wives; the mother of Tegh Bahadur (q.v.).

NANAK-PANTH. 'The way of Nanak,' a term commonly used for the entire pre-Khalsa Sikh Panth (qq.v.) or for those post-Khalsa Sikhs who do not follow the Rahit (q.v.). 'Nanak-panthi' was frequently used for any Sikh prior to 1699, and the term is still sometimes used for a sahaj-dhari Sikh (q.v.).

NANAKSAR. A Sikh movement which originated with Nand Singh (d. 1943) of Kaleran village in Ludhiana District. Nand

Singh, a Ramgarhia (q.v.), spent some time at Hazur Sahib in Nander (qq.v.) and then travelled around the Punjab for many years, living a life of extreme austerity. He eventually returned to Kaleran in 1918 and stayed in the nearby wilderness where Nanaksar now stands. There he continued his life of austerity, practicing **nām simaraṇ** (q.v.) in **bhore** (holes, caves) and refusing to allow any building to be erected. He believed that Nanak (q.v.) had physically appeared to him out of the Guru Granth Sahib (q.v.). Nand Singh was succeeded by his devoted follower Ishar Singh, a Jat (q.v.), under whom the Nanaksar movement rapidly expanded. In 1950 the gurdwara (q.v.) at Nanaksar was commenced, a magnificent marble structure enclosing beneath its golden dome an underground room to represent a **bhorā**. Ishar Singh nominated no successor, and the movement has now divided under several leaders. One with a substantial following in Coventry and Vancouver is Mihan Singh. Some differences distinguish the Nanaksar movement from the orthodox Khalsa (q.v.). Devotion is focused strongly on Nanak (though the other Gurus are not excluded), the emphasis on austerity is still maintained, and no nishan (q.v.) flies above the gurdwaras. The movement claims to take no interest in politics. *See also* ORTHODOXY.

NAND LAL (1633–1715). Sikh poet born in Ghazni. From there he travelled to Delhi via Multan [(q.v.) where he married a Sikh wife]. He worked as a servant of Prince Muazzam (later Bahadur Shah), but his real skill lay in composing Persian poetry. To mark this he adopted the pen name Goya ('Eloquent'). In 1689 he moved to Anandpur (q.v.), where he entered the service of Guru Gobind Singh (q.v.), and it is as a Sikh poet that his reputation was securely established. Two of his collections, his *Dīvān* and the *Zindagī-nāmā,* merit special attention. Because they are both in Persian, however, they are little-read today. After the death of Gobind Singh he retired to Multan, dying there in 1715. Like most other Khatris (q.v.), he declined to take initiation into the Khalsa (q.v.), and his poetry reads much more like the devotional works of the early Gurus. Three Punjabi rahit-namas (q.v.) are wrongly attributed to him. *See also* PRASHAN-UTTAR; TANAKHAH-NAMA.

NANDER (NANDED). A town situated in eastern Maharashtra on the Godavari river. It was here that Guru Gobind Singh (q.v.) died in 1708 following an assassination attempt. In Sikh sources the town is commonly known as Abilchalnagar (the 'Resolute City'). Hazur Sahib (q.v.), the principal gurdwara (q.v.) of Nander, is one of the five takhats (q.v.).

NANKANA MASSACRE. Because of his immoral way of life, Narain Das, custodian of the Nankana Sahib gurdwaras (qq.v.) and the wealthiest of all the mahants (q.v.), was a particular target for the Akalis (q.v.) during the Gurdwara Reform Movement (q.v.) of the early 1920s. A group of Akalis entered Gurdwara Janam-asthan (q.v.) on February 20, 1921 and were set upon by hired thugs of Narain Das. 130 were killed. Three of the killers were executed, and Narain Das was transported for life. The incident had a considerable effect upon Sikhs everywhere and greatly strengthened their resolve to free the gurdwaras from their mahant owners.

NANKANA SAHIB. The birth-place of Guru Nanak (q.v.). Formerly called Talvandi Rai Bhoi, it is in Sheikhupura District, approximately forty miles west-southwest of Lahore and now in Pakistan. It contains several gurdwaras (q.v.), including Gurdwara Janam-asthan (q.v.) which marks the birth-place of Nanak.

NARAK (hell). As with **svarag** ([q.v.] 'heaven') this term is variously understood. Those who are well acquainted with the Adi Granth (q.v.) regard it as the condition of separation from God. This is the sense in which the word is used by the Gurus, as also in their references to Yam, the god of death. Many Sikhs, however, conceive **narak** as a place where evil people go after death. The origin of this latter belief among the Sikhs is presumably Islam.

NATH TRADITION. The ascetic Nath or Kanphat tradition of India comprises a cluster of yogic sects, all claiming descent from the semi-legendary Gorakhnath (q.v.) and all promulgating hatha-yoga (q.v.) as the means of spiritual liberation. This involves physical postures and breath control of formidable difficulty. The tradition figured prominently amongst the early Sikhs for two reasons. First, the Sant tradition of Northern India (q.v.), of which Nanak (q.v.) was a conspicuous representative, was significantly influenced by Nath ideals, though the Sants (including Nanak) were strongly opposed to their theories. Nath doctrine affirms that the rigorous application of hatha-yoga induces a psycho-physical process whereby the spirit ascends to mystical bliss. The Sants rejected the physical features of hatha-yoga in favor of meditation technique but accepted the concept of a spiritual ascent to ultimate bliss. Kabir (q.v.) was a notable Sant apparently connected to the Naths, yet scorned their physical notions while accepting their belief in a wholly inward spiritual enlightenment. Secondly, the Naths were also important to the early Panth (q.v.) in that they provided considerable competition for followers. Janam-sakhi (q.v.) anecdotes give much prominence to debates between Nath masters (called Siddhs [q.v.]) and Nanak. The tradition, though greatly weakened, still survives.

NAU NIHAL SINGH (1821–40). Son of Kharak Singh and grandson of Ranjit Singh (qq.v.). A capable youth, he assumed the state's administration soon after his grandfather's death. Killed on the day of his father's funeral by a collapsing arch in Lahore (q.v.).

NEO-SIKH *see* TAT KHALSA.

NIHANG. Today the Nihangs form only a remnant of their initial strength of the eighteenth and early nineteenth centuries. At that time they were known as Akalis (q.v.) and were greatly feared as determined warriors. The origins of the Akalis or Nihangs are not known, although they claim to be the true representatives of Guru Gobind Singh (q.v.) and in consequence the true Khalsa (q.v.). In the time of the misls (q.v.) they usually fought for the Shahid misl. Under Ranjit Singh (q.v.), they were renowned both for their intrepid bravery and their total lack of discipline except when controlled by other Akalis. After the death of their famous leader Phula Singh (q.v.) in 1823, they dwindled in importance, and they survive today only as a historic relic. They are seen by others as having two main vices, namely their fondness for bhang (cannabis) and their habit of not paying for anything that they require. They are, however, generally rigorous in observing the Rahit (q.v.) as they understand it. The name Nihang ('free from care' or 'free from worldly concerns') may have been taken from the pre-initiation name of Akali Phula Singh.

NIHANG ORGANIZATION. The Nihangs (q.v.) are divided into four 'armies' (**dal**), each under its own jathedar (q.v.). Most are unmarried, believing that as true soldiers of the Khalsa (q.v.) they must remain unencumbered by family ties. For part of each year they remain in their 'camps' (**ḍerā** [q.v.]), attending to cultivation. At other times they roam around the Punjab and adjacent states on horseback, conspicuously visible in their blue garments and for the range of steel weapons which they carry. On their heads they wear a high turban known as a **damālā,** surmounted by a piece of cloth called a **pharaharā** ('standard' or 'flag'). For the festival of Hola Mahalla (q.v.) they converge on Anandpur (q.v.) to participate in mock battles.

NIL-DHARI. 'Wearer of a blue [belt]'; a small sub-sect of the Namdhari Sikhs (q.v.).

NINDAK. A slanderer, one who defames another. The term is particularly used of those who spoke ill of one of the Gurus.

NINE TREASURES. All blessings that may be conferred in this life.

NIRANJAN. 'Unspotted,' pure; an epithet of Akal Purakh (q.v.).

NIRANJANI *see* HINDALI.

NIRANKAR. 'Without form'; an epithet of Akal Purakh (q.v.).

NIRANKARI. A Sikh sect which developed in northwest Punjab during the later years of Maharaja Ranjit Singh (q.v.). The original Nirankaris were the followers of Baba Dayal (q.v.), who preached a return to the doctrine of **nām simaraṇ** (q.v.). Most were members of trading castes and were called Ni-rankaris because of Dayal's stress on the formless nature of God (**niraṅkār**). The sect includes both kes-dhari and sahaj-dhari Sikhs (qq.v.), and outwardly they are indistinguishable from most other Sikhs. The acceptance of Anand marriage (q.v.) by orthodox Sikhs settled the main issue separating them from the main body, and today the Nirankaris deviate only in that they recognize a line of continuing Gurus, beginning with Baba Dayal. With the partition of India in 1947 (q.v.), they shifted their main center from Rawalpindi to Chandigarh. They should be distinguished from the Sant Nirankaris (q.v.), a small group viewed with hostility by orthodox Sikhs and Nirankaris alike. *See also* ORTHODOXY.

NIRANKARI DARBAR *see* SANT NIRANKARI.

NIRGUNA. Without 'qualities' or attributes; doctrine of a formless Akal Purakh (q.v.). *See also* SAGUNA.

NIRMALA. 'Spotless.' By tradition, the order of Nirmala sants was founded by Guru Gobind Singh (q.v.) who despatched five Sikhs to Banaras to learn Sanskrit. This is highly improbable, and the Nirmala order is scarcely mentioned in Sikh literature until the nineteenth century. It acquired particular strength in the Malwa region (q.v.) in the nineteenth century because of patronage from the Sikh rulers of Patiala and other Phulkian states (q.v.). Although it is accepted as a part of the Panth (q.v.), its ascetic discipline deviates from Sikh teachings and practice. Its members wear saffron robes and observe celibacy, and its teachings are strongly Vedantic. As itinerant preachers they did much to commend Sikh teachings beyond the Punjab, and although some of their doctrines met with disapproval from the Tat Khalsa (q.v.), they were regarded cordially by Sanatan Sikhs (q.v.). A famous Nirmala scholar was Tara Singh Narotam (q.v.). *See also* AKHARA.

NISHAN SAHIB. The Khalsa flag which should fly above every gurdwara (q.v.). It is usually triangular in shape and saffron in color. Dark blue is also permitted. The mast will be draped in cloth of the same color (the chola). On the flag should be embroidered or printed a khanda (q.v.), and it should be surmounted by a steel spear, a two-edged sword, or another khanda. The origins are obscure. It was certainly being used in the nineteenth century, though without the khanda on it.

NISHANVALIA MISL. A small misl (q.v.). The founder was a Gill Jat (q.v.) from Firozpur District, but its territory is uncertain. Whereas some historians place it southeast of the Satluj river, others believe it was kept as a reserve force in Amritsar (q.v.). The name means 'flag-bearing.'

NIT-NEM. The daily devotional discipline for all Sikhs. Three times are appointed. 1. Between 3 and 6 a.m. after bathing: *Japjī, Jāp,* and the *Ten Savayyās,* concluding with Ardas. 2. At sunset: Raharas, with Ardas. 3. Before retiring: Kirtan Sohila (qq.v.).

O

OANKAR *see* IK-OANKAR.

OBEDIENCE. A prime virtue among the Sikhs. Children are expected to show implicit obedience to their parents, and all Sikhs should be obedient to any command which carries the sanction of the Guru.

OBSCENITY. Punjabi is a very colorful language, and, particularly in rural Punjab, it produces some very robust expressions. These expressions are sometimes used with the intention of giving insult, but normally they are harmless (if somewhat upsetting to delicate ears). Swear words center on kinship relationships. They never concern the Gurus.

ORTHODOXY. In the Panth (q.v.) there is, as one would expect, a continuum from orthodoxy through semi-orthodox to sect to heresy. Orthodox Sikhs constitute the Khalsa (q.v.). They believe in the ten Gurus (q.v.), revere the Guru Granth Sahib (q.v.), and accept the Rahit (q.v.) as set out in *Sikh Rahit Maryādā* (q.v.). Examples of those who differ in detail from the orthodox (the semi-orthodox) are the Nanaksar movement or the Bhai Randhir Singh da Jatha (qq.v.). Arguably, the Nirankaris (q.v.) would also be included in this group, because although they agree that the line of personal Gurus has ended, they nevertheless accept as leader a person who is called a Guru. They could, however, be regarded as a sect. This term can be applied to those who differ in some fundamental respect from the orthodox. The Namdharis (q.v.) are a sect, as they believe in the continuing line of personal Gurus yet explicitly maintain the Rahit. Many Sikhs would also regard Sahaj-dharis (q.v.) as a sect, accepting as they do the Gurus and the scripture but rejecting the Rahit. Heresy means that a group with Sikh origins has departed in a radical sense from orthodoxy. The Sant Nirankaris (q.v.), with their belief in a scripture larger than the Guru Granth Sahib, are regarded as committing heresy.

P

PAG, PAGARI *see* **TURBAN.**

PAHUL *see* **KHANDE DI PAHUL.**

PAINDA KHAN (d. 1635). A Muslim who entered the service of Guru Hargobind (q.v.). His enormous physical strength turned him to insolence, and having been detected in deceit, he was dismissed. He became the Guru's enemy and was slain by Hargobind at Kartarpur.

PAKHYAN CHARITRA. A lengthy series of 404 anecdotes in the Dasam Granth (q.v.), many of which tell of the skills which women bring to the art of seduction. This section is also known as the *Charitro-pākhyān.* The language is

Braj (q.v.), and the total number of verses is 7,558. These stories are drawn from a wide range of sources (Epic, Puranic,
Rajput, Persian, and native Punjabi). *Benatī Chaupaī,* included in Sodar Raharas (q.v.), appears as an epilogue. Because the Dasam Granth is generally regarded as a sacred
scripture, the collection is usually interpreted as a series of
cautionary tales to protect careless men from the perils of lust.
See also ANUP KAUR; TRIA CHARITRA.

PALKI. 'Palanquin.' A litter in which the Guru Granth Sahib
(q.v.) is carried; the canopied structure in a gurdwara (q.v.)
where the Guru Granth Sahib is placed.

PANCH KHALSA DIVAN *see* BHASAUR SINGH SABHA.

PANCHAMI. The fifth day of each half of the lunar calendar. *See
also* AMAVAS; SANGRAND; PURAN-MASHI.

PANGAT. 'Line.' The lines in which the sangat (q.v.) must sit in the
gurdwara (q.v.) and particularly in the langar (q.v.). The convention is anti-caste, no one being able to claim superior status
by sitting forward or to acknowledge inferiority by sitting back.

PANJ GRANTHI. A book which contains five favorite works of
the Sikhs. *Japjī* is always included, plus such compositions
as *Sodar Raharas, Kīrtan Sohilā, Āsā dī Vār, Anand Sāhib,
Jāp, Akāl Ustati,* and *Bachitar Nāṭak* (qq.v.). *See also* DAS
GRANTHI.

PANJ HATHIAR *see* FIVE WEAPONS.

PANJ ISHNAN (PANJ ISNAN, PANCH SNAN). The 'five
washings' (two hands, two feet, and mouth) to be undertaken
before meditation or before entering a gurdwara (q.v.) when
full bathing is not practicable. *See also* ISHNAN.

PANJ KAKKAR, PANJ KAKKE *see* FIVE Ks.

PANJ KHAND. The five 'realms' which Nanak (q.v.) describes
in *Japjī* (q.v.). These are stages of developing spiritual aware-

ness through which one must pass, by means of regular **nām simaran** (q.v.), to union with the divine. The five realms are **dharam khaṇd** (moral duty), **giān khaṇd** (knowledge), **saram khaṇd** (humility or effort), **karam khaṇd** (grace, action, or fulfillment), and **sach khaṇd** (truth) (q.v.). Debate continues regarding the nature of the third and fourth realms. The origins of this pattern have been the subject of various theories. One traces it to the Sufis (q.v.). Another holds that it represents Nanak's adaptation of hatha-yoga doctrine (q.v.), with the five **khaṇds** replacing the **chakkars** of the Naths (q.v.). There is no suggestion, however, that Nanak actually accepted Nath theory. *See also* NANAK: DOCTRINE.

PANJ MEL. The five reprobate groups which members of the Khalsa (q.v.) must swear to spurn. The identity of the five has never been settled. The Minas and the Masands (qq.v.) are in every list; the Dhir Malias and Ram Raias (qq.v.) are usually included. The fifth group is much disputed, however. The earliest list names the Masandias (followers of the Masands). Other candidates are those who kill female infants (**kuṛī-mār** [q.v.]), those who observe the head-shaving ritual (**bhadaṇī**), users of the hookah (**naṛī-mār**), and amrit-dhari Sikhs (q.v.) who subsequently cut their hair (**sir-gum**). During the Singh Sabha (q.v.) period much attention was paid to the question, and the list which was finally agreed upon included the four usual groups together with those who are **sir-gum**. Today's rahit-nama, *Sikh Rahit Maryādā* (q.v.), avoids the issue by naming seven groups as 'transgressors' (**tanakhāhīe** [q.v.]) to be avoided by amrit-dhari Sikhs. In addition to the usual four these are the **naṛī-mār**, the **kuṛī-mār**, and the **sir-gum**.

PANJ PIARE. The 'Cherished Five' or 'Five Loved Ones'; the first five to volunteer at the inauguration of the Khalsa (q.v.). These were Daya Singh, Dharam Singh, Himmat Singh, Sahib Singh, and Muhakam Singh (respectively a Khatri, a Jat, a Jhinvar, a Nai, and a Chhimbar [qq.v.]). Presumably the name 'Singh' (q.v.) was added when they were initiated. Today the term designates five amrit-dhari Sikhs (q.v.) who are chosen to represent a sangat (q.v.) at a Khalsa initiation or for any other function. For Khalsa initiation they must be physically sound, possessing both eyes, ears, legs, and arms. In theory, women may serve as Panj Piare, though in practice men are almost always chosen. *See also* AMRIT SANSKAR; KHALSA INAUGURATION.

PANJ THAG. 'The five thugs': power, wealth, high caste, youth, and beauty. Five desires which seduce man from remembrance of the divine Name (q.v.).

PANJA SAHIB. 'The Holy Palm.' A location near Hasan Abdal in Attock District where Nanak (q.v.) is said to have stopped with his hand a boulder rolled down the hill by a jealous Muslim dervish called Vali Qandhari. Vali Qandhari became enraged when Nanak opened a spring at the foot of the hill, thereby cutting off his own spring further up the hill. The anecdote is a late entrant into the *Bālā* janam-sakhis (q.v.), owing its origins to a story which dates from the time of Maharaja Ranjit Singh (q.v.). Until 1940 the 'impression' of Nanak's palm projected from the rock, and only in that year was it carved into it. There is a famous gurdwara (q.v.) on the spot.

PANTH. The Sikh community. The Sanskrit word **panth** (literally 'path') is used in India to designate groups following particular teachers or doctrines. The early Sikh community was thus known as the Nanak-panth (q.v.) or 'followers of Nanak.' After the Khalsa (q.v.) was established, Nanak's name was dropped, and the community came to be known simply as 'the Panth.' Doubt still remains concerning who belongs to the Panth, though the term tends to be used for kes-dhari Sikhs (q.v.). Many Sahaj-dharis (q.v.) still prefer the title 'Nanak-panth,' using 'Khalsa Panth' for the Kes-dharis. When using a script which employs capital letters, 'panth' designates any of the innumerable religious groups in India, whereas 'Panth' is reserved for the Sikh community alone. As such, the capitalized form is an extremely important word, one which deserves to be a part of normal English usage. The Sikh community is the Panth just as Christians constitute the Church.

PANTHIC. Concerning the Panth (q.v.).

PAONTA SAHIB. A small town in the Shivalik Hills (q.v.) near Nahan. Here, on the banks of the Yamuna river, Guru Gobind Singh (q.v.) lived from 1685 to 1688.

PARAMATMA. The universal or cosmic spirit with which the individual **ātmā** (q.v.) should seek to blend; God.

PARCHIAN SEVADAS. A collection of anecdotes by Seva Das Udasi concerning the ten Gurus, with a heavy emphasis on Guru Gobind Singh (q.v.). It is said to have been completed in 1708.

PARIKARAMA. Used in the Hindu tradition for making a clockwise circuit of an idol. For the Sikhs, it designates the walkway around a pool surrounding a gurdwara (q.v.). Pilgrims always approach Harimandir Sahib (q.v.) or any other gurdwara by walking clockwise around the parikarama.

PARKASH KARNA. Installing the Guru Granth Sahib (q.v.) in a gurdwara (q.v.) early each morning. The sacred volume is carried respectfully on the head by a Sikh into the gurdwara from the resting place where it has been placed for the night. While all present sing hymns, the rumalas (q.v.) in which it was wrapped for the night are changed for fresh ones. *See also* SUKHASAN.

PARMANAND. Little is known of this poet except that he lived in Sholapur District. There is one work by him in the Adi Granth (q.v.).

PARTITION. When India gained independence from Britain in 1947, the country was divided into Bharat (India) and Pakistan. For the Sikh population in the Pakistan portion of the Punjab it involved a tremendous upheaval. Virtually all the Sikhs from this area, together with a large majority of the Hindus, crossed to India, the Muslims from India moving in the opposite direction. The savage killings which took place on both sides of the border have left memories which still live on in all three communities. The estimated number of Sikhs who were massacred is estimated as 200,000. The number of Hindus and Muslims slaughtered was likewise high. *See also* MUSLIM RELATIONS; PUNJAB.

PATH. A reading of any portion of scripture. *See also* AKHAND PATH; SADHARAN PATH; SAPTAHIK PATH.

PATIT. A 'fallen' Sikh; an apostate; an Amrit-dhari (q.v.) who knowingly commits one of the kurahits (q.v.). The term is also loosely applied to Kes-dharis (q.v.) who trim or cut their hair.

PATKA. The patka is a recent addition to male Sikh dress, one that has quickly secured widespread popularity. It is a piece of cloth measuring approximately two feet by two feet which has four cloth ties of the same material, one at each corner. Boys wear them in place of the rumal (q.v.) while still too young for the turban (q.v.). Sportsmen also commonly wear them in sports where there is a risk of entangling the turban. The patka fits snugly over the head, covering almost all the hair. Amrit-dhari males (q.v.) and all females are not permitted to wear the patka.

PATNA. The capital city of Bihar state. Guru Gobind Singh (q.v.) was born in Patna, which now has one of the five takhats (q.v.).

PATRIARCHY. Guru Nanak (q.v.) gave to women a share in the process of religious liberation which places them on the same level as men. Women have the same privileges and the same duties as men. They too must meditate on the divine Name (q.v.) and can hope that in so doing they will attain the condition of sahaj (q.v.) or perfect bliss. All of life is, moreover, dependent upon women, for without them how can mankind continue? A stanza which well expresses this is Var Asa 19:2 (*AG,* p. 473). This belief is, however, set within the society in which Nanak lived. It is a patriarchal structure which allowed no share of ancestral property to women and which assumed that when married they would move from their parents' home to that of their husband. This pattern has been maintained ever since and has involved the Sikh religion in a situation at once uneasy and hopeful. The situation is uneasy in that social practice seems clearly at variance with the Guru's teaching. It is hopeful in that Sikhs possess the appropriate doctrine to provide a way out of the difficulty as societies move towards greater equality between the sexes. *See also* GENDER.

PAURI. 'Step'; a stanza from one of the Adi Granth vars (qq.v.) or other longer works.

PEPSU. The Patiala and East Punjab States Union which was formed following partition between India and Pakistan in 1947 (q.v.). The state was centered on Patiala and had a Sikh majority. The Maharaja of Patiala was the Raj Pramukh (Governor), and Gyan Singh Rarewala was the Chief Minister. In 1956 PEPSU was united with the Punjab (q.v.) which at that time had a Hindu majority.

PHERUMAN, DARSHAN SINGH *see* DARSHAN SINGH PHERUMAN.

PHULA SINGH (c.1761–1823). His original name was Nihang Singh, changed to Phula Singh when he took Khalsa initiation (q.v.). He was a Jat (q.v.), son of an attendant at Akal Takhat (q.v.), and joining the Akalis (q.v.) became their most famous leader. He first attracted attention by leading a group of Akalis in an unsuccessful raid on Metcalfe's escort in Amritsar (q.v.) and then by appearing before Maharaja Ranjit Singh (q.v.) with drawn sword, demanding vengeance on the strangers who had humiliated him. Ranjit Singh treated him tactfully, and thereafter Phula Singh entered his service, paying no heed to attempts to discipline him but fighting with conspicuous bravery in many battles. In 1823 he was killed in the Battle of Nushahira against the Afghans, and the strength of the Akalis then began to dwindle. In accordance with the rule of celibacy generally observed by the early Akalis (the later Nihangs [q.v.]), he was unmarried.

PHULKIAN. Descendants of Baba Phul, a Sidhu Jat (q.v.) of the Malwa region (q.v.). The princely houses of Patiala, Nabha, and Jind were all Phulkian.

PHULKIAN MISL. A large misl (q.v.) founded by the descendants of Baba Phul with territories south of the Satluj river. During the Afghan invasions of Ahmad Shah Abdali (q.v.), their chieftain, Ala Singh, frequently sided with the invader against the remainder of the Khalsa (q.v.). Following his death the misl was divided into a number of groups and became a confederacy. These were saved from Ranjit Singh (q.v.) by the advancing British who, placing Malwa (q.v.) under their protection at the beginning of the nineteenth century, permitted the Phulkian chieftains to retain their territories as princes. The principal one was Patiala.

PILGRIMAGE. Guru Nanak (q.v.) taught that external religious practices, including pilgrimage, were fruitless. The impulse to conduct pilgrimages was, however, too strong, and during the time of Guru Amar Das (q.v.) provision was evidently made for distinctively Sikh pilgrimages. A **baoli** (sacred well) was dug in Goindval (q.v.), and Sikhs were encouraged to visit both it and the Guru. Since then the number of sacred sites has greatly multiplied. They are always places associated with one of the Gurus, Harimandir Sahib in Amritsar (qq.v.) being the leading one. Pilgrimages to visit a selection of these has long been a regular custom. *See also* GURDWARA; TIRATH.

PIPA. Traditionally a Rajput chieftain of Gagaraun, born in 1425. From being a follower of the goddess Durga he is said to have changed to Ramanand (q.v.). There is one work by him in the Adi Granth (q.v.).

PIR. The head of a Sufi (q.v.) order; a renowned Sufi.

POLITICAL PARTIES: PRE-PARTITION. Sikh political parties date from the Chief Khalsa Divan (q.v.) or CKD, founded as a merger of the Amritsar and Lahore Singh Sabhas (q.v.) in 1902. By the end of World War I, ardent Sikhs, particularly those influenced by the Tat Khalsa (q.v.), wanted more radical political expression. In 1919 the Central Sikh League (q.v.) was founded and stridently demanded that the gurdwaras (q.v.) should be returned to the Panth (q.v.). In 1920 two new organizations were begun under its auspices, the Akali Dal (q.v.), to take over the gurdwaras, and the Shiromani Gurdwara Parbandhak Committee (q.v.), to administer them once they were in Sikh hands. Following the success of the Gurdwara Reform Movement (q.v.) in 1925, the Akali Dal continued as the principal political party of the Panth. On the right the CKD formed the Khalsa National Party after 1935 and joined the Unionist Party (a multi-communal landlord party) to form the government of the Punjab (q.v.). On the left were several small parties. Between them were many more Sikhs supporting either the Akali Dal (the majority) or the Congress Party (a minority). The latter comprised those Sikhs who preferred Congress's all-India strategy rather than the explicitly Sikh policy of the Akali Dal. During this period the dominant figure in Akali affairs, and indeed in all Sikh politics, was Tara Singh (q.v.), who retained his authority until partition in 1947 (q.v.) and for almost two decades after it.

POLITICAL PARTIES: POST-PARTITION. Tara Singh and the Akali Dal (qq.v.) survived the experience of partition in 1947 (q.v.), casting in their lot with India. The Punjab that survived was, however, a Hindu-majority state, and the Akalis had no hope of ever ruling it. Attention was turned to securing Punjabi Suba (q.v.), an appreciably smaller state with a majority of Sikhs. After vigorous campaigns this was eventually secured in 1966, though by that time Tara Singh had been eclipsed as leader by Fateh Singh (q.v.). Although the Punjab now had a majority of Sikhs, the Akali Dal still found power elusive. It was able to form the government of the Punjab for brief periods, but each time its authority was undermined (usually by the Congress). In the 1980s the situation in the Punjab deteriorated, with power increasingly passing from Harchand Singh Longowal to the militant Jarnail Singh Bhindranvale (qq.v.). In 1984 the Central Government ordered the army to attack Bhindranvale and his followers in the Golden Temple (q.v.) and its precincts which they had occupied; his death was followed by the avenging assassination of Mrs. Gandhi, the Prime Minister. The result of this period was disastrous for the Akali Dal. It split into several different groups, each claiming the name of the Akali Dal. The dominant group still continues to exist, however, and it may eventually regain at least a measure of its lost authority. *See also* POLITICS; RECENT HISTORY.

POLITICS. Much Sikh energy has been channelled into political activity during the twentieth century. The results have scarcely been rewarding but leaders of the principal Sikh party, the Akali Dal (q.v.), have always insisted that politics and faith are intimately bound together. Political activity is, they maintain, directly concerned with a Sikh's duty as a member of the Khalsa (q.v.). Tara Singh (q.v.) was particularly identified with this view. The Sikh faith inescapably involves politics, and all politics should be conducted with the interests of the Khalsa paramount. In spite of results, the Akalis have carried with them a very substantial portion of the Panth (q.v.), particularly in their morchas (q.v.). Their brand of politics still commands a wide following. *See also* POLITICAL PARTIES; RECENT HISTORY.

POPULATION. In 1985 Sikhs were estimated to total approximately sixteen million worldwide. Of these, roughly fourteen million lived in the Punjab and immediately adjacent areas; one million lived elsewhere in India; and one million lived in other countries. Outside India the largest Sikh population was in the United Kingdom, where in 1987 they were estimated to total 269,600 out of a South Asian population of 1,271,000. Canada and the United States both have numbers which are extremely difficult to estimate, recent immigration having complicated the issue. Each is thought to have (very roughly) 175,000. Malaysia, Singapore, Sri Lanka, Thailand and Kenya all have more than 10,000 Sikhs. All of these totals (particularly the foreign ones) include the several varieties of Sikhs, not just kesdhari Sikhs who are easily recognizable. *See also* IDENTITY.

POTHI. Volume; tome.

PRAHILAD SINGH (or RAI) *see* RAHIT-NAMA PRAHILAD SINGH.

PRAJA MANDAL. The Tenants' Association formed in the princely states of the Punjab in 1928, affiliated to the Indian

National Congress. It comprised both Sikh and Hindu members. *See also* SEVA SINGH THIKRIVALA.

PRAN SANGALI. 'The chain of the breath.' A lengthy apocryphal work attributed to Nanak (q.v.) which shows clear evidence of Nath (q.v.) influence. The janam-sakhis (q.v.) of the *Purātan* tradition (q.v.) claim that Nanak composed it while visiting Raja Shiv-nabh (q.v.). *See also* KACHCHI BANI.

PRASAD (PRASHAD). Either 'grace' (q.v.) or 'food.' The two meanings are linked by the fact that **prasād** also means food offered to a god or the leavings of a person of great piety. The common Adi Granth (q.v.) formula **gur prasād** (or **sat-gur prasād**), "by the (True) Guru's grace," is a central doctrine of Gurmat (q.v.). *See also* KARAH PRASAD.

PRASHAN-UTTAR. A brief rahit-nama (q.v.) in simple Punjabi verse attributed to Nand Lal (q.v.). It is, however, most unlikely that it can be traced to him. The date is uncertain, but is probably late eighteenth century. *See also* TANAKHAH-NAMA.

PRATAP SINGH KAIRON (1901–65). A Jat (q.v.), he was educated at the University of Michigan and then joined the Congress Party in 1929. His politics, prior to independence in 1947, were mainly Akali (q.v.), but in 1956 he became the Congress chief minister of the Punjab, remaining in the position until 1964 when he was forced to resign over corruption charges. As chief minister he was very effective, successfully opposing Punjabi Suba (q.v.) as long as he was in the position. In 1965 he was assassinated.

PREM SUMARG. A lengthy prose rahit-nama (q.v.) composed in the early or mid-nineteenth century. The author is unknown. It is also referred to as the Param Sumarg.

PRITHI CHAND (1558–1618). The older brother of Arjan (q.v.) and unsuccessful contender for the title of Guru. *See also* MINA; SULHI KHAN.

PUJARI. The person who was responsible for ritual in major Sikh shrines. The term is not currently in common use.

PUNJAB. Punjab means 'five waters,' from the five rivers which flow through it, together with the Indus in the west in which they all merge. The five rivers are (from the Indus eastwards) the Jhelum, the Chenab, the Ravi, the Beas, and the Satluj. These rivers have conferred on the Punjab extensive areas of highly productive soils, with irrigation in recent times adding much more. Modern Punjab comprises adjacent portions of India and Pakistan, divided by partition in 1947 (q.v.). The Indian portion was more narrowly defined by the creation of Punjabi Suba (q.v.) in 1966. Undivided Punjab was the homeland of the Sikhs, and before 1947 the vast majority lived within its borders, ranging from comparative scarcity in the northwest to relative density in the areas of Manjh, Doaba, and Malwa (qq.v.). Nanak (q.v.) was born in the Punjab, and there the Gurus carried out the greater part of their labors. According to the 1921 census, only eleven percent of undivided Punjab was Sikh. Because they had ruled the Punjab prior to annexation by the British they occupied a disproportionate share of the land, and of the so-called 'leading families' approximately half were Sikh. Even so the Government of India Act of 1919 granted the Sikhs only nineteen percent of the seats in the new constitution, and in 1947 partition proceeded without serious consideration of their interests. Forced to choose, they opted for India, thereby swinging more of central Punjab to India than would otherwise have been the case. At partition in 1947 (q.v.) virtually every Sikh in Pakistan, together with the vast majority of Hindus, crossed to India. Muslims moved the other way. At this stage the Punjab was still distinct from the former princely states which formed the Sikh-dominated PEPSU (q.v.). When the two were brought together in 1956 Hindus were sixty-two percent of the united state. As a result of the Punjabi Suba agitation (q.v.), the Sikhs succeeded in having the boundaries of the Punjab more narrowly drawn, excluding those areas where the majority had declared Hindi to be their mother tongue instead of Punjabi. This at last gave them a Punjab with fifty-six percent of the people Sikhs, though as it turned out it did not give them control of the parliamentary process. *See also* POPULATION.

PUNJABI SUBA. The Punjabi-language state. Sikhs, led by the Akali Dal (q.v.), agitated for it from partition in 1947 (q.v.).

Following vigorous Sikh participation in the 1965 Indo-Pakistan war the Government of India granted a separate Punjabi-speaking state in 1966 by separating Haryana from the existing Punjab.

PURAN SINGH (1881–1931). Trained in glass technology and pharmaceutical chemistry at Tokyo University, Puran Singh worked as an industrial chemist when he returned to India. His chief distinction, however, was as a poet in both Punjabi and English. Influenced by Walt Whitman, he produced blank verse which stressed the universal appeal of the Sikh Gurus.

PURAN-MASHI. The day of the full moon; the end of a lunar month. An important festival for the Panth (q.v.). *See also* AMAVAS; PANCHAMI; SANGRAND.

PURATAN JANAM-SAKHI TRADITION. The *Purātan* tradition forms a small group of immensely influential janam-sakhis (q.v.). Scholarly Sikhs during the late nineteenth century were uneasy that the *Bālā* tradition (q.v.), with its strong emphasis on the miraculous and the bizarre, provided the material for life of Nanak (q.v.). In 1872 Trumpp (q.v.) discovered a different janam-sakhi in London and declared it to be probably the origin of all janam-sakhis. When it was examined in the Punjab, scholarly Sikhs agreed, and the manuscript was termed the *Purātan* or 'Ancient' janam-sakhi. This has since been shown to be in error, for although the manuscript is certainly old, the janam-sakhi which it records is well structured. The anecdotes which relate the travels of Nanak are organized into four major missionary journeys in four directions (plus one minor one), a feature of a comparatively late janam-sakhi. The two main manuscripts of the tradition are the *Colebrooke* (the London one) and the *Hafizābād* (now destroyed). Biographies of Nanak written during the twentieth century are normally based on the *Purātan* tradition. The tradition is, however, no more reliable than other traditions.

PURDAH. The influence of Muslim social tradition has been powerful in the Punjab, a result of which is that many Sikh women (particularly in villages) used to veil themselves in the presence of strange men. Purdah is, however, forbidden for Sikh women. According to *Sikh Rahit Maryādā* (q.v.), they should not cover their faces with a veil, including when they are in a sangat (q.v.). The custom is fast waning in the Punjab.

PURITY/POLLUTION. In a sense Sikhs are little bothered by concepts of purity or pollution. They do, however, generally observe the rules of caste marriage, and strict members of the Khalsa (q.v.) will not eat with non-members. The attitude towards Dalits (q.v.) is distinctly ambivalent. Whereas they do recognize that the Gurus spoke against discrimination, they nevertheless maintain a clear awareness of who is an Outcaste. They also commonly absorb other less weighty customs from their Indian background, such as distinguishing their use of the right (pure) and left (polluted) hand or always circling a sacred object clockwise.

Q

QAUM. 'A people who stand together'; [the Sikh] community.

QAZI (QADI). A Muslim judge; administrator of Islamic law. Qazis are cast as unsympathetic interlocutors of Nanak (q.v.) in the janam-sakhis (q.v.).

R

RABAB. A musical instrument like a rebeck.

RADHASOAMI. A Sant movement (q.v.) which traces its origins to a parent movement founded in Agra by Swami Shiv Dayal in 1861. The Agra movement later divided, and a branch was established beside the Beas river in Amritsar District by Jaimal Singh, a Jat Sikh (q.v.). This came to be called the Beas Radhasoami Satsang, as distinct from the parent group which continued in Agra. In 1903 he was succeeded by Sawan Singh, the 'Great Master,' another Jat Sikh. A line of Masters was thus established, teaching the threefold message of **simaraṇ** (repetition of the Lord's many Names until attention is focused on the Third Eye which lies within), **dhyān** (contemplation of the immortal form of the Master), and **bhajan** (hearing the celestial music within us). The movement is led by Sikh Masters, and many Sikhs have been attracted to it. To orthodox Sikhs, however, it is unacceptable. This is partly because of the differences between Sikh doctrine and the teachings of the Satsang and partly because the Satsang consists predominantly of Hindus.

RAG (RAGA). A series of five or more notes upon which a melody is based; melody. Different rags are held to be appropriate for various times of the day. The works in the Adi Granth (q.v.) and other collections of hymns are divided according to their rags.

RAGI. A professional singer of kirtan (q.v.). Normally employed by a gurdwara (q.v.), ragis are also available for singing kirtan at private functions.

RAG-MALA. The list of rags (q.v.) at the very end of the Adi Granth (q.v.), pages 1429–30. Because of its apparent mistakes, *Rāg-mālā* is regarded with doubt, and its status as a part of the Adi Granth is undecided. Santokh Singh, Gian Singh, Kahn Singh Nabha, Teja Singh Bhasaur, and Randhir Singh (qq.v.) were among those who doubted or wholly rejected it. According to *Sikh Rahit Maryādā* (q.v.) the question is left open, though *Rāg-mālā* is not normally recited in Akhand Paths at Harimandir Sahib (qq.v.).

RAHARAS *see* SODAR RAHARAS.

RAHIT. The code of belief and discipline which all amrit-dhari Sikhs (q.v.) vow to observe at initiation into the Khalsa (q.v.).

Recorded versions are known as rahit-namas (q.v.). According to tradition, the Rahit was promulgated by Gobind Singh (q.v.) when he instituted the Khalsa in 1699. If so, this must have been a Rahit different from the modern version. During the eighteenth century the Rahit continued to change, principally in accordance with the predominantly Jat constituency of the Panth (qq.v.) and its conflict with Muslim enemies. It continued to alter at a slower rate during the nineteenth century and towards the end of the century was taken up by the reforming Singh Sabha (q.v.). After a lengthy debate a modern version of the Rahit was finally published in 1950. The Rahit is binding only on amrit-dhari Sikhs, not on Sahaj-dharis (q.v.). Strictly speaking it does not apply either to Kes-dharis (q.v.) who are not Amrit-dharis, though they are strongly encouraged to observe it as far as possible. 'Rahit' is a very important term and deserves to be a part of regular English usage. *See also* SIKH RAHIT MARYADA.

RAHIT BIBEK. The rahit-nama (q.v.) observed by the Bhai Randhir Singh da Jatha (q.v.). It deletes **kes** from the Five Ks, instead substituting **keskī** (qq.v.) which it requires women as well as men to wear. Also, it commands complete vegetarianism and insists on the use of **sarab loh** ('all iron') whenever possible. Members of the Jatha reject the manual *Sikh Rahit Maryādā* (q.v.) as mistaken in these important respects.

RAHITIA. A Sikh from the Chamar (leather-working) caste; an Outcaste Sikh. *See also* CASTE; DALIT; RAMDASIA.

RAHIT-NAMA. A manual which records any version of the Rahit of the Khalsa (qq.v.). The original Rahit is attributed to Guru Gobind Singh (q.v.), and the early rahit-namas all purport to reproduce his actual words. Although there is considerable uncertainty concerning sequence and dates, it seems that the earliest of the formal rahit-namas emerged during the mid-eighteenth century. These were prose collections of numerous injunctions attributed to Chaupa Singh and Nand Lal (qq.v.). Subsequently there appeared at least two more lengthy ones in prose (the *Prem Sumārg* and the *Sau Sākhīan* [qq.v.]), four shorter rahit-namas in verse, and one short one in prose. Two of the verse products are attributed to Nand Lal, one to Prahilad Rai (or Singh), and one to Desa Singh (qq.v.). Both of the long prose works are anonymous, and the short one bears the name of Daya Singh (q.v.), the first of five Sikhs to receive Khalsa initiation. These attributions have been attached to them spuriously. The attributions were, however, accepted by Singh Sabha (q.v.) scholars, and from these sources they attempted to distil the original Rahit. In 1915 they published their reformist views as an entirely new rahit-nama. This manual, the *Gurmat Prakāsh Bhāg Sanskār,* failed to win acceptance. Not until *Sikh Rahit Maryādā* (q.v.) was issued in 1950 did an authoritative and accepted rahit-nama appear. *See also* PRASHAN-UTTAR; TANAKHAH-NAMA.

RAHIT-NAMA DAYA SINGH. Daya Singh was the first Sikh to offer his head to Guru Gobind Singh (q.v.) at the inauguration of the Khalsa (q.v.), and there exists a brief prose rahit-nama (q.v.) attributed to him. The nature of its contents and language indicates a nineteenth-century provenance.

RAHIT-NAMA DESA SINGH. A brief verse rahit-nama (q.v.) which claims to record the words of Guru Gobind Singh (q.v.) but which dates from at least the late eighteenth century.

RAHIT-NAMA PRAHILAD SINGH. A brief rahit-nama (q.v.) in simple Punjabi verse said to have been composed at Nander (q.v.) shortly before Guru Gobind Singh (q.v.) died. This cannot have been the case. The rahit-nama was probably composed in the late eighteenth century. It contains some very important lines concerning both the Panth and the Granth as Guru (qq.v.).

RAI BHOI DI TALVANDI *see* NANKANA SAHIB.

RAI BULAR. The village landlord of Talvandi Rai Bhoi when Nanak (q.v.) was young. Traditionally, he is regarded as warm admirer of the youthful Nanak.

RAIDAS *see* RAVIDAS.

RAJ KAREGA KHALSA. At the conclusion of Ardas (q.v.) the following couplet is recited: "The Khalsa (q.v.) shall rule (**rāj karegā khālsā**), no enemy shall remain. All who endure suffering and privation shall be brought to the safety of the Guru's protection." This is a quotation from the *Tanakhāh-nāmā*, attributed to Nand Lal (qq.v.). It probably dates from the middle or late eighteenth century. Certainly it reflects the increasing self-confidence of the Khalsa (q.v.) in its contest for power in the Punjab.

RAKAB-GANJ GURDWARA. The gurdwara (q.v.) in New Delhi marking the place where the headless body of Guru Tegh Bahadur (q.v.) was secretly cremated by Lakkhi Shah who, with his son, managed to carry it away from the place of execution in Delhi (q.v.) to his house in the village of Rakab-ganj (or Rikab-ganj). To avoid suspicion, Lakkhi Shah's whole house, with the body inside, was burnt. A gurdwara was built on the spot in 1790 by Baghel Singh, one of the raiding chieftains who had briefly taken Delhi. In 1913, during the construction of New Delhi, its outer wall was demolished by the government in order to provide a straight road to the Viceregal Lodge. This raised widespread protest. The issue was shelved during the war but broke out again after it was over and was one of the reasons for the foundation in 1919 of the Central Sikh League (q.v.). A band of prospective martyrs led by Sardul Singh Caveeshar (q.v.) marched on Delhi to reconstruct the wall. Before they arrived, the government, realizing it had stirred up something which it did not consider essential, had rebuilt the wall and handed the gurdwara over to the Khalsa Divan of Delhi. *See also* JAITA.

RAKHI. One-fifth of the harvest taken by misls (q.v.) in return for protection of villages (including from government officials).

RAKHRI (RAKSHA BANDHAN). A festival celebrated by Hindus and Sikhs held on the full moon day of the month of Saun (August), on which a girl ties a ribbon on her brother's wrist, and he promises to defend her honor throughout his life.

RAM. One of the most common names for God in the Adi Granth, as in Hindu usage also. *See also* AKAL PURAKH; HARI; VAHIGURU.

RAM DAS, GURU (1534–81). Fourth Guru. Born in Lahore (q.v.), a member of the Sodhi subcaste of Khatris (qq.v.). Known as Jetha until he became a Sikh, he was married in 1554 to Bhani (q.v.), the daughter of Guru Amar Das (q.v.). Before Amar Das died in 1574 at the advanced age of 95, his choice as successor and fourth Guru fell upon Ram Das. Sources for the life of Guru Ram Das are sparse (as they are for all Gurus from the second to the eighth), and although it is clear that he should undoubtedly be associated with the founding of Amritsar (q.v.), it is not certain whether he did so on his own initiative or in response to instructions from Amar Das. Amritsar was nevertheless established by Ram Das and known first as Chak Guru, then as Ramdaspur. The first act of the Guru was to excavate the pool which ultimately gave the site its name of Amritsar ('pool of nectar'). Guru Ram Das is credited with having established the masands (q.v.), representatives who acted for the Guru in his absence. Composing hymns was a particular skill of his, and many of his works have been recorded in the Adi Granth (q.v.). In the early Panth (q.v.) the singing of hymns in praise of the divine Name (q.v.) was the dominant activity, an emphasis which continues to the present day. Guru Ram Das is very important as a contributor to this tradition. He chose his youngest son Arjan (q.v.) to succeed him as the fifth Guru, passing over his two older sons Prithi Chand (q.v.) and Mahadev. All the Sikh Gurus were thereafter his direct male descendants.

RAM RAI (1646–87). The elder son of Guru Har Rai (q.v.). Because Har Rai had supported Dara Shikoh in the Mughal war of succession, the successful contender Aurangzeb (q.v.) required him to send Ram Rai to the court in Delhi as a hostage. The intention was to educate the hostage in Mughal ways, converting him into a supporter of the throne. In this regard Aurangzeb was evidently successful. Sikh tradition explains it by describing a particular incident. It records that Ram Rai successfully ingratiated himself by his answer to what Aurangzeb held to be a demeaning reference in the Adi Granth. How did he explain the claim that earthenware pots were made from **miṭṭī musalamān kī** ('the dust which is formed by Muslim [bodies]')? Ram Rai replied that the words were miscopied, the original text reading **miṭṭī beīmān kī** ('the dust which is formed by [the bodies] of faithless people'). Upon hearing this Guru Har Rai declared that Ram Rai, having presumed to amend the words of Guru Nanak (q.v.), should never again appear before him. His younger brother Har Krishan (q.v.) should instead succeed Har Rai as Guru. The tradition can be presumed to be accurate, at least to the extent that it describes relations between Aurangzeb and Ram Rai. Aurangzeb granted revenue-free land in the Dun Valley to Ram Rai, the town there subsequently known as Dehra Dun because Ram Rai set up a **dehrā** (shrine) on his estate. Ram Rai proved to be a rival to the orthodox line for the allegiance of the Sikhs. For this reason, his followers, known as Ram Raiyas (q.v.), were included in the Panj Mel (q.v.).

RAM RAIYA. A member of the schismatic group led by Ram Rai (q.v.). The group is usually included as one of the Panj Mel (q.v.).

RAM SINGH (1816–85). The second and most influential Guru of the Kuka or Namdhari sect (q.v.), believed by members of the sect to be the reincarnation of Gobind Singh (q.v.). Ram Singh was a Ramgarhia (q.v.), and under him the Namdharis became a predominantly rural sect largely comprising Ramgarhias and poorer Jats (q.v.). In 1871 and 1872 there were disturbances involving the Namdharis which the British rulers treated as a prelude to revolution. Because no court would have convicted Ram Singh, he was deported without trial to Rangoon. He died there in 1885.

RAMANAND (? c. 1400). A religious figure particularly associated with Vaishnava bhakti (q.v.) in North India. The tradition that he was Kabir's (q.v.) guru is spurious. One work in the Adi Granth (q.v.) is attributed to him.

RAMDASIA. A Sikh of the Chamar (leather-working) caste; an Outcaste Sikh. *See also* CASTE; DALIT; RAHITIA.

RAMGARHIA. A Sikh artisan caste comprising predominantly Tarkhans (carpenters) together with small numbers of Sikh masons, barbers, and blacksmiths. Sikh Tarkhans, seeking to elevate their position in the caste hierarchy, abandoned the Tarkhan identity, choosing instead the name Ramgarhia from Jassa Singh Ramgarhia (q.v.), who was also a Tarkhan. Their success has, however, been markedly less than that of the Ahluvalias (q.v.) who also adopted the name of a famous misldar (q.v.) as part of a campaign to elevate their caste. Ramgarhias were extensively employed by the British on building the railways of East Africa, and from there many have migrated to Britain and North America. *See also* CASTE; MIGRATION.

RAMGARHIA MISL. A misl (q.v.) led by Jassa Singh Thoka (a Tarkhan by caste) who, taking his name from the fort known as Ramgarh outside Amritsar (q.v.), became Jassa Singh Ramgarhia. His territory spread eastward from Batala across the Beas river. Jassa Singh frequently adopted positions which conflicted with other chieftains, including occasional support for the Afghan invader Ahmad Shah Abdali (q.v.). The misl came to an effective end when it joined the alliance which Ranjit Singh (q.v.) overcame at Bhasin in 1799.

RANDHIR SINGH (1878–1961). A Grewal Jat (q.v.) from Narangwal near Ludhiana who spent lengthy periods in British jails, where he created considerable problems by his rigorous interpretation of the Khalsa faith (q.v.). In particular he insisted on **sarab loh** ('all iron') and refused to eat anything which had not been cooked in an iron vessel. For a lengthy period he was associated with Teja Singh of Bhasaur and the Panch Khalsa Divan (qq.v.) but parted company when Teja Singh was banished from the Panth (q.v.). His followers are known as the Bhai Randhir Singh da Jatha (q.v.).

RANGHRETA. A section of the Mazhabi Sikh outcastes (q.v.) who claim an elevated status on the grounds that Jaita (q.v.), one of their number, carried the severed head of Guru Tegh Bahadur (q.v.) to his son Gobind Singh (q.v.).

RANJIT SINGH (1780–1839). Sikhs remember Maharaja Ranjit Singh with respect and affection as their greatest ruler. He was born a Jat (q.v.), son of the leader of the Shukerchakia misl (q.v.) at a time when the misls (q.v.) were still confronted by Afghan invasions. In 1792 he succeeded his father, when control of the Punjab was moving strongly in favor of the misls. By means of marriages, alliances, and open wars Ranjit Singh was able to reduce all the other misls west of the Satluj river and to emerge in 1801 as Maharaja of most of the Punjab. Those east of the Satluj were protected by the advancing British. During the next two decades he enlarged his territories, capturing Multan, Peshawar, and Kashmir. He took a particular interest in his army, bringing in several Europeans to train it in the western style. He was much less able in economics, however, and the finances of the kingdom were never put on a sound footing. Ranjit Singh was small, marked from smallpox, and illiterate. In spite of the latter feature, he was able to choose competent servants, favoring the Sikhs but nevertheless balancing the three communities which dominated the Punjab. When he died the kingdom rapidly descended into murderous strife, and after two wars fought with the British the Punjab was annexed to British India in 1849. *See also* ANNEXATION OF THE PUNJAB; DULEEP SINGH; JINDAN; KAHNAIYA MISL; KHARAK SINGH, MAHARAJA; SADA KAUR; SHER SINGH, MAHARAJA.

RATAN SINGH BHANGU (d. 1846). Mahtab Singh, one of the assassins of Massa Ranghar (q.v.), had a grandson who was called on to relate the history of the Sikhs. This was Ratan Singh Bhangu. In 1809 Bhangu was invited to tell the story of the Sikhs to the Englishman Captain Murray in Ludhiana; in 1841 he issued his account in Braj/Punjabi (qq.v.) under the title of *Panth Prakāsh* (subsequently known as *Prāchīn Panth Prakāsh* to distinguish it from the later work of the same name by Gian Singh [q.v.]). Although he retained the same emphasis of earlier writers on destiny and struggle, the focus is strongly on the creation of the Khalsa (q.v.). The Khalsa was created to rule. All who acknowledge its discipline must be prepared to assert that right. He gives the date of the founding of the Khalsa as 1695.

RAVIDAS (c. 1500). An outcaste (Chamar) bhagat of Banaras, also known as Raidas. There are forty of his works in the Adi Granth (q.v.). The inclusion of the works of a Chamar in the Adi Granth shows that no importance was attached to caste (q.v.) by the Gurus.

RECENT HISTORY. For several years prior to 1984 there had been growing hostility between the Government of India and the Akali Dal (q.v.). The Akali claim centered on the Anandpur Sahib Resolution of 1973 (q.v.). This document asserted the right of the Akali Dal to represent the Sikhs and embodied several claims, some religious and some economic. The Congress Party (which controlled the central government) evidently sought to provoke disruption within the Akali Dal, promoting the interests of a young militant called Jarnail Singh Bhindranvale (q.v.) without him being aware of the fact. He soon proved himself much more radical than the leadership of the Akali Dal, insisting on a thoroughly fundamentalist approach. With his followers he occupied the buildings around Harimandir Sahib (q.v.) and, threatened with further hostilities, Prime Minister Indira Gandhi decided to send in the Army. The attack (Operation Blue Star) began on June 5th, 1984. So determined was the resistance that it was not until the following day that Bhindranvale was killed and the opposition subdued. The Army had largely managed to avoid attacking Harimandir itself, but in other respects the damage was considerable. The Sikh Reference Library had been burnt, and Akal Takhat (q.v.) lay in ruins. In October 1984 Mrs. Gandhi was assassinated by her Sikh bodyguards, and for several days mobs in Delhi (q.v.) and elsewhere killed Sikhs unchecked. The Punjab became the scene of warfare, Sikh militants fighting Government of India forces. Not until 1992, with the killing of several militant leaders, did the Government of India secure effective control over the state. Meanwhile, an accord signed in 1985 by the new Prime Minister Rajiv Gandhi and Harchand Singh Longowal (q.v.) remains unfulfilled. Three items in particular are outstanding. The city of Chandigarh should be transferred to the Punjab; the question of contiguous villages needs to be settled; and the distribution of river waters must be determined. Until these are definitively decided, discontent will remain. *See also* POLITICAL PARTIES; POLITICS.

RITES OF PASSAGE. Prior to the Singh Sabha movement (q.v.) in the late nineteenth century, the Panth (q.v.) had observed rituals similar to, or identical with, those of the Hindus. The rise of the Tat Khalsa (q.v.), however, produced a determination to observe only Sikh rituals, and for several decades a struggle between Tat Khalsa and Sanatan Sikhs (q.v.) took place within the Panth. The most significant victory of the Tat Khalsa was the passing of the Anand Marriage Act in 1909 (q.v.), one which set out a Sikh form of marriage. The victory was eventually total. Other rites of passage which date from this period are ceremonies for birth, naming, initiation, and death. Hindu ceremonies such as the **shrādh** (for deceased forbears) are forbidden, although they had previously been practiced by Sikhs. *See also* RITUALS.

RITUALS. Nanak (q.v.) taught that rituals were mere external practices and as such were useless. Sikhs, however, observe a limited number of rituals. The principal ones are amrit sanskar, anand marriage, and the funeral service (qq.v.). *See also* RITES OF PASSAGE.

RUCHI RAM SAHNI. A prominent Sahaj-dhari Sikh and member of the Brahma Samaj in the late nineteenth/early twentieth centuries.

RUMAL. 'Handkerchief.' A small piece of cloth covering the topknot, which was commonly worn without a turban by sportsmen and by boys too young for a turban. During the 1980s and 1990s it has been progressively supplanted by the patka (q.v.).

RUMALA. A cloth (normally ornate) in which the Guru Granth Sahib (q.v.) is wrapped when not being read; a portion of the 'robes' of the Guru Granth Sahib. Each set of robes contains three items, of which the rumala is the center piece. Two side-pieces (the **pālakān**) complete the set.

S

SACH *see* SAT.

SACH KHAND. The condition of ineffable sahaj (q.v.) attained at the climax of **nām simaraṇ** (q.v.). This is the meaning of **sach khaṇḍ** as used by Nanak in *Japjī* (qq.v.). For many Sikhs, however, **sach khaṇḍ** is conceived as a 'heavenly abode,' a place to which one's spirit goes at physical death, rather than a mystical condition transcending death. *See also* PANJ KHAND.

SACH KHAND GURDWARA *see* HAZUR SAHIB.

SACHA PATISHAH. 'True King,' a form of address used for God by Nanak (q.v.). Later Gurus came to be addressed by their Sikhs in the same way, as they were seen as the representatives of God.

SACRAMENT. Sikhs recognize no sacraments. The word belongs to western religious practice and, like 'clergy' (q.v.), is inappropriate in the Sikh context.

SACRED AREAS. According to *Sikh Rahit Maryādā* (q.v.) only Amrit-dharis (q.v.), loyal in their observance of the Rahit (q.v.), are permitted to enter particular areas of a takhat (q.v.). Other parts of a takhat are open to all, Sikh or non-Sikh, except for patits and tanakhahie (qq.v.). Gurdwaras (q.v.) are open to all.

SADA KAUR (d. 1832). The widow of Gurbakhsh Singh, heir to the chieftainship of the Kahnaiya misl (q.v.), who was killed in 1782. She was recognized as the effective leader of the misl and for some time was able to prevent Ranjit Singh (q.v.) from absorbing it by marrying her daughter Mahtab Kaur to him. Relations became increasingly strained, however, and in 1821 Ranjit Singh confiscated the Kahnaiya territories, keeping her in custody until her death in 1832.

SADH SANGAT. The congregation of believers.

SADHANA. A bhagat (q.v.). One work of his appears in the Adi Granth (q.v.).

SADHARAN PATH. 'Ordinary reading.' A complete reading of the Guru Granth Sahib (q.v.) with gaps between installments. The reading may be completed in a week, a month, or with an indefinite conclusion and no preordained date for the bhog (q.v.). It is also called a sahaj path. *See also* AKHAND PATH; KULLA PATH; SAPTAHAK PATH.

SADHU. Mendicant; renunciant; ascetic.

SAGUNA. The doctrine that God possesses visible 'qualities' or attributes. *See also* NIRGUNA.

SAHAJ. The condition of ineffable bliss which is the climax of **nām simaraṇ** (q.v.); eternal bliss in union with Akal Purakh (q.v.). The word is taken from the usage of the Naths (q.v.).

SAHAJ-DHARI. A Sikh who does not observe the Rahit (q.v.) and, in particular, cuts his or her hair. The etymology of the term is disputed. Singh Sabha scholars (q.v.) believed it to mean 'slow-adopter' and to designate those Sikhs who were on the path to full Khalsa membership (q.v.). A much more likely origin is that the term derives from sahaj (q.v.), meaning the ineffable bliss of union which climaxes the process of **nām simaraṇ** (q.v.). Practically all Sahaj-dharis are members of the Khatri/Arora/Ahluvalia group of urban castes (qq.v.). This is the group which commonly used to have one son of a family initiated into the Khalsa while the rest of the family remained Sahaj-dharis. *See also* IDENTITY.

SAHAJ PATH *see* SADHARAN PATH.

SAHIB. 'Sir'; a title for Akal Purakh (q.v.) or one implying great respect for places of religious significance. The Golden Temple, for example, is always called Harimandir Sahib or Darbar Sahib (qq.v.), and Amritsar (q.v.) is often known as Amritsar Sahib. Sahib is also applied to men to denote respect.

SAHIB KAUR. The third wife of Gobind Singh (q.v.). Originally called Sahib Devan, she was childless and for this reason, according to tradition, she was designated Mother of the Khalsa (q.v.).

SAHIB SINGH BEDI (1756–1834). A direct descendant of Nanak (q.v.) and as such greatly venerated by the Sikhs. From his father he inherited property at Una in Hoshiarpur district. A vigorous man, he led armed Sikhs in forays across the Satluj river. He developed a considerable reputation as a Sikh preacher and gathered a large following in central Punjab. Amongst his disciples Maharaja Ranjit Singh (q.v.) figured conspicuously, and in 1801 Sahib Singh Bedi conducted his coronation ceremonies in Lahore (q.v.).

SAHIB-ZADE. 'Offspring of the Master': Ajit Singh, Jujhar Singh, Zoravar Singh, and Fateh Singh, sons of Guru Gobind Singh (q.v.). The two elder sons were killed by Mughals in 1704 while defending Chamkaur (q.v.). The two younger ones were executed in 1705 by the Mughal administrator of Sirhind, Vazir Khan (q.v.), bricked up alive and so dying the death of shahids (q.v.). *See also* SUCHANAND.

SAIDPUR. A small town eight miles south east of Gujranwala which was sacked by Babur in 1520. The janam-sakhis (q.v.) all record that Nanak (q.v.) was present on the occasion. The town was subsequently rebuilt by the emperor Akbar and renamed Eminabad.

SAIN. Believed to have been a barber of Rewa who lived in the late fourteenth/early fifteenth centuries. He is reputed to have been a disciple of Ramanand (q.v.). The Adi Granth (q.v.) contains one of his hymns.

SAINAPATI. Author of *Gur-sobha,* 'Radiance of the Guru,' a narrative poem completed in either 1711 or 1745. The work is significant as it provides rare testimony to the beliefs and practices of the Khalsa (q.v.) in the early eighteenth century. It gives the date of the founding of the Khalsa as 1695. *See also* KHALSA DATE.

SAKHI. An anecdote concerning the life of Nanak (q.v.); a story from a janam-sakhi (q.v.).

SAKHI SARVAR. An exceedingly popular semi-legendary fig-ure among the rural people of the Punjab, widely worshipped by Sikhs and Hindus as well as by Muslims. It was in the late nineteenth century that Sakhi Sarvar attracted attention, par-ticularly from British scholars. His real name was, by tradi-tion, Sayyid Ahmad, and he is said to have lived in the twelfth century. He practiced austerities in the area of Multan (q.v.) and by his reputation for working miracles attracted a vast following.

SALUTATIONS. An early form of salutation was "Pairi pavana," loosely translated as 'I fall at your feet.' "Kartar Kartar," '[Hail to] the Creator,' was also common. Later "Sat Sri Akal" ('True is the Immortal One') (q.v.) became dominant as the common salutation, used by Sikhs and non-Sikhs ad-dressing Sikhs. Among Sikhs a more formal greeting is "Vahiguruji ka Khalsa" ('Hail to the Guru's Khalsa') to which the response is "[Siri] Vahiguruji ki fateh" ('Hail the Guru's victory') (q.v.).

SAMMAT DATING. Vikrami dating (or Bikrami dating, i.e. ac-cording to the era of Vikramaditya), which is approximately fifty-six years and nine months ahead of Common Era dating. For example, the equivalent of the first nine months of S. 1957 is AD 1900 (or 1900 CE). The equivalent of the last three months is equivalent to the first three months of AD 1901. In such dating S. stands for Sammat (or Sanvat). Prior to the British annexation of the Punjab in 1849, Sikh dates were either Sammat or Hijari (the Muslim era). In the period of the Singh Sabha (q.v.) Hijari dating was abandoned, and Sikh dates were given as either Sammat or San (q.v.) or both.

SAN DATING. Dating according to the Christian (or Common) Era. *See also* SAMMAT DATING.

SANATAN SIKHS. 'Traditional Sikhs,' conservative Sikhs within the Singh Sabha (q.v.), as opposed to the radical Tat Khalsa (q.v.). The term assumed an inclusive view of the Sikh faith, accepting beliefs drawn from a wide range of Hindu and Muslim tradition (beliefs in the Vedas, Hindu epics, idolatry, Sufi pirs [q.v.], etc.). Sanatan Sikhs, comprising largely the landed aristocracy and those of similar views, were largely responsible for the founding of the first Singh Sabha in Amritsar (q.v.) in 1873. They retained their hold on Amritsar but were soon opposed by the more ardent followers of the Tat Khalsa in Lahore (q.v.) and elsewhere who stressed the exclusive nature of the Sikh faith. The two groups shared membership in the Chief Khalsa Divan (q.v.) which they co-founded in 1902, but the Tat Khalsa found that it largely reflected the views of the Sanatan Sikhs. During the early decades of the twentieth century influence in the Panth (q.v.) passed increasingly to the Tat Khalsa, leaving the Sanatan Sikhs with a rapidly declining strength. Among the prominent Sanatan Sikhs were Khem Singh Bedi and Avtar Singh Vahiria (qq.v.).

SANDHANVALIA FAMILY. A family of Jat Sikhs (q.v.), the principal rivals for power of the Dogra family (q.v.) in the turbulent years immediately following the death of Maharaja Ranjit Singh (q.v.) in 1839. The principal members were Lahna Singh, Attar Singh, and Ajit Singh. Their most conspicuous success was the assassination of Sher Singh (q.v.), his son Partap Singh, and Dhian Singh Dogra in 1843. This was followed by the revenge killing of Lahna Singh and Ajit Singh shortly after. Attar Singh was killed the following year. *See also* THAKUR SINGH SANDHANVALIA.

SANGAT. Being together; a congregation. The sangat is of central importance in the Sikh faith, the assembly of believers being the venue where the divine Name (q.v.) is remembered by the singing of kirtan (q.v.). The terms 'satsang' (the company of truth) or 'sadhsang' (the company of the pious) are also used.

SANGRAND. The first day of the month according to Bikrami dating (q.v.). Sangrands are observed as highly auspicious by the Panth (q.v.). Bathing in the pool surrounding Harimandir Sahib (q.v.) is particularly popular as many Sikhs believe that this confers health and prosperity during the remainder of the month. *See also* AMAVAS; PANCHAMI; PURAN-MASHI.

SANSAR. The cycles of transmigration. According to Gurmat (q.v.), a person can escape sansar by regular meditation on the divine Name (q.v.), leading finally to permanent bliss. *See also* MUKTI; SAHAJ.

SANT. Originally applied to followers of the Sant Tradition (q.v.), either as religious poets or as ordinary believers. The word derives from **sat** (q.v.), 'truth,' the sant being 'a person who knows the truth.' Following the end of the line of personal Gurus within the Panth (q.v.) in 1708, the ancient master/disciple tradition survived, though the master could never be called a guru. Many Sikhs attached themselves to preceptors who had acquired reputations as teachers or exemplars and who eventually acquired the title of Sant. They continue to flourish within the Panth, particularly among its rural members, and some of them command substantial influence. Recent examples with considerable political prestige include Sant Fateh Singh, Sant Harchand Singh Longoval, and Sant Jarnail Singh Bhindranvale (qq.v.).

SANT BHASHA *see* ADI GRANTH LANGUAGE.

SANT NIRANKARI. Founded by Avtar Singh in the 1940s as a break-away from the Nirankaris (q.v.). The principal differences between the Sant Nirankaris and orthodox Sikhs are the former's addition of other works to the Adi Granth (q.v.) and the exalted homage paid to their leader as Guru. In 1978 there was conflict with orthodox Sikhs over holding of a Sant Nirankari conference in Amritsar (q.v.), an incident which led to a fatal police shooting and to the emergence of Jarnail Singh Bhindranvale (q.v.) as a leader of the orthodox. Bhindranvale's violent denunciations were widely reported, and in 1980 the leader of the Sant Nirankaris, Gurbachan Singh, was assassinated. After more than a decade of serious discord with the orthodox Sikhs, the sect largely faded from sight.

SANT TRADITION. A religious movement in Northern India, one which draws heavily on Bhakti (q.v.) antecedents but also has other roots. Two major sources can be identified. Vaishnava Bhakti (devotion to one of the avatars or 'incarnations' of the god Vishnu, particularly Krishna or Rama) is one of these, and for most Sant poets is clearly the dominant source. To it must be added the Nath tradition (q.v.), a source which is particularly evident in the works of Kabir (q.v.) (probably c. 1440–1518). Sufi influence (q.v.) may also have contributed to the development of Sant ideals, though its influence was appreciably less than the first two sources. As with believers in Bhakti, the Sants stress devotion as essential to liberation. They differ in their insistence that God is **nirgun** (without form) and can be neither incarnated nor represented iconically as can the **sagun** (with form) concept. They evidently owe their stress on a wholly interior response to the Naths. God, immanently revealed, is contemplated inwardly, and all exterior forms are spurned. Sants are commonly (but wrongly) included in Vaishnava Bhakti. The connection with the Sant tradition of Maharashtra is closer. Most Sant poets were of humble backgrounds, as with the weaver Kabir or the outcaste leather-worker Ravidas (q.v.). Nanak (q.v.) and his successor Gurus, though certainly within the tradition, were exceptions to this rule as all were high-caste Khatris (q.v.). The tradition still thrives, a modern representative being the Radhasoami movement (q.v.).

SANTOKH SINGH (1788–1844). The most prominent of all Sikh hagiographers. A Chhimba (q.v.) by caste, he was born near Amritsar (q.v.) but spent most of his working life in Malwa (q.v.), where he lived in Buria and Kaithal under the patronage of their respective sardars (q.v.). Santokh Singh wrote in-different verse in a mixture of Punjabi and Braj (qq.v.). He was strongly influenced by the heretical ideas of the Hindalis and by the Vedantic doctrines of the Udasis and Nirmalas (qq.v.) but earned considerable popularity owing to the fact that he covered the complete range of Gurus. His account of Nanak (q.v.), *Gur Nānak Prakāsh* (or the *Nānak Prakāsh*), which was completed in 1823, takes as its principal source the *Bālā* tradition (q.v.), supplemented by the *Gyān-ratanāvalī* and by other janam-sakhis (qq.v.). The other Gurus he covered in his lengthy *Gur Partāp Sūray* (the *Sūraj Prakāsh*), completed in 1844. *See also* ANAND GHAN; BUNGA.

SANT-SIPAHI. The ideal Sikh. Spiritual qualities are summed up in the first word. A Sikh should be humble and pious like a sant (q.v.), devoted to the **nām** (q.v.) and willing to be the dust under everyone's feet. A Sikh should also possess the martial qualities of a sipahi (soldier), ever courageous and bravely prepared to fight gallantly for justice even if it should mean death. The term applies to both male and female Sikhs, though in actual usage it is largely confined to men.

SAPTAHAK PATH. 'Seven-day reading,' the most common period for an intermittent reading of the complete Guru Granth Sahib (q.v.). The reading concludes with a bhog (q.v.). *See also* AKHAND PATH; PATH; SADHARAN PATH.

SARAB LOH. 'All Steel.' From the time of Guru Gobind Singh (q.v.) onwards, an epithet for God. The term is also used as a description for Mahakal or Shiv (Siva). *See also* AKAL US-TATI.

SARAB LOH GRANTH. A work by an unknown poet, probably dating from the late eighteenth century, which concerns an avatar of Sarab Loh (q.v.) or Shiv (Siva). Traditionally (but mistakenly), it has been regarded as the work of Guru Gobind Singh (q.v.). Amongst the Nihangs (q.v.) it has been particularly popular. Tara Singh Narotam, the Nirmala scholar (qq.v.), claimed it to be by Sukkha Singh, the granthi of Patna Sahib. Because it contains verses in praise of the Khalsa (q.v.), it is at least thought to derive from a Sikh origin. The work has been little studied.

SARBARAH. Official appointed by the British to manage Harimandir Sahib (q.v.) until it was taken over by the SGPC (q.v.) in 1926.

SARBAT DA BHALLA. "[May] all be blest," the three closing words of Ardas (q.v.) commonly uttered as a blessing.

SARBAT KHALSA. The 'entire' or 'plenary Khalsa' (q.v.), a term which emerged during the later eighteenth century to describe the temporary unity accomplished by the linking of misls (q.v.) for some shared purpose, such as campaigns against the Afghan invader. Today it means a representative body of Sikhs summoned by the Jathedar of Akal Takhat (qq.v.), acting on instructions from the SGPC (q.v.), for an important matter concerning the Panth (q.v.).

SARDAR. 'Chieftain.' In the eighteenth century a title applied to the leader of a misl or jatha (qq.v.). Today it is invariably applied to all kes-dhari Sikhs (q.v.). The form for women is Sardarni.

SARDUL SINGH CAVEESHAR (1886–1963). Prominent radical journalist during the early decades of the twentieth century.

SAROPA. 'Head and feet'; robe of honor. Saropas are given to individuals for piety or meritorious service to the Panth (q.v.). The quality of the saropa reflects the status of the recipient, ranging from saffron head-coverings to resplendent robes.

SAROVAR. The pool for bathing which is sometimes part of a gurdwara (q.v.). The name 'Amritsar' is a combination of **amrit** ('nectar') and **sar[ovar]** ('pool'). The term is frequently and ineptly translated by the ugly word 'tank.'

SAT (also SATI, SATYA, SACH, SACHA). 'True,' that which genuinely exists. The word is both immensely important in the Sikh tradition (and in other Indian traditions also) and impossible to translate satisfactorily.

SAT SRI AKAL. "True is the Immortal One." The common greeting used when at least one person is a Sikh. It is also used as a triumphal shout in Sikh assemblies. A leader cries "Bole so nihāl ('Blessed is the one who utters . . .') to which all who are present reply with a fervent "Sat Srī Akāl!" *See also* SALUTATIONS; VAH GURUJI KA KHALSA, VAHIGURUJI KI FATEH.

SATGURU. 'True Guru'; 'Guru' expressed with particular reverence.

SATI (SUTTEE). The burning of a widow on her deceased husband's funeral pyre. The practice was denounced by the Gurus.

SATI DAS (d. 1675). One of three Sikhs executed in Delhi (q.v.) with Guru Tegh Bahadur (q.v.). *See also* DAYAL DAS; MATI DAS.

SATIYUG *see* KALIYUG.

SAT-NAM. "True [is] the divine Name." A common form for **nām japan** (q.v.), i.e. for practicing **nām simaran** (q.v.) by means of the simple repetition of a single word or mantra.

SATSANG *see* SANGAT.

SATTA AND BALVAND *see* BALVAND AND SATTA.

SAU SAKHIAN. 'The Hundred Sayings.' A lengthy prose rahitnama (q.v.) composed in the mid-nineteenth century. One version of this work was particularly popular with the Namdharis (q.v.), containing a prophecy which they claimed pointed to their leader Ram Singh (q.v.).

SAVA LAKH. 'A lakh and a quarter'; the Khalsa (q.v.). Gobind Singh (q.v.) traditionally declared that in place of the tiny number of Sikhs who had stood by his father at the time of his execution he would create a highly visible host numbering 125,000 (**savā lakh**).

SAVAYYA, SAVAIYA. A kind of meter; a song in this meter; a panegyric.

SELI. The woollen cord which Nanak (q.v.) is thought to have worn in his turban. It is traditionally believed to have been passed down to his successors until Hargobind (q.v.) put it aside as inappropriate to the **mīrī/pīrī** role (q.v.) which he was assuming.

SEPIDARI. The Punjabi system of granting customary shares of each harvest to members of various castes (agricultural laborers, carpenters, barbers, sweepers, etc.) tied to a particular patron in a hereditary service arrangement. In most of northern India this system is known as jajmani.

SEVA. 'Service.' This may be rendered to the Guru, either in money or kind or duties performed, or it may be directed to ordinary people. In the former case, it is normally focused on the gurdwara (q.v.) and involves cash donations, contributions of food to the langar (q.v.), or such unpaid duties as reading the scripture, cleaning the premises, polishing the shoes of worshippers, or helping in the langar. The word can also be given a wider connotation to mean service to the community in the general sense.

SEVA PANTH. Followers of Ghahnaiya Ram (q.v.) who formed an order dedicated to service of the wider community. The order was formed largely by Addan Shah, a Sindhi disciple converted by Bhai Ghahnaiya early in the eighteenth century, and until the partition of India in 1947 (q.v.) its chief center was at Nurpur in Sindh. Seva-panthis are sahaj-dhari Sikhs (q.v.) and must earn their keep by labor, not by begging. Their distinctive clothing is simple, and their way of life austere. Celibacy is enjoined and borrowing money forbidden. The size of the order is very small.

SEVA SINGH THIKRIVALA (c.1882–1935). An Akali (q.v.) who was the moving spirit behind the Praja Mandal (q.v.)

(Tenants' Association) of the princely states. In 1935 he succumbed to treatment received in a Patiala jail.

SEVADAR. Servant, attendant at a gurdwara (q.v.).

SGPC *see* SHIROMANI GURDWARA PARBANDHAK COMMITTEE.

SHABAD (SABAD). 'Word.' Shabad has two related meanings. 1. For Nanak (q.v.) it was the revelation which communicates the message of the **nām** (q.v.). The Word is uttered by the mystical Guru (q.v.) to the believer who thereby perceives the **nām** (the divine Name) around and within him/her. 2. As Nanak himself came to be regarded as the inspired communicator of the **shabad** his hymns were treated as its actual expression. This belief was extended to his successors as Guru and **shabad** thus came to mean a hymn recorded in the Adi Granth (q.v.). *See also* SHALOK.

SHAHADAT. 'Martyrdom,' a term which shares the same importance for the Sikh faith as shahid (q.v.). It is justified on the grounds that it becomes inevitable when the Panth (q.v.) is resolutely involved in protecting the weak from oppression and the defenseless against tyrants. Sikhs who avow martyrdom as a supreme virtue insist that at no point have the Gurus ever been quietist or pacifist.

SHAHID. 'Martyr.' The concept of martyrdom, evidently borrowed from the Islamic culture of the Punjab, is extremely important in Sikh history and tradition. Before the arrival of the British, all martyrs met their deaths at Muslim hands. Two Gurus, Arjan and Tegh Bahadur (qq.v.), are held to have been martyred, and the shahid-ganj (place of martyrdom) in each case is endued with a special sanctity. In later history three martyrs who exercise a particular fascination are the two Sahib-zade, the younger children of Gobind Singh (qq.v.) who are believed to have been bricked up alive in Sirhind; and Dip Singh (q.v.). The two older children of the Guru are also regarded as martyrs, as is Banda Bahadur (q.v.). The concept has continued to play a central part in the history of the Panth (q.v.). Jarnail Singh Bhindranvale (q.v.) is widely regarded as a modern martyr, and there are many more besides him.

SHAHID MISL. A small misl (q.v.) with territory in the Malwa area (q.v.) around Damdama Sahib (q.v.). Dip Singh (q.v.) is believed to have belonged to this misl. It was renowned for keeping alive the traditions of the Khalsa (q.v.), later maintained by the Nihangs (q.v.).

SHALOK. **Shlok,** normally a couplet; any short composition contained in the Adi Granth (q.v.). *See also* SHABAD (SABAD).

SHASTAR NAM-MALA. 'An inventory of weapons.' A portion of the Dasam Granth (q.v.) which lists seven weapons and relates the deeds of some who used them. The weapons are the sword, the **katār** dagger, the lance, the quoit, the arrow, the noose, and the gun. The seven names are cryptically expressed as puzzles.

SHER SINGH, MAHARAJA (1807–43). Second son of Ranjit Singh (q.v.). He succeeded his half-brother Kharak Singh (q.v.) in 1840 but with his son Partap Singh was assassinated by the Sandhanvalia brothers (q.v.) in 1843. His palace still stands in Batala.

SHIROMANI or SHROMANI. Great; supreme; paramount.

SHIROMANI AKALI DAL *see* AKALI DAL.

SHIROMANI GURDWARA PARBANDHAK COMMITTEE. After World War I radical Sikhs became much more militant in demanding control of all gurdwaras (q.v.). In 1920 the Central Sikh League (q.v.) formed a committee of 175 members known as the Shiromani Gurdwara Parbandhak Committee (usually abbreviated to SGPC), the intention being that it should launch a movement on behalf of the Panth (q.v.) for liberating gurdwaras from their existing custodians, the mahants (q.v.). This was followed by the formation of the Akali Dal (q.v.) the same year. The Akali Dal was to attempt to gain control of the gurdwaras, and the SGPC was then to administer them. For five years the struggle was maintained. Eventually the Sikhs won, and the Sikh Gurdwaras Act of 1925 (q.v.) provided for a committee elected by Sikhs to manage the gurdwaras. Sikh leaders conferred this responsibility on the SGPC which thereafter possessed a statutory function. As manager of almost all the major gurdwaras in undivided Punjab, it controls considerable estates and patronage, much of which is used for political purposes. Since 1925 it has remained in the hands of the Akalis. *See also* DELHI SIKH GURDWARA MANAGEMENT COMMITTEE; GURDWARA REFORM MOVEMENT; POLITICAL PARTIES.

SHIVALIK HILLS. Foothills of the Himalayas, forming the northeastern boundary of the Punjab. A section of the hills have been very important in the history of the Sikhs, from the time of Guru Hargobind to that of Guru Gobind Singh (qq.v.). The Mughal Empire did not extend far into them, and they were ruled by hill chieftains who acknowledged the suzerainty of the Mughals. Kiratpur and Anandpur (qq.v.) are situated on the edge of the Shivaliks, overlooking the Punjab plains across the Satluj river. *See also* MUGHAL DYNASTY.

SHIV-NABH (SIVANABH). A raja whom Nanak (q.v.), according to the janam-sakhis (q.v.), is said to have converted. Traditionally he is placed in Sri Lanka. There is no evidence for his existence.

SHRADH. A Hindu ceremony performed annually on behalf of deceased forbears, the purpose being to assist their passage to Paradise or to whatever destination has been determined by their karma (q.v.). Before the late nineteenth century the custom was observed by many Sikhs. Reformers of the Tat Khalsa within the Singh Sabha (qq.v.), fortified by scriptural injunctions, mounted a generally successful attack on the practice of the ceremony by Sikhs.

SHUKERCHAKIA MISL. A misl (q.v.) with territories to the north and west of Lahore. In the late eighteenth century it won total supremacy in western and central Punjab, developing into the Kingdom of the Punjab under Ranjit Singh (q.v.).

SIDDH (SIDDHA). Eighty-four venerable men believed to have attained immortality through the practice of yoga and to be dwelling deep in the Himalayas. In the Adi Granth (q.v.) and the janam-sakhis (q.v.) Siddh and Nath (q.v.) are used inter-changeably.

SIDH GOSHTI. 'Discourse with the Siddhs (q.v.).' A lengthy work by Nanak (q.v.) in the Adi Granth (q.v.), pages 938–46.

SIKH. A Sikh is defined by *Sikh Rahit Maryādā* (q.v.) as "any per-son who believes in Akal Purakh, in the ten Gurus (Guru Nanak to Guru Gobind Singh), in Sri Guru Granth Sahib, other writings of the ten Gurus and their teachings, in the Khalsa initiation ceremony instituted by the tenth Guru, and who does not believe in any other system of religious doc-trine" (qq.v). This definition is an enlarged version of what was written into the Sikh Gurdwaras Act of 1925 (q.v.). That Act, however, marked the victory of the Tat Khalsa (q.v.) over others who took a more relaxed view of the Panth (q.v.), particularly the Sahaj-dharis (q.v.). The latter could scarcely agree that a Sikh had to 'believe in' (**nischā rakhdā**) the Khalsa initiation ceremony or that there was no place for other religious systems. The definition is rather that of a Khalsa Sikh. A definition of a Sikh which would embrace all who claim the title would have to omit these two items and add a reference to the ideal of **nām simaraṇ** (q.v.). At the same time it must be acknowledged that this latter definition would be rejected by many members of the Khalsa as inade-quate and that an agreed definition is impossible. *See also* IDENTITY.

SIKH DHARMA OF THE WESTERN HEMISPHERE. Founded in 1971 in the United States by Harbhajan Singh Khalsa Yo-giji (commonly called Yogi Bhajan [q.v.]), the sect now claims several thousand Western adherents scattered over seventeen countries. Its strength is concentrated in the United States. Members are distinguished by white apparel (including turbans for women as well as men) and by a rigorous discipline of meditation and what is called kundalini yoga. The movement is also distinctive in that it possesses an ordained ministry. Relations with the orthodox Khalsa (q.v.) are cautious, though in general members are punctilious in observing the Rahit (q.v.). The movement is best known as 3HO (Healthy Happy Holy Organisation), strictly the name of its educational branch. Members all take Punjabi names but adopt the name Khalsa as their surname.

SIKH GURDWARAS ACT, 1925. Enacted by the Legislative Council of the Punjab, this Act marked the triumph of the Akalis (q.v.) and the end of the Gurdwara Reform Movement (q.v.). A list of the major gurdwaras (q.v.) of the Punjab was appended to the Act, and a committee elected by Sikhs was given the right to manage them, giving it considerable powers of patronage. According to a later amendment Sahaj-dharis (q.v.) could be enrolled as electors. The Act's definition of a Sikh, however, was particularly important as it lent considerable support to the view, advocated by the Tat Khalsa (q.v.), that a Sikh was one who had 'no other religion.' A later amendment made this still clearer, specifying that all persons elected to the committee had to be either Amrit-dhari or Kes-dhari (qq.v.). They were also required to certify that they did not take alcoholic drinks, a restriction which still applies in theory. To this committee the Akalis transferred the name of their own Shiromani Gurdwara Parbandhak Committee (q.v.), and since then it has been supreme in Sikh affairs. *See also* DELHI SIKH GURDWARA MANAGEMENT COMMITTEE.

SIKH KANYA MAHAVIDYALA. A school founded in Firozpur by Takht Singh (q.v.) in 1890 and taken over by the local Singh Sabha (q.v.) in 1892 as an exclusively girls' school. Female education was at that time a novelty, but the school soon became a model for other Sikh schools run by the Tat Khalsa (q.v.). The objective was to train each girl to read and write Gurmukhi (q.v.), to be knowledgeable about the Sikh past, and to perform all household duties. She should be respectful and obedient to her husband and should bring up her children in accordance with the Tat Khalsa conception of the Sikh faith.

SIKH RAHIT MARYADA. The title of the definitive statement of the Khalsa Rahit (qq.v.), first issued in 1950. The unsatisfactory state of the extant rahit-namas (q.v.) was first faced by Singh Sabha reformers (q.v.) at the end of the nineteenth century, and slow progress was made amidst the political activities which engaged the Panth (q.v.). Finally, a committee was appointed in 1931 with Principal Teja Singh as convener, and by 1932 a draft was complete. Further obstructions occurred, and it was not until 1950 that the work appeared as a small booklet. (Teja Singh did, however, include an English translation of most of the Rahit as a chapter in his *Sikhism: Its Ideals and Institutions,* published in 1938.) *Sikh Rahit Maryādā* has stood the test of time since 1950. The work is divided into two parts: personal discipline and panthic discipline (q.v.). The first part covers such topics as behavior in a gurdwara (q.v.) and reading of the Guru Granth Sahib (q.v.). It also details the order to be followed in the rituals for birth and naming, marriage, and death (qq.v.). The second section largely comprises the order for Khalsa initiation (q.v.). An English translation is available.

SIKHI. The wider Sikh faith as opposed to the Khalsa belief of Singhi (qq.v.).

SIKHISM. There are conflicting definitions attached to the word 'Sikh' (q.v.), and it is consequently impossible to define 'Sikhism' to the satisfaction of everyone. It may mean the wider body of all who embrace the teachings of Nanak (q.v.) and revere the Adi Granth (q.v.); it may be confined to the Khalsa (q.v.); or it may be located somewhere between the two. Usually the term assumes the Tat Khalsa (q.v.) meaning which centers firmly on the Khalsa. There is also a problem when one contrasts the normative Sikhism of the intellectual elite with the operative beliefs and customs of the vast majority of the Panth (q.v.). In describing Sikhism one should be clearly aware that it is normally the former which is placed under scrutiny. Most Sikhs prefer the word Gurmat (q.v.) ('the teachings of the Guru') to Sikhism. *See also* IDENTITY.

SIKHISM: SEPARATE FAITH. Although Nanak (q.v.) was born a Hindu and an overwhelming majority of early Sikhs were from Hindu backgrounds, the way of **nām simaraṇ** (q.v.) was open to anyone of any faith, specifically Muslim as well as Hindu. All that was required was the Sant belief (q.v.) in the inward nature of faith, devoid of any outward symbols and practices. The third Guru, Amar Das (q.v.), introduced a rudimentary discipline to hold the community of his followers together; at a later date the establishment of the Khalsa (q.v.) by the tenth Guru, Gobind Singh (q.v.), required those who joined it to observe outward symbols which proclaimed their identity. This led to the conviction that the Sikhs (at least the Sikhs of the Khalsa) were distinctively different, and eventually there developed the conviction that they were a completely separate community. This conviction owed much to the success of the Tat Khalsa (q.v.) in propagating their distinctive view of the Sikh faith.

SIKKHAN DI BHAGAT-MALA *see* BHAGAT-RATANAVALI.

SINGH. 'Lion.' All male Amrit-dharis (q.v.) must add Singh to their first name. The custom is also followed by most Kes-dharis (q.v.) and those with a Khalsa (q.v.) background and is thus borne by a large majority of male Sikhs. The word is also used in a general sense to designate Khalsa Sikhs. *See also* AMRIT SANSKAR; IDENTITY; KAUR; NAMING CEREMONY.

SINGH SABHA MOVEMENT. The first Singh Sabha was founded in 1873 to restore the credibility of the Sikhs following Kuka disturbances (q.v.) and also to stem what seemed to be clear signs of decay in the Panth (q.v.). After the annexation of the Punjab in 1849, (q.v.) the Panth appeared to be declining rapidly, and there were numerous forecasts of its demise. In actual fact the condition of the Panth was little changed, but educated Sikhs were learning to see it in a dis-

tinctively western mode. The readiness of many Sikhs to indiscriminately adopt Hindu life styles was one cause of increasing dismay. Christian missions also seemed to be a
threat, and in 1873 the decision of four pupils of the Amritsar Mission School to accept Christian baptism prompted the
foundation of the Singh Sabha (Singh Society) in that city.
Another branch was formed in Lahore in 1879, and others followed in areas populated by Sikhs, all supporting a general
reformist policy with strong emphasis on the recovery of distinctive Sikh values. This policy was applied through literature, education, religious assemblies, preaching, and public
controversy. Two distinct trends soon emerged, with what
have been termed the Sanatan Sikhs prominent in Amritsar
and the Tat Khalsa dominant in Lahore (qq.v.). A split appeared between the two, with each supported by satellites of
smaller sabhas. The need for reform was seen as comparatively little by Amritsar, much greater by Lahore. A third
group, much more radical than the other two, emerged in the
village of Bhasaur (q.v.). Although a fragile unity between
Amritsar and Lahore was achieved in 1902 by the formation
of a joint body, the Chief Khalsa Divan (q.v.), this organization proved much too cautious for the Tat Khalsa. The Tat
Khalsa progressively assumed complete dominance in Sikh
affairs, introducing newly-fashioned rituals, stressing Khalsa
forms, and reinterpreting Sikh history. In 1920 it issued in the
Akali movement (q.v.). This Tat Khalsa dominance has continued through the twentieth century. Whenever general reference is made to the Singh Sabha nowadays, it is usually the
Tat Khalsa which is meant.

SINGHALADIP. Sri Lanka; the land where Raja Shiv-nabh (q.v.)
was believed to rule.

SINGHI. The faith or spirit of the Khalsa (q.v.). *See also* SIKHI.

SINGHPURIA MISL. A small misl (q.v.), also known as the
Faizulapuria misl, with territories on either side of the Satluj
river. This misl was associated with Nawab Kapur Singh
(q.v.) and must therefore have been taking shape before the
Afghan invasions of Ahmad Shah Abdali (q.v.) which began

in 1747. Later in the eighteenth century it gave way to stronger misl neighbors.

SIRI CHAND (trad. 1494–1629). One of two sons of Nanak (q.v.), believed to have opposed his father's appointment of Angad (q.v.) as second Guru. He lived a celibate life and is traditionally regarded as the founder of the Udasi panth (q.v.). The title Baba is usually attached to his name. *See also* GURU-VANS; LAKHMI DAS.

SIROPA *see* SAROPA.

SIS GANJ. 'The place [where the Guru's] head [was struck off].' The large gurdwara (q.v.) in Chandni Chauk, Delhi (q.v.), which marks the spot where Guru Tegh Bahadur (q.v.) was beheaded on orders from the emperor Aurangzeb (q.v.) in 1675.

SMOKING *see* HOOKAH; TOBACCO.

SODAR RAHARAS. *Sodar* comes from **so dar,** the words which begin the first of the relevant five hymns recorded in the liturgical section at the beginning of the Adi Granth, pp. 8–10 (q.v.); *raharās*, 'straight path,' now bears the meaning 'supplicatory prayer.' These hymns, together with the following four known as the *so purakh* group (pp. 10–12), are sung by devout Sikhs every day at sundown. The nine hymns are repeated under their appropriate ragas later in the Adi Granth. To them are added the *Benatī chaupaī, Savayyā, and Doharā* from the Dasam Granth (qq.v.), the first five and the last stanzas of the *Anand* (q.v.), and the *Mundavaṇī* and *Shalok* by Guru Arjan (q.v.). *See also* SOHILA.

SODHI. The sub-caste of the Khatris (q.v.) to which Ram Das (q.v.) and all subsequent Gurus belonged. Membership in this sub-caste conferred honor on all who belonged to it. Two important lineages were the Sodhis of Kartarpur and those of Anandpur (qq.v.). The former, descended from Dhir Mal (q.v.), have in their possession the copy of the Adi Granth (q.v.) said to have been dictated by Guru Arjan to Bhai Gurdas (qq.v.). *See also* CHHOTE MEL; GURU-VANS.

SOHAGAN. A deserving wife who is cherished by her husband. Used as a metaphor for the loving believer who wins approval from God.

SOHAN KAVI. Pseudonym of the anonymous author of *Gurbilās Chhevīn Pātshāhī*, the heroic story of Guru Hargobind (q.v.). It is said to be an eighteenth century work but actually originates in the early or mid-nineteenth century. *See also* DEVI WORSHIP; GUR-BILAS.

SOHILA or KIRTAN SOHILA. The five hymns which are sung or chanted by devout Sikhs prior to retiring at night. The hymns are recorded at the end of the liturgical portion of the Adi Granth, pp. 12–13 (q.v.) and again under their appropriate rags (q.v.). The order is also sung at the conclusion of a Sikh cremation. *See also* SODAR RAHARAS.

SOURCES. Prior to the nineteenth century sources for the study of Sikh history and religion are comparatively few. For the teachings of the first five Gurus and the ninth Guru there is the incomparable Adi Granth (q.v.), aided by the works of Bhai Gurdas (q.v.). The janam-sakhis (q.v.) are important, though considerable care is required with them as they serve as sources for later periods than that of Nanak (q.v.). The *Dabistān-i-Mazāhib* (q.v.) also provides an interesting account of the time of Guru Hargobind (q.v.). For the later Gurus and for the founding of the Khalsa (q.v.) the sources are both sparser and more difficult to use. During the eighteenth century there are the Dasam Granth, the early rahit-namas, and the early gur-bilas literature (qq.v.). These mainly focus on Gobind Singh (q.v.) and the Khalsa, yet they present the historian with considerable problems and relatively little attention has been devoted to their critical analysis. One such problem is language, many of the eighteenth-century sources being written in Braj (q.v.). Another is dating. Several sources (particularly the rahit-namas) are much later than their purported dates. During the nineteenth and particularly the twentieth centuries the sources become much more plentiful. For the reign of Ranjit Singh (q.v.) Persian sources now add much information. Europeans were also in the Punjab, and their observations are of increasing value. After the appearance of the Singh Sabha movement (q.v.) in 1873 there was a considerable interest in Sikh history and religion, and some important scholars (such as Vir Singh and Kahn Singh Nabha) emerged within the Panth (qq.v.). Two basic problems confront the researcher with regard to sources. The first is that piety frequently leads to some sources being exalted while others are ignored. The second arises from the continuing influence of the Singh Sabha (q.v.). Most scholars are Singh Sabha products, their approach to Sikh history and religion shaped by the philosophy of the Tat Khalsa (q.v.). This influence continues today, with the result that a critical treatment of Sikh history and religion must expect to encounter strenuous opposition.

SPORT. Sikhs occupy a major position in Indian sport, particularly those involving physical strength. In addition to Indian sports such as kabaddi they have figured prominently in international hockey, cricket, wrestling, and athletics.

SUBA. A province or state of an empire or federation. The Mughal empire was divided into subas.

SUCHANAND. A Hindu who was a member of the retinue of Vazir Khan (q.v.) of Sirhind. When Zoravar Singh and Fateh Singh, two of the children of Guru Gobind Singh (q.v.), fell into Vazir Khan's hands Suchanand urged that they should be executed. This advice was accepted, and the two children were bricked up alive. In 1710 Banda (q.v.) wrought terrible vengeance on Sirhind and on Suchanand. Sikhs sometimes refer to him as Jhuthanand, **jhūṭhā** meaning 'false' whereas **suchā** means 'true' or 'faithful.' *See also* SAHIB-ZADE.

SUFI. A member of one of the mystical Sufi orders of Islam. *See also* PIR.

SUICIDE. No official guidance is given on the subject of suicide, though it meets with disapproval from Sikhs as life is believed to be the gift of God. Suicide must be distinguished from the willing death of the martyr (**shahīd** [q.v.]) which is certainly accepted.

SUKHASAN. The procedure whereby in gurdwaras (q.v.) the Guru Granth Sahib (q.v.) is closed at night, wrapped in rumalas (q.v.), and transported respectfully to a place of rest. *See also* PARKASH KARNA.

SUKHMANI SAHIB. A lengthy poem by Guru Arjan (q.v.) included in the Adi Granth, pp. 262–96 (q.v.). The title can mean either 'The Pearl of Peace' or 'Peace of Mind.' A work of supreme lyricism, it extols the beauty of the divine Name (q.v.) and repeatedly declares its crucial importance in the individual's quest for liberation. It is immensely popular among Hindus as well as Sikhs.

SUKKHA SINGH (1766–1838). Author of *Gur-bilās Dasvīn Pātshāhī,* the heroic story of Guru Gobind Singh (q.v.), completed in 1797. Sukkha Singh shows considerable sympathy with the Udasis (q.v.). His is the earliest Sikh work to give 1699 as the date of the founding of the Khalsa (q.v.). The language tends strongly towards Gurmukhi Braj (qq.v.). *See also* DEVI WORSHIP; GUR-BILAS.

SULAKHANI. Wife of Guru Nanak. She was a Chona Khatri (q.v.) from Pakhoke, near Batala, and is commonly referred to as Mata Choni.

SULHI KHAN. A Muslim friend of Prithi Chand, leader of the Minas (qq.v.). At Prithi Chand's instigation he attacked Guru Arjan (q.v.) but was killed when his horse fell into a brick kiln.

SULTANPUR (SULTANPUR LODHI). A town in southern Doaba (q.v.) near the confluence of the Satluj and Beas rivers. Guru Nanak (q.v.), as a young man, was employed here by Daulat Khan Lodi (q.v.). It was evidently here that he experienced the call to go out and preach the doctrine of the divine Name (q.v.).

SUNDAR. Author of a work of six stanzas entitled *Sadu,* composed in memory of his grandfather Guru Amar Das (q.v.) and acknowledging Ram Das (q.v.) as the successor. It is included in the Adi Granth, pp. 923–24 (q.v.).

SUNDARI. The second of the three wives of Guru Gobind Singh (q.v.), married in 1684; the mother of Ajit Singh. *See also* SAHIB-ZADE.

SUNDER SINGH MAJITHIA (1872–1941). Active in the Singh Sabha and Chief Khalsa Divan (qq.v.). The first secretary of the latter. Proved too moderate for many in the Panth (q.v.) and saw the Chief Khalsa Divan overtaken by the more radical Akali movement (q.v.).

SUPERSTITIONS. The Tat Khalsa reformers (q.v.) were strongly opposed to what they regarded as the superstitious practices of many Hindus and have written prohibitions into *Sikh Rahit Maryādā* (q.v.). Gurmat (q.v.), it states, requires Sikhs "to reject caste distinctions and untouchability, magical amulets, mantras, and spells; auspicious omens, days, times, planets and astrological signs; the ritual feeding of Brahmans to sanctify or propitiate the dead; oblation for the dead, the superstitious waving of lights; [traditional] obsequies; fire sacrifices; ritual feasting or libations; sacred tufts of hair or ritual shaving; fasting for particular phases of the moon; frontal marks, sacred threads and sanctified rosaries; worshipping at tombs, temples or cenotaphs; idol worship (q.v.); and all other such superstitions."

SURAJ MAL (b. 1617). The son of Guru Hargobind and his third wife Mahadevi (qq.v.). The line descending from Suraj Mal came to be known as the **vaḍḍe mel** ('greater relationship') and formed the Sodhi family of Anandpur (qq.v.). *See also* CHHOTE MEL.

SURDAS. The blind bhagat (q.v.). Two works of his appear in the Adi Granth (q.v.).

SURNAMES. These are a comparatively recent introduction to Sikh society, the result of a western-style administration which required each person to be identified in terms of his/her father's name. For strict members of the Khalsa (q.v.) there can be no name following the given name of the individual apart from 'Singh' for men and 'Kaur' for women (qq.v.).

Many feel, however, that this does not differentiate people sufficiently, and third names have commonly been added by Sikh men. Usually this is their caste or (much more frequently) sub-caste name (Ahluvalia, Arora, Bedi, Grewal, Siddhu, etc.). Sometimes it is the name of the village or area with which they are associated (Jhabal, Kairon, Longowal, etc.). For others it is a poetic name which has been deliberately chosen (Musafir, Rahi, etc.). During the twentieth century whatever name has been selected by a male has increasingly come to be regarded as the family surname. Outside India those men who adhere to Singh as a last name normally use it as a surname, with the result that their wives and unmarried daughters also adopt Singh.

SVARAG ('heaven'). The concept of **svarag** or **baikunth** has different meanings for different Sikhs. For the Gurus recorded in the Adi Granth (q.v.) it referred to escape from transmigration to the perfect serenity which climaxed the discipline of **nām simaran** in the experience of sahaj (qq.v.). As such it was a condition, not a place, and those who are well acquainted with the Adi Granth assimilate this meaning. The Adi Granth also specifies the congregation of believers (the **sādh sangat** [q.v.]) as the location of **svarag,** and this would be the meaning attached to by most devout Sikhs. Influenced by the Muslim concept, however, many Sikhs evidently conceive it indistinctly as a place of ease and plenty to which the individual soul travels after death. To "go to one's heavenly abode" is an expression frequently used when a person dies.

SWORD. The sword (together with steel in general) has been a powerful symbol for the Khalsa (q.v.), at least since the time of Guru Gobind Singh (q.v.). The Guru commanded the Khalsa to bear arms as a religious duty, and for them the sword became the chief weapon in the battles of the eighteenth century. Today it figures prominently in the khanda (q.v.) and plays a central role in amrit sanskar (q.v.). *See also* ARMY, ARMED FORCES; BHAGAUTI; SARAB LOH.

SYMBOLS. As with all the great religions, Sikhism is particularly rich in symbols, both intangible and visible. The primary symbol is Akal Purakh or Vahiguru (qq.v), and Sikhs will normally affirm that their faith is, like Christianity and Islam, strictly monotheistic. The mystical 'voice' of Akal Purakh is the Guru (q.v.), appearing in human form as the ten historic Gurus and embodied thereafter in the sacred scripture which becomes the Guru Granth Sahib (q.v.). Each of the Gurus taught the supremely-important **nām** (q.v.), communicated through the **shabad** (q.v.). The tenth Guru constituted the Khalsa (q.v.). Sikhs who choose to enter the Khalsa do so by the ceremony of **khaṇḍe dī pāhul** (q.v.) at which they receive **amrit** (q.v.) and are required to wear the Five Ks (q.v.). Other important visible symbols are the gurdwara (q.v.), signifying sacred ground; the **nishān sāhib** (q.v.), which denotes the presence of a gurdwara; and **karāh prasād** (q.v.), which marks a visit to a gurdwara or presence at a devotional occasion.

T

TAKHAT (TAKHT). 'Throne'; a center of Sikh worldly authority as opposed to the spiritual authority of the gurdwara (q.v.). There are five takhats. Akal Takhat in Amritsar (qq.v.) is paramount, and from it decisions of the whole Panth (q.v.) (or what is represented as the whole Panth) are made. The others are Kesgarh Sahib at Anandpur, Harimandir Sahib in Patna, Hazur Sahib in Nander, and Damdama Sahib in southern Punjab (qq.v.). These four are all located at sites associated with Guru Gobind Singh (q.v.), and the first three have been recognized as takhats for an indeterminate period. The status of Damdama was in doubt until it was definitively declared a takhat in 1966. The origins of the role and primacy of Akal Takhat seem evident, its pre-eminence due to the practice of the Sarbat Khalsa (q.v.) meeting before it during the later eighteenth century.

TAKHT SINGH (1860–1933). A prominent Tat Khalsa (q.v.) leader of the Malwa region (q.v.). Founder of the Sikh Kanya

Mahavidyala (q.v.), a girls' school in Firozpur. Because of the difficulties he encountered he was termed a zinda shahid (q.v.).

TAKSAL. 'Mint.' A group or 'school' seeking to impart a particular version of Gurmat (q.v.). The most famous is the Damdami Taksal (q.v.).

TALVANDI RAI BHOI *see* NANKANA SAHIB.

TALVANDI SABO *see* DAMDAMA SAHIB.

TANAKHAH. A penance or fine imposed by a sangat on any member of the Khalsa who violates the Rahit (qq.v.). The person so convicted is known as a tanakhahia (q.v.). The two words evidently acquired their present meaning during the early eighteenth century. 'Tanakhah' means 'salary.' In an attempt to shore up their crumbling authority in the Punjab, the Mughals made grants of money to some of those who assisted them, and the Khalsa viewed such a person as a hireling. From here the word shifted to mean a Sikh guilty of an offence against the Rahit, and the offence came to be called a tanakhah. The rahit-namas (q.v.) commonly have lengthy lists of tanakhahs which merit discipline.

TANAKHAHIA. A Sikh who is convicted of a tanakhah (q.v.).

TANAKHAH-NAMA. A brief rahit-nama (q.v.) in simple Punjabi verse attributed to Nand Lal (q.v.). It is most unlikely that it can be traced to him. The date is uncertain, but is probably late eighteenth century. *See also* PRASHAN-UTTAR.

TARA SINGH (1885–1967). A Sikh political leader, invariably known as Master Tara Singh because he spent his early years as a teacher. Born into a Hindu Khatri family (q.v.), Tara Singh formally became a Sikh at the age of seventeen. He participated in the Akali movement (q.v.) of the early 1920s, earning for himself a position of leadership in the Akali Dal (q.v.). He maintained this position throughout the remainder of British rule, leading the Sikhs in the events prior to Partition in 1947 (q.v.). After independence he worked vigorously for Punjabi Suba (q.v.) (a Punjabi-language state), launching several **morchās** (q.v.) (campaigns) in support of it. Before it was attained in 1966 he was finally overthrown within the Akali Dal by Sant Fateh Singh (q.v.). His political career had lasted for more than four decades, and for most of the period his power was unchallenged. Throughout it all, he maintained the ideal that for Sikhs there can be no separation of politics and religion, that to be true to their faith Sikhs must necessarily fight political battles. *See also* POLITICAL PARTIES; POLITICS.

TARA SINGH NAROTAM (1822–91). A distinguished Nirmala scholar (q.v.). His books included a defense of the Sanatan position (q.v.), a description of 508 major gurdwaras, and a learned etymological dictionary of the Adi Granth (q.v.).

TARA SINGH OF VAN (d. 1725). Killed by Mughal forces during the disturbed times of Abdus Samad Khan and Zakariya Khan (qq.v.) and since regarded as a Sikh martyr.

TARU SINGH (d. 1743). For sheltering fugitive Sikhs, he was executed by Zakariya Khan (q.v.) by having his scalp scraped. He is regarded as a martyr by Sikhs.

TARUNA DAL. The 'young army.' When the Sikhs were regrouping their scattered military strength in the 1730s, a decision was evidently reached to divide the Dal Khalsa (q.v.) into two. Men under forty should fight in the Taruna (or Tarun) Dal, and the rest should be organized as the Buddha Dal (q.v.) ('older men's army').

TAT KHALSA. 'Pure Khalsa.' Originally the name given to a section of the Panth (q.v.) which opposed the Sikh leader Banda (q.v.) in the early eighteenth century. Since the late nineteenth century, however, the name describes the radical group within the Singh Sabha (q.v.) which pressed to have its exclusivist interpretation of the Sikh faith accepted by the Panth (q.v.). Within the Singh Sabha it was opposed by the conservative Sanatan Sikhs (q.v.), who believed that Sikhism was merely one of the many varieties of Hindu tradition. The Tat Khalsa vigorously contested this, maintaining that Sikhism was an entirely separate religion. Eventually it gained ascendancy over the Sanatan Sikhs, and ever since the early twentieth century its interpretation has been accepted as orthodox. Prominent members of the Tat Khalsa included Gurmukh Singh, Dit Singh, Vir Singh, and Kahn Singh Nabha (qq.v.). *See also* CHIEF KHALSA DIVAN.

TAZKIRA. A hagiographic anecdote concerning a Sufi pir (q.v.).

TEGH BAHADUR (1621–75). Ninth Guru. One of the sons of the sixth Guru Hargobind, born of his second wife Nanaki (qq.v.). Tradition regards him as a retiring person, a view which receives support from his works which were later added to the Adi Granth (q.v.). In 1632 he married Gujari (q.v.), but had no children for thirty-four years. At the death of Hargobind in 1644, he moved to his mother's village of Bakala, near Amritsar (q.v.), where he is said to have been chiefly occupied with meditation. Tradition records that he became the ninth Guru when his predecessor, the child Har Krishan (q.v.), uttered the words "Baba Bakale" ('the Baba [who is] in Bakala' [q.v.]) just before his death in 1664. The hagiographic story of Makhan Shah (q.v.) relates how his identity was recognized from among the others who descended on Bakala, hoping to become the next Guru. For some months he remained in Bakala but encountered opposition from his nephew Dhir Mal in neighboring Kartarpur (qq.v.) and from another relative, the Mina leader Harji, in Amritsar (qq.v.). Leaving the plains, he shifted to Kiratpur (q.v.) at the edge of the Shivalik Hills (q.v.), but there his presence was unwelcome to his half-brother Suraj Mal (q.v.). He moved to the neighboring village of Makhoval, crossing from the territory of the chief of Hindur into that of Kahlur. There a new center called Chak Nanaki (later Anandpur [q.v.]) was developed. In 1665 he departed on an extended journey to the east of India, where in Patna his only son, Gobind Rai (later Gobind Singh [q.v.]), was born in December 1666. The surviving hukam-namas (q.v.) which he sent to the various Khatri Sikh sangats (q.v.) along the way show that he was received with great enthusiasm. Returning to Chak Nanaki he spent time touring on the plains, visiting those Sikhs who had remained faithful to him. This was the period when rival Gurus exercised considerable influence, and there was marked hostility from other contenders to the title. In 1675 he was arrested by the Mughals and beheaded in Delhi. *See also* MUGHAL DYNASTY.

TEGH BAHADUR'S EXECUTION. In 1675 Guru Tegh Bahadur (q.v.) was arrested in circumstances which are disputed. According to Muslim sources he was taken as a brigand. Sikh sources, however, vigorously resist this claim. The dominant Sikh view attributes it to the Guru's intercession on behalf of a group of Kashmiri Brahmans threatened with conversion to Islam. A minority interpretation maintains that the reason was a request put to the Mughal authorities by one of the Guru's rivals, Dhir Mal (q.v.). Later in the same year, having refused the choice of Islam, he was beheaded in Delhi. Gurdwara Sis Ganj (q.v.) on Chandni Chauk now marks the site of his execution. *See also* JAITA; RAKAB-GANJ.

TEJA SINGH BHASAUR (1867–1933). A Jat, commonly known as Babu Teja Singh or as Teja Singh Overseer. He was drawn into the Singh Sabha and the Chief Khalsa Divan (qq.v.), becoming one of the most controversial of modern Sikh leaders. In 1893 he founded a branch of the Singh Sabha in his village of Bhasaur (Patiala state) and from 1907 developed it as the Panch Khalsa Divan (q.v.). His efforts to change certain Sikh doctrines, rituals, and the Rahit (q.v.) involved him in strenuous disputes. Brahmanical customs and caste were rejected, and members of other faiths were converted to his rigorous version of Sikhism. In 1928 he was banished from the Panth by order of Akal Takhat (qq.v.) for the changes which he had introduced. *See also* BHASAUR SINGH SABHA.

TEJA SINGH, PROFESSOR (1894–1958). An eminent product of the Singh Sabha (q.v.), important in education and writing. He was by far the most active member of the panel which anonymously produced *Shabadārath,* a four-volume text and commentary on the Adi Granth (q.v.). In the 1930s he was the convener of the committee which considered the Rahit for the SGPC (qq.v.) and personally wrote much of the text of *Sikh Rahit Maryādā* (q.v.).

TEJA SINGH SAMUNDARI (1881–1926). A prominent Akali leader (q.v.) at the time of the Rakab-ganj affair (q.v.) and during the early 1920s. Teja Singh Samundari was a Jat (q.v.).

TEJA SINGH SAMUNDARI HALL. The offices of the SGPC (q.v.) situated adjacent to Harimandir Sahib in Amritsar (qq.v.).

TEN SAVAYYAS. A portion of *Akāl Ustati* (q.v.), appointed as a part of the early morning order for nit-nem (q.v.). In the Dasam Granth (q.v.) the verses are preceded by the heading *tav-prasād savayye,* literally 'By your grace savayyas' (q.v.) or 'Invocatory Quatrains.' They are sometimes known by this name.

THAG. Strictly, a member of the cult of ritual murderers who strangled and robbed in the name of the goddess Kali, but used for any highwayman or violent robber. According to the janam-sakhis Nanak (qq.v.) converted a thag called Sajjan. The English word 'thug' is a borrowing from **thag**.

THAKUR SINGH SANDHANVALIA (1837–87). A member of an important family and the first president of the Singh Sabha (q.v.). The Sandhanvalias (q.v.) had been extremely powerful in the Sikh kingdom prior to its annexation in 1849 (q.v.) but were stripped of much of their influence by the annexing British. Thakur Singh did not let this stand in the way of a notable career. A supporter of Sanatan views (q.v.), he vigorously managed the affairs of the Amritsar Singh Sabha for ten years. In 1885 he persuaded his cousin the ex-Maharaja Duleep Singh (q.v.) to renounce Christianity and to seek the Punjab throne once again. He escaped from the British to the French territory of Pondichery and there conducted the affairs of Duleep Singh until his death in 1887.

3HO MOVEMENT *see* SIKH DHARMA OF THE WESTERN HEMISPHERE.

TIKKE DI VAR. A paean written in praise of the first two Gurus, with three supplementary verses concerning the third, fourth, and fifth Gurus. The authors were Rai Balvand and Satta the Dum (q.v.). The work is included in the Adi Granth, pp. 966–68 (q.v.).

TIRATH. A Hindu pilgrimage center. Nanak (q.v.) taught that the only tirath is within a person. The idea of visiting pilgrimage centers proved too strong to be eliminated, but for Sikhs the places were to be locations associated with one of the Gurus. *See also* AMAR DAS; GURDWARA; PILGRIMAGE.

TOBACCO. Using tobacco is one of the four kurahits (q.v.) which amrit-dhari Sikhs (q.v.) must swear at initiation to avoid. They should also promise not to associate with other Sikhs who smoke. The word which is used in the earliest rahit-nama (q.v.) is **bikhiā,** 'poison,' which in the Adi Granth (q.v.) means anything which befuddles the mind. This may include alcohol, drugs, or poison. In later Punjabi usage, **bikhiā** was increasingly used to mean tobacco which had recently been brought from Europe (where it had arrived from America) by Muslims and was smoked by them in hookahs (q.v.). It is difficult to determine precisely when it acquired the specific meaning of tobacco. At the founding of the Khalsa (q.v.), **bikhiā** was proscribed for all who took initiation. A likely reason for the ban is that hookah smoking was widespread among the Muslims who were the Khalsa's enemies, and Guru Gobind Singh (q.v.) was determined that his followers should avoid practices associated with them. This also explains the Khalsa ban on consuming meat killed in the Muslim fashion (**kutthā** [q.v.]). An alternative possibility is that hookahs would be too cumbersome for the fighting Khalsa to carry with them.

TRADITION. In Sikh history and religion tradition plays an immensely important part. In this *Historical Dictionary of Sikhism* the word 'tradition' is used to mean anything which is handed down from the past and is implicitly believed but which lacks adequate historical credentials. The janam-sakhis (q.v.), for example, are widely believed, but because most parts of them lack historical proof those parts must be labelled traditional. The terms 'tradition' and 'traditional' appear frequently in this *Dictionary*. Wherever either is used, the material it describes cannot be proved historically. It must have a considerable measure of doubt attached to it, and often it is clearly impossible.

TRANSCENDENCE. According to Sikh doctrine, Akal Purakh is both immanent and transcendent. *See also* IMMANENCE.

TREHAN. The Khatri (q.v.) sub-caste to which Guru Angad (q.v.) belonged.

TRIA CHARITRA. 'The deeds of women.' The correct name is *Charitro-pākhyān* or *Pakhyān Charitra* (q.v.).

TRILOCHAN. Said to have been a Vaishya from Sholapur area in Maharashtra and a contemporary of Namdev (q.v.). There are five works by him included in the Adi Granth (q.v.).

TRIPATA (TRIPTA). Wife of Kalu and mother of Guru Nanak (qq.v.).

TRUMPP (1828–85). Ernest Trumpp was a German philologist and missionary who was twice in India (in Sindh and Peshawar) working on languages before ill health compelled him to return to Europe. There he taught Indian languages at Tubingen. In 1869 he was asked to translate the Sikh sacred scriptures by the India Office in London. After spending fifteen months in the Punjab (q.v.) he concluded that the Adi Granth (q.v.) was not worth translating in full (the same few ideas, he thought, being endlessly repeated) and the Dasam Granth (q.v.) not worth translating at all. Eventually a translation of approximately one third of the Adi Granth was published in 1877, together with translations of *Purātan* and *Bālā* janam-sakhis (qq.v.), the lives of the later Gurus, and an account of their teachings. The translations were dull and stilted. The introductory portion of *The Adi Granth* was sometimes very perceptive, but this portion was expressed in terms which were highly insulting to the Sikhs and caused great offence which is still felt today. In the course of his research Trumpp had, however, discovered the first known manuscript of the *Purātan* janam-sakhi tradition in the India Office Library in London. Some Sikhs persuaded Aitcheson, the Lieutenant Governor of the Punjab, to have it sent to Lahore for inspection, where it was copied by a zincographic process. This is the copy variously known as the Colebrooke or Vilait-vali manuscript.

TURBAN. The turban is mandatory for all male Kesh-dhari Sikhs (q.v.) except small boys. *Sikh Rahit Maryādā* (q.v.) makes it optional for women, but in practice very few women wear it except for those who regard it as compulsory for both sexes. These include members of the Bhai Randhir Singh da Jatha (where women wear it in the form of a keski [qq.v.]) and of the American Sikh Dharma movement (q.v.). Many Sikhs display particular identities by the color or shape of their turban. Members of the Akali Dal (q.v.) wear a distinctive dark blue. White is usually associated with old men, but has been adopted by members of the Congress Party. Supporters of Khalistan (q.v.) commonly adopt saffron. Bhapa Sikhs (q.v.) often wear 'beaked' turbans with the crest pointing forward. Patterned turbans frequently indicate that the wearer is from a Southeast Asian country. A turban with the peak off center signifies East Africa. A Namdhari (q.v.) always wears one of white homespun cloth, tied horizontally across the forehead. Some punctilious Sikhs also wear them tied this way on the grounds that it accords with older tradition. Other Sikhs wear a band or a keski underneath the turban with a portion exposed where the two sides meet as a vertex. In western countries the turban has sometimes been proscribed for police, military, or other uniforms, but the Sikhs have always won the right to have the ban lifted. In the United Kingdom they have also been exempted from wearing a helmet when motorcycling or a hard hat on building sites.

U

UDASI. Detachment, sadness. (1) Used by the *Purātan* janam-sakhis for Nanak's journeys (qq.v.) ; and (2) for a follower of the way attributed to Siri Chand (q.v.), the son of Nanak. The latter meaning designates a group who regard themselves as Sikhs, differing from the Khalsa (q.v.) by their celibacy, asceticism, and refusal to acknowledge such practices as keeping their hair uncut. In actual fact, they were very like ascetic Sahaj-dharis (q.v.). Never uniform in terms of organization or doctrine the Udasis numbered more than a dozen orders by the end of Sikh rule in 1849. By this time they had more than 250 akharas (q.v.) or centers. Each center claimed connection with a traditional dhuan or bakhshish (qq.v.). They were respected by the early Panth (q.v.), particularly as Gurditta (the son of Guru Hargobind [qq.v.]) evidently favored them. During the eighteenth century they were not targeted by the rulers as were the orthodox Khalsa, with the result that many gurdwaras (q.v.) evidently passed into their care. Certainly the mahants (q.v.) of the late nineteenth/early twentieth centuries frequently claimed an Udasi descent, though their lifestyle was by this time very different from that of the traditional Udasis. Khalsa Sikhs became increasingly uneasy about their control of gurdwaras. The crucial turning point in relations with the Khalsa came in 1921 when the mahant of Nankana Sahib (q.v.), who had declared himself to be an Udasi, arranged the massacre of a large group of Akalis (q.v.). *See also* ANAND GHAN; DHUAN; GURDWARA REFORM MOVEMENT.

UPDESHAK. 'Preacher'; a person appointed by Singh Sabhas (q.v.) as an itinerant preacher.

V

VADDA GHALLUGHARA. The 'great holocaust.' An occasion in 1762 when the Afghan army of Ahmad Shah Abdali (q.v.) caught up with a large body of Sikhs near Malerkotla, including many women and children, and killed large numbers of them. Estimates of the dead vary between 5,000 and 30,000.

VAHIGURU. The term **vāh gurū** first appears in the janam-sakhis (q.v.) where it means 'Praise to the Guru' and is used to signal the conclusion of a sakhi (q.v.). At this early stage it was also an appropriate expression repeated as **nām japaṇ** (q.v.). The two words eventually coalesced to form one of the characteristic names of God, and for Sikhs it is the most popular of all such names today. The term occurs at only two places in the Adi Granth (q.v.), both of them in panegyrics to the Guru by the bards. *See also* AKAL PURAKH; GENDER OF GOD; HARI; RAM.

VAHIGURUJI KA KHALSA, VAHIGURUJI KI FATEH. "Hail to the Guru's Khalsa! Hail the Guru's victory!" The greeting of the Khalsa (q.v.), normally given only to other Sikhs. It may all be uttered by one person, or he/she may utter the first half, with the second part being the response. Sikhs commonly use it as a greeting to the whole sangat (q.v.) when they enter a gurdwara (q.v.). It is also uttered as an invocation before speaking in a gurdwara or to any gathering of Sikhs. *See also* SALUTATIONS; SAT SRI AKAL.

VAISHANAVA. A believer in bhakti (q.v.) addressed to Vishnu.

VAK LAINA *see* HUKAM LAINA.

VAL GUNDAN *see* BAL GUNDAN.

VANI *see* BANI.

VAR. Normally the word var applies to lengthy poems such as those composed by Bhai Gurdas (q.v.). In the Adi Granth (q.v.), however, it designates a series of stanzas (**pauṛī** [q.v.]), each of which is preceded by a number of couplets or subordinate stanzas called **shaloks** (q.v.). With one exception, the vars are all composite structures embodying selections from the work of the Gurus whose works are included in the Adi Granth. The **pauṛīs** of any particular var are all by one Guru, but the **shaloks** can be by any of the Gurus with a few by bhagats (q.v.). The most famous is Nanak's *Āsā kī Vār* (qq.v.) which has acquired a liturgical function and is sung in gurdwaras (q.v.) in the early morning.

VARAN BHAI GURDAS. The thirty-nine Punjabi vars (lengthy poems) of Bhai Gurdas (q.v.). Because of their content and the significance of their author they are traditionally regarded as 'the key to the Guru Granth Sahib' (q.v.). Some of them relate events from his own time and from the lives of the Gurus. Others are doctrinal, helping to explain what the Gurus actually taught. A fortieth var is attached to the collection, written by an eighteenth-century Gurdas. *See also* GURDAS II.

VARNA. 'Color'; the four groups into which castes are conventionally organized as a hierarchy (Brahman, Kshatriya, Vaisha, and Shudra).

VAZIR KHAN. The Mughal subadar (governor) of Sirhind who in 1704 attacked Gobind Singh in Anandpur (qq.v.) and later executed the Guru's two younger sons. An agent of his may have been responsible for the assassination of the Guru in 1708. *See also* SAHIB-ZADE.

VEGETARIANISM. Opinions within the Panth (q.v.) differ strongly over vegetarianism, some arguing that passages from the Adi Granth (q.v.) can be interpreted as upholding it and others asserting that the Gurus granted freedom from it to their Sikhs. The latter add that Indian tradition, not Sikh teaching, is the source. Goat and chicken are freely consumed in Punjab villages, and provision in the Rahit for jhatka meat (qq.v.) certainly implies that the Khalsa (q.v.) at least is free to choose. Sections of the Panth are, however, strongly opposed to eating meat, and in the langar (q.v.) only vegetarian food is served. *See also* ALCOHOL.

VIKRAMI *see* SAMMAT DATING.

VIR SINGH (1872–1957). An Arora of Amritsar (qq.v.), the leading intellectual of the Singh Sabha movement (q.v). He was the author of novels, poems, hagiography, religious history, religious biography, pamphlets, newspaper articles, and tracts, all of them bearing strong testimony to his faith. Social reform and the question of Sikh identity also received prominent attention. Vir Singh was an adherent of the Tat Khalsa (q.v.), doing much to formulate and propagate its ideal of Sikhism. His father, Charan Singh, began the Punjabi newspaper *Khālsā Samāchār* in 1899, and as its editor Vir Singh maintained a high standard of Punjabi prose and religious discussion. He also promoted the Khalsa Tract Society (q.v.), using its numerous publications to further his concern for the Sikh faith. Vir Singh still commands considerable respect for his many literary productions.

W

WAZIR KHAN *see* VAZIR KHAN.

WOMAN *see* GENDER *and* PATRIARCHY.

WORD *see* SHABAD (SABAD).

WORSHIP. Sikh worship consists largely of kirtan (q.v.), normally to the accompaniment of three musicians (two with hand-pumped harmoniums and one with drums). In formal worship katha (q.v.) is sometimes included. The order of worship concludes with Ardas (q.v.) and the distribution of karah prasad (q.v.). The Adi Granth (q.v.) is always present. Worship is normally followed by a meal in the langar (q.v.). *See also* GURDWARA PROCEDURE.

Y

YAM. The god of the dead who determines the fate after death of each individual. *See also* DHARAM-RAJ.

YOGI BHAJAN (b. 1929). The name by which Harbhajan Singh Puri, founder of the Sikh Dharma movement (q.v.), is always known.

Z

ZAFAR-NAMA. The 'Letter of Victory,' attributed to Guru Gobind Singh (q.v.) and addressed to the Mughal emperor Aurangzeb (q.v.). The letter, which is in Persian verse, was composed after the Guru's withdrawal from Anandpur (q.v.). After detailing infamous deeds by the Mughals, it declares that God is just and that justice requires the sword to be drawn when order is threatened. The *Zafar-nāmā* is now in the Dasam Granth (q.v.), although its inclusion was only fixed towards the end of the nineteenth century. Sikhs generally regard it as unquestionably authentic, which may be correct but is certainly not established. The lengthy period of transmission may well have produced changes both in language and content. *See also* FATEH-NAMA.

ZAIL SINGH (b. 1916). Congress Chief Minister of the Punjab 1972–77, Home Minister in the Government of India 1980–82, and President of India from 1982. He was President when the Indian Army invaded the Golden Temple complex in 1984 and for this reason has never been forgiven by many of his fellow Sikhs. *See also* RECENT HISTORY.

ZAKARIYA KHAN (d. 1745). The son of Abdus Samad Khan (q.v.) and Mughal governor of Lahore (q.v.) from 1726 until his death. He was also governor of Multan (q.v.) from 1737. Zakariya Khan endeavored to confirm his hereditary title to these Mughal provinces and was pragmatic in his loyalties, siding with the Afghan Ahmad Shah Abdali (q.v.) if it was to his advantage. His policy with regard to Khalsa Sikhs (q.v.) varied, but at times was fiercely oppressive. This has been represented in subsequent Sikh accounts as a determination to exterminate them.

ZAT (JATI). Caste; endogamous caste grouping.

ZINDA SHAHID. 'Living martyr,' a title informally conferred by
the Panth (q.v.) upon individuals who have faced fierce opposition (but not actual death) in their attempts to achieve objectives on its behalf. The title is very rarely given. Two who
earned it were Takht Singh of Firozpur and Baba Kharak
Singh (qq.v.).

BIBLIOGRAPHY

This bibliography is selective; it comprises only books, and those books are only in English (apart from one section entitled 'Principal sources for Sikhism in Punjabi'). It is selective because otherwise the volume would be altogether too weighty. An attempt has been made to include most books published in English during the last fifty years, but those published before have been recorded only if they are (for whatever reason) important. The reader is referred to other published bibliographies for books which have been omitted, together with articles relating to Sikhism. The best one to consult is Rajwant Singh, *The Sikhs: Their Literature on Culture, History, Philosophy, Politics, Religion and Traditions* (Delhi: Indian Bibliographies Bureau, 1990). For Punjabi books the most appropriate work is *Pañjābī Pustak Kosh* (Patiala: LDP, 1971). Ganda Singh has published two separate volumes, *A Select Bibliography of the Sikhs and Sikhism* (Amritsar: SGPC, 1965) and *A Bibliography of the Punjab* (Patiala: Punjabi University, 1966). These are both useful in that they cover books in all the principal languages.

One problem was the question of how lengthy a work needed to be before it was included. Partly for this reason and partly because of guidance to potential readers, where a work has less than fifty pages the number of pages has been indicated.

Another problem was how to incorporate authors' names in the alphabet. In Rajwant Singh's bibliography (and in the vast majority of other works published in India), where an author's final name is Singh (e.g. Fauja Singh) or Kaur (e.g. Madanjit Kaur) he/she is included according to his/her first name. This means that for the two examples given the names would be listed under F and M. Only when the individual used a third name (e.g. Surindar Singh Kohli) would that name be used as a surname and included as such in the bibliography (e.g. Kohli, Surindar Singh).

This contrasts with the western method, which is to record in alphabetical order the final name, classifying Fauja Singh under **S** and Madanjit Kaur under **K**. The problem could not be easily solved simply by adopting this so-called western method, for many books published in the West actually use the standard Indian method. This is in fact the case with all bibliographies given at the back of books by the present author, books which have been published by the Clarendon Press in Oxford or Columbia University Press in New York. It is a method generally preferred by Indian readers, and for that reason it is frequently adopted in western countries.

Reluctantly, however, the decision was finally taken to use the standard western form. Many users of this bibliography will want to consult particular works in western libraries where the western method of classification is invariably used and being quite unused to the Indian style would sometimes be baffled by it. Those accustomed to the Indian method will regrettably have to make the necessary adjustment when seeking a book by a Singh or a Kaur.

In this bibliography books are grouped according to the following divisions.

I. General
    A. Encyclopedias and Reference
    B. Bibliographies
    C. General works
II. The Gurus
    A. The Gurus: General
    B. Guru Nanak
    C. Guru Angad to Guru Har Krishan
    D. Guru Tegh Bahadur
    E. Guru Gobind Singh
III. History
    A. General Historical
    B. The Eighteenth Century
    C. Maharaja Ranjit Singh and His Successors
    D. Early British Interest and Administration
    E. The Singh Sabha, the Gurdwara Reform Movement, and Independence, 1873–1947
    F. The Period Since Independence
IV. Doctrine and Symbols
    A. Doctrine: General
    B. Ethics
    C. Symbols, Rituals, and Customs

ABBREVIATIONS FOR THE BIBLIOGRAPHY

APH	Asia Publishing House
CKD	Chief Khalsa Divan
CRRID	Centre for Research in Rural and Industrial Development
CUP	Cambridge University Press
DGPC	Delhi Gurdwara Parbandhak Committee
DSGMC	Delhi Sikh Gurdwara Management Committee
GGSF	Guru Gobind Singh Foundation
GNDU	Guru Nanak Dev University
GNF	Guru Nanak Foundation
GPC	Gurdwara Parbandhak Committee
IIAS	Indian Institute of Advanced Study
IOL	India Office Library
LDP	Languages Department, Punjab
NBO	National Book Organisation
NBS	National Book Shop
NBSM	Niraguna Balik Satsang Mandal
NPH	National Publishing House
OUP	Oxford University Press
PWCIS	Punjab Writers' Cooperative Industrial Society
SGPC	Shiromani Gurdwara Parbandhak Committee
SGTBCT	Sri Guru Tegh Bahadur Charitable Trust
SOAS	School of Oriental and African Studies
UBSPD	UBS Publishers' Distributors Ltd.
VVRI	Vishveshvaranand Vedic Research Institute

General

Encyclopedias and Reference

Bakshi, S.R., ed. *Encyclopaedia of Punjab,* 10 vols. New Delhi: Rima, 1994.

Cole, W. Owen, and Piara Singh Sambhi. *A Popular Dictionary of Sikhism.* London: Curzon, 1990.

Dogra, Ramesh Chander, and Gobind Singh Mansukhani. *Encyclopaedia of Sikh Religion and Culture.* New Delhi: Vikas, 1995.

Johar, Surinder Singh. *Handbook on Sikhism.* Delhi: Vivek, 1977.

Kaur, Manmohan. *Encyclopaedia of India,* vol. XVIII *Punjab.* New Delhi: Rima, 1994.

Kohli, Surindar Singh. *A Conceptual Encyclopaedia of the Adi Granth.* New Delhi: Manohar, 1992.

————. *Dictionary of Guru Granth Sahib.* Amritsar: Singh Brothers, forthcoming.

————. *Dictionary of Mythological References in Guru Granth Sahib.* Amritsar: Singh Brothers, 1993.

Ralhan, O.P., and Suresh K. Sharma, eds. *Documents on Punjab,* 15 vols. New Delhi: Anmol, 1994.

Shackle, C. *A Guru Nanak Glossary.* London: SOAS, University of London, 1981.

Singh, Harbans, ed. *The Encyclopaedia of Sikhism,* 4 vols. Patiala: Punjabi University, 1992-.

Singha, H. S. *Concise Encyclopedia of Sikhism.* New Delhi: Madhuban, 1986.

Singha, H. S. *Junior Encyclopaedia of Sikhism.* New Delhi: Vikas, 1985.

Bibliographies

Barnett, L.D., comp. *Printed Punjabi Books in the British Museum.* London: British Museum, 1961.

Barrier, N. Gerald. *The Sikhs and their Literature.* Delhi: Manohar, 1970.

Deora, Man Singh, comp. *Guru Gobind Singh: A Literary Survey.* New Delhi: Anmol, 1989.

Gulati, S. P., and Rajinder Singh, comp. *Bibliography Sikh Studies.* Delhi: NBS, 1989.

Kaur, Ganesh, comp. *Catalogue of Punjabi Printed Books Added to the India Office Library 1902–1964.* London: IOL, 1975.

Malik, Ikram Ali, comp. *A Bibliography of the Punjab and its Dependency (1849–1910).* Lahore: University of the Punjab, 1968.

Rai, Priya Muhar, comp. *Sikhism and the Sikhs: An Annotated Bibliography.* New York: Greenwood, 1989.

Ramdev, Jagindar Singh, comp. *Guru Gobind Singh: a descriptive bibliography.* Chandigarh: Panjab University, 1967.

Shackle, Christopher, comp. *Catalogue of Punjabi and Sindhi Manuscripts in the India Office Library.* London: IOL, 1977.

Singh, Ganda, comp. *A Bibliography of the Punjab.* Patiala: Punjabi University, 1966.

———, comp. *A Select Bibliography of the Sikhs and Sikhism.* Amritsar: SGPC, 1965.

Singh, Hakam, comp. *Sikh Studies: A Classified Bibliography of Printed Books in English.* Patiala: Punjab Publishing House, 1982.

Singh, Kirpal, comp. *Guru Nanak's Japuji: A Descriptive Bibliography.* Patiala: Punjabi University, 1990.

Singh, Rajwant, comp. *The Sikhs: Their Literature on Culture, History, Philosophy, Religion and Traditions.* Delhi: Indian Bibiliographies Bureau, 1990.

Tatla, Darshan Singh, and Eleanor M. Nesbitt, comp. *Sikhs in Britain: An Annotated Bibliography.* Coventry: Centre for Research in Ethnic Relations, University of Warwick, 1987.

Verma, Devinder Kumar, and Jatinder Singh, comp. *A Biobibliography of Dr. Ganda Singh.* Rajpura: Aman, 1989.

General Works

Anand, Balwant Singh. *The Sikhs and Sikhism.* Delhi: DSGMC, 1982.

Baird, Robert D., ed. *Religion in Modern India.* 2nd rev. ed. New Delhi: Manohar, 1991.

Besant, Annie. *Sikhism: A Convention Lecture.* Adyar: Theosophical Publishing House, 1920. Repr. 1947. 40 pp.

Bloomfield, M. *The Sikh Religion.* New York, 1912.

Cole, W. Owen. *Teach Yourself Sikhism.* London: Hodder & Stoughton, 1994.

Cole, W. Owen, and Piara Singh Sambhi. *Sikhism.* London: Ward Lock Educational, 1973. 48 pp.

———. *The Sikhs: Their Religious Beliefs and Practices.* London: Routledge & Kegan Paul, 1978.

Dhillon, Dalbir Singh. *Sikhism: Origin and Development.* New Delhi: Atlantic, 1988.

Duggal, K. S. *Philosophy and Faith of Sikhism.* Honesdale, Pennsylvania: Himalayan, 1982.

Dulai, Surjit, and Arthur Helweg, eds. *Punjab in Perspective.* East Lansing, Michigan: Asian Studies Center, Michigan State University, 1991.

Field, Dorothy. *Religion of the Sikhs.* London: John Murray, 1914. Reprint, New Delhi: Ess Ess, 1976.

Guilford, E. *Sikhism.* London: Lay Readers, 1915. 39 pp.

Jain, Nirmal Kumar. *Sikh Religion and Philosophy.* Delhi: Sterling, 1979.

Jain, S. C. *A Panorama of Sikh Religion and Philosophy.* Delhi: Bahubali, 1985.

Johar, Surinder Singh. *The Sikh Religion.* Delhi: NBS, 1988.

Juergensmeyer, Mark, and N. Gerald Barrier, eds. *Sikh Studies: Comparative Perspectives on a Changing Tradition.* Berkeley, California: Berkeley Religious Studies Series, 1979.

Kapoor, S. S. *The Sikh Religion and the Sikh People.* New Delhi: Hemkunt, 1992.

Kaur, Manjit [P. M. Wylam]. *Introduction to Sikh Belief.* London: Sikh Cultural Society, n.d.

Kohli, Surinder Singh. *The Sikh and Sikhism.* New Delhi: Atlantic, 1993.

Macauliffe, M., et al. *The Sikh Religion: A Symposium.* Contains contributions by M. Macauliffe, H. H. Wilson, F. Pincott, J. Malcolm, and Kahan Singh. Calcutta: Susil Gupta, 1958.

McLeod, W.H. *The Sikhs of the Punjab*. Auckland: Graphic Educational Publications, 1968. 32 pp.

————, trans. *Textual Sources for the Study of Sikhism*. Manchester: Manchester University Press, 1984. Reprint, Chicago, Illinois: University of Chicago Press, 1990.

Madan, T. N. *Religion in India*. New Delhi: OUP, 1991.

Mansukhani, Gobind Singh. *Aspects of Sikhism*. New Delhi: PW-CIS, 1982.

————. *Introduction to Sikhism*. New Delhi: India Book House, 1967.

O'Connell, Joseph T., et al, eds. *Sikh History and Religion in the Twentieth Century*. Toronto: Centre for South Asian Studies, University of Toronto, 1988. Reprint, New Delhi: Manohar, 1990.

Parry, R. E. *The Sikhs of the Punjab*. London: Drains, 1921.

Raj, Hormise Nirmal. *Evolution of the Sikh Faith*. New Delhi: Unity, 1987.

Sacha, Gurinder Singh. *The Sikhs and their Way of Life*. Southall, London: Sikh Missionary Society, 1983.

Scott, George Batley. *Religion and Short History of the Sikhs, 1469–1930*. London: Mitre Press, 1930. Reprint, Patiala: LDP, 1970.

Shackle, Christopher. *The Sikhs*. London: Minority Rights Group, 1984. Rev. ed. 1986.

Singh, Dalip. *Sikhism: A Modern and Psychological Perspective*. New Delhi: Bahari, 1979.

Singh, Daljit, and Angela Smith. *The Sikh World*. London: Macdonald, 1985.

Singh, Dharam, ed. *Sikhism and Secularism: Essays in Honour of Professor Harbans Singh*. New Delhi: Harman, 1994.

Singh, Fauja, et al. *Sikhism*. Patiala: Punjabi University, 1969.

Singh, Ganda. *A Brief Account of the Sikh People*. Patiala: Sikh History Society, 1956.

——. *The Sikhs and Sikhism*. Patiala: Sikh History Society, 1959.

——. *The Sikhs and Their Religion*. Redwood City, California: Sikh Foundation, 1974.

Singh, Gopal. *The Religion of the Sikhs*. Bombay: APH, 1971.

——. *The Sikhs: Their History, Religion, Culture, Ceremonies and Literature*. Madras: Seshachalam, and Bombay: Popular Prakashan, 1970.

Singh, Gurcharan. *Studies in Punjab History & Culture*. New Delhi: Enkay, 1990.

Singh, Harbans. *Berkeley Lectures on Sikhism*. New Delhi: GNF, 1983.

——. *Heritage of the Sikhs*. Bombay: Asia Publishing House, 1964. 2nd edition, New Delhi: Manohar, 1983.

Singh, Harbans. [Different from previous author.] *Degh Tegh Fateh: A Book on Socio-Economic and Religio-Political Fundamentals of Sikhism*. Chandigarh: Alam, 1987.

Singh, Khazan. *History and Philosophy of the Sikh Religion*. 2 vols. Lahore: Newal Kishore, 1914.

Singh, Khushwant. *Religion of the Sikhs*. Madras: University of Madras, 1969. 38 pp.

——. *The Sikhs*. London: George Allen & Unwin, 1953.

————. *The Sikhs Today*. Bombay: Orient Longmans, 1959. Revised edition, 1964.

Singh, Khushwant, and Raghu Rai. *The Sikhs*. Varanasi: Lutra, 1984.

Singh, Mohinder, ed. *History and Culture of Panjab*. New Delhi: Atlantic, 1988.

Singh, Nikki-Guninder Kaur. *Sikhism*. New York: Facts on File, 1993.

Singh, Sher. *Glimpses of Sikhism and the Sikhs*. New Delhi: Metropolitan, 1982.

————. *Philosophy of Sikhism*. Lahore: Sikh University Press, 1944. Reprint, Delhi: Sterling, 1966.

Singh, Sudarshan. *Sikh Religion: Democratic Ideals and Institutions*. New Delhi: Oriental, 1979.

Singh, Teja. *Sikhism: its ideals and institutions*. Calcutta: Orient Longmans, 1951.

Singh, Trilochan. *Historical Sikh Shrines in Delhi: Fundamental Beliefs of Sikh Religion: the Ten Masters*. Delhi: DSGMC, 1972.

Singh, Wazir, ed. *Sikhism and Punjab's Heritage*. Patiala: Punjabi University, 1990.

Thomas, Terry. *Sikhism: the voice of the Guru*. Milton Keynes: Open University Press, 1978.

Thompson, M. R. *Sikh Belief and Practice*. London: Edward Arnold, 1985.

Thursby, Gene R. *The Sikhs*. New York: E. J. Brill, 1992.

Webster, John C. B., ed. *Popular Religion in the Punjab Today*. Delhi: Christian Institute of Sikh Studies, Batala, 1974.

The Gurus

The Gurus: General

Ahuja, Roshan Lal, and Gurdial Singh Phul. *Our Masters: Life Sketch of Ten Gurus*. Allahabad: Vishwa Vidhyalaya, 1956.

Banerjee, Anil Chandra. *Guru Nanak to Guru Gobind Singh*. Allahabad: Rajesh, 1978.

————. *The Sikh Gurus and the Sikh Religion*. New Delhi: Munshiram Manoharlal, 1983.

Banerjee, Indubhushan. *The Evolution of the Khalsa*. 2 vols. Calcutta: University of Calcutta, 1936. Reprint, Calcutta: A. Mukherjee, 1979 and 1970.

Bhattacharya, Vivek Ranjan. *Secular Thoughts of the Sikh Gurus*. Delhi: Gian, 1988.

Dass, J. R. *Economic Thought of the Sikh Gurus*. Delhi: NBO, 1988.

Deol, Gurdev Singh. *Social and Political Philosophy of Guru Nanak Dev and Guru Gobind Singh*. Jullundur: New Academic, 1976.

Duggal, Kartar Singh. *The Sikh Gurus: Their Lives and Teachings*. New Delhi: Vikas, 1980.

Gandhi, Surjit Singh. *History of the Sikh Gurus: A Comprehensive Study*. Delhi: Gur Das Kapur, 1978.

Grewal, K. S. *Understanding Sikhism*. New Delhi: Inter-India, 1991.

Gupta, Hari Ram. *History of the Sikh Gurus*. New Delhi: Uttam Chand Kapur, 1973.

Hansrao, Gurdev Singh. *Ideology of the Sikh Gurus*. Ropar: Hans Rao Publishers, 1990.

Kaur, Gurdeep. *Political Ideas of the Sikh Gurus*. New Delhi: Deep & Deep, 1990.

Khosla, D. N. *Sikh Gurus on Education*. Delhi: Adi-Jugadi, 1989.

Macauliffe, Max Arthur. *The Sikh Religion: Its Gurus, Sacred Writings and Authors*. 6 vols in 3. Oxford: Clarendon. 1909. Reprint, Delhi: S. Chand, 1985.

Makin, Gurbachan Singh. *Philosophy of Sikh Gurus*. Chandigarh: Guru Tegh Bahadur Educational Centre, 1994.

Nayyar, Gurbachan Singh. *The Sikhs in Ferment: Battles of the Sikh Gurus*. New Delhi: NBO, 1992.

Ray, Niharranjan. *The Sikh Gurus and the Sikh Society: A Study in Social Analysis*. Patiala: Punjabi University, 1970.

Sikh Religion. Detroit: Sikh Missionary Center, 1990.

Singh, Attar, trans. *Travels of Guru Tegh Bahadur and Gobind Singh*. Lahore: N.p., 1876.

Singh, Darshan. *Indian Bhakti Tradition and Sikh Gurus*. Chandigarh: Panjab Publishers, 1968.

Singh, Ganda. *The Lives of Sikh Gurus and Basic Principles of Sikhism*. Ipoh, Malaysia: Khalsa Diwan Malaya, 1962.

Singh, Gurdev. *Punjab Politics: Socio-Politico Orientations of the Sikh Gurus*. Delhi: B. R. Publications, 1986.

Singh, Jagdish. *The Founders of Sikh Religion: Selected Episodes from the Life History of the Ten Gurus*. New Delhi: GNF, 1989.

Singh, K. *Sikh Gurus: Brief Life Story of the Ten Sikh Gurus*. Bangkok: Sri Guru Singh Sabha, 1969.

Singh, Kanwarjit. *Political Philosophy of the Sikh Gurus*. New Delhi: Atlantic, 1989.

Singh, Kartar. *Sikh Gurus and Untouchability.* Amritsar: JS & JS, 1936. 40 pp.

Singh, Khazan. *Miracles of the Sikh Gurus.* Sialkot: author, 1932.

Singh, Narain. *Guru Nanak and his Images.* Vol. 2. Amritsar: author, 1970.

Singh, Puran. *The Book of the Ten Masters.* Amritsar: CKD, N.d. (1920).

Singh, Ranbir. *Glimpses of the Divine Masters: Guru Nanak–Guru Gobind Singh 1469–1708.* New Delhi: International Traders, 1965.

Singh, Teja. *Religion of the Sikh Gurus.* Amritsar: SGPC, 1957. 30p.

Singh, Tharam. *The Story of the Sikhs Covering the Lives of the Sikh Gurus.* Singapore: N.p., 1975.

Guru Nanak

Ahuja, N. D. *The Great Guru Nanak and the Muslims.* Chandigarh: Kirti, 1971.

Anand, Balwant Singh. *Guru Nanak: His Life Was His Message.* New Delhi: GNF, 1983.

Bal, Sarjit Singh. *Life of Guru Nanak.* Chandigarh: Panjab University, 1969.

———, comp. *Guru Nanak in the Eyes of Non-Sikhs.* Chandigarh: Panjab University, 1969.

Banerjee, Anil Chandra. *Guru Nanak and his Times.* Patiala: Punjabi University, 1971.

Bedi, P. L. *Guru Baba Nanak.* New Delhi: New Light, 1971.

————. *Prophet of the Full Moon: Guru Baba Nanak, the Founder Master of Sikhism*. New Delhi: New Light, 1976.

Bhatia, S. *Sant Kavi Nanak: a Harbinger of Peace and Goodwill*. New Delhi: Anoopum, 1989.

Brar, Gurdip Kaur. *Guru Nanak's Philosophy of Politics*. Goniana Mandi: Mahant Bhai Tirath Singh 'Sewapanthi' Tikana Bhai Jagta Ji Sahib, 1994.

Chawla, Harbans Singh. *Guru Nanak: the Prophet of the People*. New Delhi: Gurdwara Sri Guru Singh Sabha, 1970.

Cole, W. Owen. *Sikhism and its Indian Context 1469–1708: the Attitude of Guru Nanak and Early Sikhism to Indian Religious Beliefs and Practices*. London: Darton, Longman & Todd, 1984.

Francis, Eric. *Guru Nanak*. Bombay: Purohit, 1970.

Gill, Pritam Singh. *The Doctrine of Guru Nanak*. Jullundur: New Book Co., 1969.

Grewal, J. S. *Guru Nanak and Patriarchy*. Shimla: IIAS, 1993. 47 pp.

————. *Guru Nanak in History*. Chandigarh: Panjab University, 1969.

————. *Guru Nanak in Western Scholarship*. Shimla: IIAS, 1992. New Delhi: Manohar, 1993.

Gupta, Hari Ram. *Life Sketch of Guru Nanak*. Delhi: NPH, 1968. 32 pp.

Guru Nanak. New Delhi: Publications Division, Government of India, 1969.

Iyengar, K. R. Srinivasa. *Guru Nanak: a Homage*. New Delhi: Sahitya Academy, 1973.

Johar, Srinder Singh. *Guru Nanak: a Biography*. Jullundur: New Book Co., 1969.

Kapur, B.L. *The Message of Shri Guru Nanak Dev in the Context of the Ancient Sanatanist Tradition*. Patiala: Punjabi University, 1967.

Kapur, Prithipal Singh, ed. *The Divine Master: Life and Teachings of Guru Nanak*. Jalandhar: ABS Publications, 1988.

Kaur, Madanjit, ed. *Guru Nanak and his Teachings*. Amritsar: GNDU, 1989.

Kaur, Premka. *The Life and Teachings of Guru Nanak: Guru for the Aquarian age*. San Rafael, CA: Spiritual Community, 1972.

Kohli, Surindar Singh. *Philosophy of Guru Nanak*. Chandigarh: Panjab University, 1970.

———. *Travels of Guru Nanak*. Chandigarh: Panjab University, 1969.

Lorenzen, David N. (ed.), *Bhakti Religion in North India: Community Identity and Political Action*. Albany, New York: State University of New York Press, 1994.

McLeod, W. H. *Gurū Nānak and the Sikh Religion*. Oxford: Clarendon, 1968. 2nd edition, Delhi: OUP, 1976.

Mansukhani, Gobind Singh. *Gurū Nānak: World Teacher*. New Delhi: India Book House, 1968.

———. *Life of Guru Nanak*. New Delhi: GNF, 1974.

Paul, Dharam. *Guru Nanak and Religion Today*. Amritsar: SGPC, 1969. 16p.

Puri, Sunita. *Advent of Sikh Religion*. Delhi: Munshiram Manoharlal, 1993.

Raghavachar, S. S., and K. B. Ramakrishna Rao, eds. *Guru Nanak: His Life and Teachings*. Mysore: University of Mysore, 1971.

Sagoo, Harbans Kaur. *Guru Nanak and the Indian Society*. New Delhi: Deep & Deep, 1992.

Sarna, J. S. *Flora and Fauna in Guru Nanak's Bani*. Gangyal, Jammu: Gujral, 1991.

Seetal, Sohan Singh. *Prophet of Man Guru Nanak*. Ludhiana: Lyall, 1968.

Sekhon, Sant Singh, ed. *Guru Nanak Today: An Anthology*. Jandiala: Guru Gobind Singh Republic College, 1970.

Shan, Harnam Singh. *God as Known to Guru Nanak*. Delhi: Guru Nanak Vidya Bhandar Trust, 1971.

———. *Guru Nanak's Moral Code as Reflected in his Hymns*. Chandigarh: GGSF, 1970.

Singh, Ajit, and Rajinder Singh, comp., *Studies in Guru Nanak*. 3 vols. Delhi: NBS, 1984–87.

Singh, Balbir. *Some Aspects of Guru Nanak's Mission*. Guru Nanak Lectures 1970–71. Madras: Madras University, 1971.

Singh, Dalip. *Guru Nanak Dev and his Teachings*. Jullundur: Raj, 1969.

Singh, Daljit. *Guru Nanak*. Ludhiana: Guru Nanak Mission Society, 1971.

Singh, Darshan. *The Religion of Guru Nanak*. Ludhiana: Lyall, 1970.

Singh, Diwan. *Guru Nanak and the Indian Mystic Tradition*. Ludhiana: Lahore Book Shop, 1981.

Singh, Diwan. *The Revolution of Guru Nanak*. Chandigarh: People's Publishing House, 1993.

Singh, Fauja, and A. C. Arora, eds. *Papers on Guru Nanak*. Patiala: Punjabi University, 1970.

Singh, Fauja, and Kirpal Singh. *Atlas [:] Travels of Guru Nanak*. English and Punjabi. Patiala: Punjabi University, 1976.

Singh, G. *Divine Master: Life and Teachings of Guru Nanak*. New Delhi: Gian, 1989.

Singh, G. N., ed. *Guru Nanak: Life and Times*. New Delhi: GNF.

Singh, Ganda. *Guru Nanak: His Life and Teachings*. Singapore: Sikh Missionary Tract Society, 1940.

————, ed. *Sources on the Life and Teachings of Guru Nanak*. Guru Nanak's Birth Quincentenary volume of *The Panjab Past and Present* III (1969). Patiala: Punjabi University, 1969.

Singh, Gopal. *Guru Nanak*. New Delhi: National Book Trust, 1967.

Singh, Gurmit. *Guru Nanak's Relationship with the Lodis and the Mughals*. New Delhi: Atlantic, 1987.

————. *The Versatile Guru Nanak*. Sirsa: Usha Institute of Religious Studies, 1972.

Singh, Gurmukh Nihal, ed. *Guru Nanak: His Life, Time and Teachings*. Delhi: NPH, 1969.

Singh, Harbans. *Guru Nanak*. Patiala: Punjabi University, 1979.

————. *Guru Nanak and the Origins of the Sikh Faith*. Bombay: APH, 1969.

————, ed. *Perspectives on Guru Nanak*. Patiala: Punjabi University, 1975.

Singh, Harnam. *Guru Nanak's Philosophy of Divine Life*. Chandigarh: Juneja, 1969.

Singh, Ishar. *Nanakism: A New World Order, Temporal and Spiritual*. New Delhi: Ranjit, 1976.

————. *The Philosophy of Guru Nanak: A Comparative Study*. New Delhi: Ranjit, 1969. Enlarged edition, 2 vols. Delhi: Atlantic, 1985.

Singh, Jodh. *Guru Nanak Lectures*. Madras: Madras University, 1969.

————. *Teachings of Guru Nanak*. Delhi: NPH, 1969. 26 pp.

————. *The Religious Philosophy of Guru Nanak: A Comparative Study with Special Reference to Siddha Gosti*. Varanasi: Sikh Philosophical Society, 1983.

Singh, Jogendra, and Daljit Singh. *The Great Humanist Guru Nanak*. Patiala: LDP, 1970.

Singh, K. *Nanak My Master: Gleanings from the Life of Guru Nanak Dev*. Bangkok: Guru Singh Sabha, 1969.

Singh, Kapur. *Guru Nanak's Life and Thought*. Edited by Madanjit Kaur and Piar Singh. Amritsar: GNDU, 1991.

Singh, Kartar. *Life of Guru Nanak Dev*. 1st edition 1937. Revised edition, *Guru Nanak: life and teachings*. Ludhiana: Lahore Book Shop, 1958.

Singh, Khushdeva. *At the Feet of Guru Nanak*. Patiala: Guru Nanak Foundation Committee, 1969. 41p.

Singh, Mrigendra. *Miraculous Guru Nanak*. New York: Robert Spencer & Sons, 1977.

Singh, Narain. *Guru Nanak and his Images*. Vol. 1. Amritsar: author, n.d.

————. *Guru Nanak Re-interpreted*. Amritsar: author, 1965.

————. *Guru Nanak's View of Life*. Amritsar: author, 1969.

Singh, Ravinder G. B. *Indian Philosophical Tradition and Guru Nanak*. Patiala: Punjab Publishing House, 1983.

Singh, Sahib, and Dalip Singh. *Guru Nanak Dev and his Teachings*. Jullundur: Raj, 1969.

Singh, Sewaram. *The Divine Master*. Lahore: Gulab Singh, 1930.

Singh, Shamsher, and Narendra Singh Virdi. *Life of Guru Nanak through Pictures*. Amritsar: Modern Sahitya Academy, 1969.

Singh, Shanta Serbjeet. *Nanak the Guru*. New Delhi: Orient Longmans, 1970.

Singh, Sohan. *Guru Nanak: A Brief Biography*. Ludhiana: Lyall, 1968.

Singh, Taran. *Guru Nanak: His Mind and Art*. New Delhi: Bahri, 1992,

————. *Teachings of Guru Nanak Dev*. Patiala: Punjabi University, 1977.

————, ed. *Guru Nanak and Indian Religious Thought*. Patiala: Punjabi University, 1970.

Singh, Trilochan. *Guru Nanak: founder of Sikhism: A Biography*. Delhi: GPC, 1969.

————. *Guru Nanak's Religion*. Delhi: Rajkamal, 1969.

————. *True Humanism of Guru Nanak*. Delhi: DGPC, 1968.

Singh, Ujagar. *The Story of Guru Nanak*. Translated by M. C. Sharma. Patiala: Punjabi University, 1970. 38 pp.

Singh, Wazir. *Aspects of Guru Nanak's Philosophy*. Ludhiana: Lahore Book Shop, 1969.

———. *Humanism of Guru Nanak: A Philosophic Inquiry*. Delhi: Ess Ess, 1977.

Sodhi, T. S. *Educational Concepts of Guru Nanak in Sidh Goshti*. Ludhiana: Mukand, 1981.

———. *Educational Philosophy of Guru Nanak*. Patiala: Bawa, 1993.

Suddhasatwananda, Swami. *Thus Spake Guru Nanak*. Mylapore: Sri Rama Krishna Math, 1963.

Surma, M. S. *Guru Nanak: The Apostle of Love*. Amritsar: Jawahar Singh Kirpal Singh, 1971.

Talib, Gurbachan Singh. *Guru Nanak*. New Delhi: Sahitya Akademi, 1984.

———, ed. *Guru Nanak Commemorative Volume*. Patiala: Punjabi University.

———. *Guru Nanak: His Personality and Vision*. Delhi: Gur Das Kapur, 1969.

———. *Moral Core of Guru Nanak's Teachings*. Chandigarh: Panjab University, 1975–76. 38 pp.

Tewari, V. N. *Life of Guru Nanak*. New Delhi: National Council of Educational Research and Training, 1990.

Tiwari, Vishwa Nath. *Na ko Hindu na Musalman*. Translated by Bal Krishna. Chandigarh: Panjab University, 1973.

Vaidya, G. M. *Guru Nanak*. Poona: Vidarbha Marathwada, 1965.

Vaswani, T. L. *Guru Nanak*. Poona: Gita, 1970.

Guru Angad to Guru Har Krishan

Dhillon, Balwant Singh, ed. *Shri Guru Amar Das Abhinandan*. Amritsar: GNDU, 1985.

Jaspal, Partap Singh. *Eternal Glory of Guru Arjan*. New Delhi: Reliance, 1993.

Kaur, Balbir. *Guru Amar Das*. New Delhi: Makhan Singh, 1979. 44 pp.

Mansukhani, Gobind Singh. *Guru Ramdas: His Life, Work and Philosophy*. New Delhi: Oxford & IBH, 1979.

Nara, Ishar Singh. *Light of Guru Ram Dass Ji*. Translated by Harnam Singh. New Delhi: author, 1986.

Peace, M. L. *Guru Amar Das*. Ferozepore: D. S. Bhalla, 1960.

———. *Shri Guru Arjan Dev*. Ferozepore: D. S. Bhalla, 1961.

Singh, Fauja. *Guru Amar Das: Life and Teachings*. New Delhi: Sterling, 1979.

———, and Rattan Singh Jaggi, eds. *Perspectives on Guru Amar Das*. Patiala: Punjabi University, 1982.

Singh, Ganda. *Guru Arjan's Martyrdom Re-interpreted*. Patiala: Guru Nanak Mission, 1969.

Singh, Jodh. *Life of Guru Amar Dass Ji*. Ludhiana: Lahore Book Shop, 1953.

Singh, Kapur. *Guru Arjun and his Sukhmani*. Edited by Madanjit Kaur and Piar Singh. Amritsar: GNDU, 1992.

Singh, Narain. *The Holy Guru Arjan*. Amritsar: author, 1967.

———. *The Life Sketch of Guru Amar Dass Ji*. Amritsar: Bhagat Puran Singh, n.d.

Singh, Ranjit. *Guru Amar Das Ji: A Biography*. Amritsar: Nanak Singh Pustakmala, 1980.

Singh, Taran. *Guru Amar Das: The Apostle of Bliss*. London: Federation of Sikh Organisations, 1979.

Singh, Trilochan. *Life of Guru Hari Krishan: A Biography and History*. Delhi: DSGMC, 1981.

Singh, Wazir. *Guru Arjan Dev*. Delhi: National Book Trust, 1991.

Sodhi, Brijindra Singh. *Shri Guru Arjan Dev: The Poet and The Organiser*. Amritsar: author, 1936.

Guru Tegh Bahadur

Ahuja, Anand Mohan. *Significance of Guru Tegh Bahadur's Martyrdom: A True Perspective*. Chandigarh: Kirti, 1975. 27 pp.

Anand, Balwant Singh. *Guru Tegh Bahadur: A Biography*. New Delhi: Sterling, 1979.

Anand, G. S. *Guru Tegh Bahadur*. Agra: Agra University, 1970.

Baagha, Ajit Singh. *Palprsnavali or Guru Tegh Bahadur's Mission in Historical Perspective*. Amritsar: Faqir Singh, 1975.

Chawla, Surjeet Singh. *Martyrdom of Guru Tegh Bahadur: Message for Mankind*. Gurgaon: Harmony, 1991.

Dhawan, S. K. *Guru Tegh Bahadur: The Ninth Guru: A Chronology*. Delhi: Deepalika, 1976.

Doabia, Harbans Singh. *Sri Guru Tegh Bahadur Sahib: Life History, Sacred Hymns and Teachings*. Amritsar: Singh Brothers, 1975.

Gill, Pritam Singh. *Guru Tegh Bahadur: The Unique Martyr*. Jullundur: New Academic, 1975.

Grewal, J. S. *Guru Tegh Bahadur and the Persian Chroniclers.* Amritsar: GNDU, 1976.

Gupta, B. S. *Guru Tegh Bahadur: A Study.* Chandigarh: Panjab University, 1978.

Guru Tegh Bahadur: A Brief Account of His Life and Teachings. Patiala: Punjabi University, 1975. 24 pp.

Jaspal, Partap Singh. *Eternal Glory of Guru Tegh Bahadur.* New Delhi: Reliance, 1993.

Johar, Surinder Singh. *Guru Tegh Bahadur: A Biography.* New Delhi: Abhinav, 1975.

Kohli, Mohinder Pal. *Guru Tegh Bahadur.* New Delhi: Sahitya Academy, 1992.

Kohli, Surinder Singh. *Sword and the Spirit: An Introduction to Guru Tegh Bahadur's Life and Philosophy.* New Delhi: Ankur, 1977.

Rani, Phulan. *Life of Guru Tegh Bahadur Through Pictures.* Annotated by Shamsher Singh and Narendra Singh Virdi. Amritsar: Modern Sahit Academy, N.d.

Singh, Dalip. *Guru Tegh Bahadur.* New Delhi: Young Sikh Cultural Association, 1975. 32p.

Singh, Daljit. *Guru Tegh Bahadur.* Patiala: LDP, 1971.

Singh, Darshan. *The Ninth Nanak: A Historical Biography.* Jullundur: K. Lal, 1975.

Singh, Fauja, and Gurbachan Singh Talib. *Guru Tegh Bahadur: Martyr and Teacher.* Patiala: Punjabi University, 1975.

Singh, Ganda. *Martyrdom of Guru Tegh Bahadur.* Amritsar: GNDU, 1976.

————, ed. *Guru Tegh Bahadur Commemoration Volume*. Patiala: Punjabi University, 1975.

Singh, Harbans. *Guru Tegh Bahadur*. New Delhi: Sterling, 1982.

————. *Sri Guru Tegh Bahadur Sahib: Life History, Sacred Hymns and Teachings*. Amritsar: Singh Brothers, 1975.

Singh, Jagdish. *Guru Tegh Bahadur: An Illustrated Biography*. New Delhi: Punjab and Sind Bank, 1976. 44 pp.

Singh, Ram. *Tegh Bahadur: His Life, Teachings and Martyrdom*. Ambala Cantt: Joshi Press, 1970.

Singh, Ranbir. *Guru Tegh Bahadur: Divine Poet, Saviour & Martyr*. Amritsar: CKD, 1975.

Singh, Satbir, ed. *Guru Tegh Bahadur: Commemorative Volume*. Amritsar: Guru Tegh Bahadur Tercentenary Committee, 1975.

Singh, Trilochan. *Brief Life of Guru Tegh Bahadur*. Delhi: Sikh Gurdwara Board, 1974.

————. *Guru Tegh Bahadur: Prophet and Martyr*. Delhi: GPC, 1967.

Talib, Gurbachan Singh, ed. *Guru Tegh Bahadur: Background and the Supreme Sacrifice*. Patiala: Punjabi University, 1976.

Guru Gobind Singh

Ahluwalia, Rajendra Singh. *The Founder of the Khalsa*. Chandigarh: GGSF, 1966.

Chatterjee, Debendranath. *Guru Gobind Singh*. Chandernagar: Chatterjee, 1950.

Chatterji, Suniti Kumar. *Guru Gobind Singh, 1666–1708.* Chandigarh: Panjab University, 1967. 40 pp.

Deane, S. F. *Saint Warrior Guru Gobind Singh.* Ambala Cantt: Dass Brothers, N.d.

Dhillon, Dalbir Singh, and Shangana Singh Bhullar. *Battles of Guru Gobind Singh.* New Delhi: Deep & Deep, 1990.

Doabia, Harbans Singh. *Life Story of Siri Satguru Gobind Singh Ji Maharaj and Some of His Hymns.* Chandigarh: author, 1974.

Grewal, J. S., and S. S. Bal. *Guru Gobind Singh: A Biographical Study.* Chandigarh: Panjab University, 1967. 2nd edition, 1987.

Jaspal, Partap Singh. *Eternal Glory of Guru Gobind Singh and the Khalsa.* New Delhi: Reliance, 1994.

Johar, Surinder Singh. *Guru Gobind Singh: A Biography.* Delhi: Sterling, 1967.

————. *Guru Gobind Singh: A Study.* New Delhi: Marwah, 1979.

Kohli, Surindar Singh. *Life and Ideals of Guru Gobind Singh.* New Delhi: Munshiram Manoharlal, 1986.

Mansukhani, Gobind Singh. *Guru Gobind Singh.* Delhi: Hemkunt, 1976.

————, and Dharamjit Singh. *Guru Gobind Singh: Cosmic Hero.* New Delhi: India Book House, 1967.

————, and Surindar Singh Kohli. *Guru Gobind Singh: His Personality and Achievement.* New Delhi: Hemkunt, 1976.

Nara, Ishar Singh. *Safarnama and Zafarnama, Being an Account of the Travels of Guru Gobind Singh and the Epistle of Moral Victory Written By Him to Emperor Aurangzeb.* Abridged and translated by Joginder Singh. New Delhi: Nara Publications, 1985.

Rai, Daulat. *Sahibe Kamal Guru Gobind Singh.* Written in 1901. Abridged and translated by Surinderjit Singh. Amritsar: Gurmat Sahit Charitable Trust, 1988.

Rama, Swami. *Celestial Song/Gobind Geet: The Dynamic Dialogue Between Guru Gobind Singh and Banda Singh Bahadur.* Honesdale, Pennsylvania: Himalayan, 1986.

Ravi Batra. *Leadership in its Finest Mould: Guru Gobind Singh.* Amritsar: SGPC, 1979.

Safeer, Pritam Singh. *The Tenth Master.* New Delhi: GNF, 1983.

Seetal, Sohan Singh. *Prophet of Man: Guru Gobind Singh.* Ludhiana: Lyall, 1968.

Singh, Dalip. *Guru Gobind Singh and Khalsa Discipline.* Amritsar: Singh Brothers, 1992.

Singh, Fauja, ed. *Travels of Guru Gobind Singh.* English and Punjabi. Maps by Mehar Singh Gill. Patiala: Punjabi University, 1968.

Singh, Ganda. *Guru Gobind Singh's Death at Nanded: An Examination of Succession Theories.* Faridkot: GNF, 1972.

Singh, Gopal. *Guru Govind Singh.* New Delhi: National Book Trust, 1966. 2nd edition, New Delhi: Sterling, 1979.

———. *Prophet of Hope: The Life of Guru Gobind Singh.* Delhi: Sterling, 1967.

Singh, Harbans. *Guru Gobind Singh.* Chandigarh: GGSF, 1966.

Singh, Jagjit K. *Guru Gobind Singh: A Study.* Bombay: Pritpal Kaur, 1967.

Singh, Kartar. *Guru Gobind Singh and the Mughals.* Chandigarh: GGSF, 1967.

————. *Life of Guru Gobind Singh.* 2nd edition, Ludhiana: Lahore Book Shop, 1951.

Singh, Khushwant, and Suneet Vir Singh. *Homage to Guru Gobind Singh.* Bombay: Jaico, 1970.

Singh, Nahar, and Kirpal Singh. *Two Swords of Guru Gobind Singh in England (1666–1708 AD).* New Delhi: Atlantic, 1989.

Singh, Narain. *Guru Gobind Singh Re-told.* Amritsar: author, 1966.

————. *Guru Gobind Singh: The Warrior-Saint.* Chandigarh: GGSF, 1967. 42 pp.

Singh, Parkash, ed. *The Saint-Warrior Guru Gobind Singh.* Amritsar: Khalsa College, 1967.

Singh, Puran. *Guru Gobind Singh: Reflection and Offerings.* Chandigarh: GGSF, 1966.

————. *Life and Teachings of Guru Gobind Singh.* Amritsar: Khalsa Agency, N.d.

————. *The Tenth Master.* Ludhiana: Sahitya Sangam, 1960.

Singh, Sahib. *Guru Gobind Singh.* Jullundur: Raj, 1967.

Singh, Satbir, ed. *Guru Gobind Singh 300th Birthday Souvenir.* Patna: Takht Harimandirji, 1967.

Singh, Sher. *Social and Political Philosophy of Guru Gobind Singh.* Delhi: Sterling, 1967.

————. *Sri Guru Gobind Singh Ji, Being Some Unwritten Leaves in the Life of the Guru.* Amritsar: Jaidev Singh Jogindar Singh, 1933.

Singh, Trilochan. *Guru Gobind Singh: A Brief Life Sketch.* Delhi: GPC, 1964. 35 pp.

Talib, Gurbachan Singh. *The Impact of Guru Gobind Singh on Indian Society.* Chandigarh: GGSF, 1966.

The Tenth Master: Tributes on Tercentenary. Chandigarh: GGSF, 1967.

Uppal, S. S., ed. *Guru Gobind Singh: The Saviour.* New Delhi: SGTB Khalsa College, 1969.

History

General Historical

Azad, Mohammad Akram Lari. *Religion and Politics in India during the Seventeenth Century.* New Delhi: Criterion, 1990.

Bal, S. S. *A Brief History of the Modern Punjab.* Ludhiana: Lyall, 1974.

Birdwood, C. B. *India's Freedom Struggle: Role of Muslims and the Sikhs.* Delhi: Discovery, 1988.

Chhabra, G.S. *Advanced History of the Punjab,* vol.1, 2nd edition, Jullundur: New Academic, 1968. Vol.2, 2nd edition, Ludhiana: Parkash, 1965.

Court, Henry. *History of the Sikhs.* Translation of *Sikhan de raj di vikhia [sic. vithia].* Lahore: Civil and Military Gazette, 1888.

Data, Piara Singh. *The Sikh Empire (1708–1849 A.D.)* Delhi: NBS, 1986.

Dewey, Clive. *The Settlement Literature of the Greater Punjab: A Handbook.* New Delhi: Manohar, 1991.

Dhillon, Sukhwinder Kaur. *Religious History of Early Medieval Punjab.* New Delhi: NBO, 1991.

Dilgeer, Harjinder Singh, and Awatar Singh Sekhon. *The Sikhs' Struggle for Sovereignty: An Historical Perspective.* Edited by A. T. Kerr. Edmonton: Sikh Educational Trust, 1992.

George, W. L. M. *History of the Sikhs.* Allahabad: R. S. Publications, 1979.

Gill, Pritam Singh. *History of Sikh Nation: Foundation, Assassination, Resurrection.* Jullundur: New Academic, 1978.

Grewal, Gurdial Singh. *Freedom Struggle of India by Sikhs and Sikhs in India.* Ludhiana: Sant Isher Singh Rarewala Education Trust, 1993.

Grewal, J. S. *From Guru Nanak to Maharaja Ranjit Singh: essays in Sikh history.* Amritsar: GNDU, 1972. Revised edition, 1982.

————. *Miscellaneous Articles.* Amritsar: GNDU, 1974.

————. *The Sikhs of the Punjab.* Vol. II.3 of *The New Cambridge History of India.* Cambridge: CUP, 1990.

————, ed. *Studies in Local and Regional History.* Amritsar: Guru Nanak University, 1974.

Gupta, Hari Ram. *History of the Sikhs.* 6 vols. New Delhi: Munshiram Manoharlal, 1978–91.

————. *A History of the Sikhs from Nadir Shah's Invasions to the Rise of Ranjit Singh (1739–1799).* 3 vols. Simla: Minerva, 1939–44.

————. *Short History of the Sikhs*. Ludhiana: Sahitya Sangam, 1970.

Gustafson, W. Eric, and Kenneth W. Jones, eds. *Sources on Punjab History*. Delhi: Manohar, 1975.

Hans, Surjit. *Reconstruction of Sikh History from Sikh Literature*. Jullundur: ABS Publication, 1988.

Khilnani, N. M. *Rise of the Sikh Power in Punjab*. Delhi: Independent, 1990.

Lal, Shiv. *Dateline Punjab Lifeline Sikhs*. New Delhi: Election Archives, 1994.

Latif, Syad Muhammad. *History of the Panjab from the Remotest Antiquity to the Present Time*. Calcutta: Central Press, 1891. Reprint, Delhi: Eurasia, 1964.

Malik, Ikram Ali. *The History of the Punjab 1799–1947*. Delhi: Neeraj, 1983.

Narang, Gokul Chand. *Transformation of Sikhism*. Lahore: Tribune Press, 1914. Revised and enlarged 2nd edition, 1945. Republished as *Glorious History of Sikhism*. New Delhi: New Book Society of India, 1972.

Narang, K. S., and H. R. Gupta, eds. *History of the Punjab (1526–1857)*. Delhi: Uttar Chand Kapur, N.d.

Nijjar, Bakhshish Singh. *Punjab under the British Rule*. 3 vols. New Delhi: K. B. Publications, 1974.

Payne, C. H. *Short History of the Sikhs*. London: Thomas Nelson, 1915. Reprint, Patiala: LDP, 1970.

Singh, Chetan. *Region and Empire: Panjab in the Seventeenth Century*. Delhi: OUP, 1991.

Singh, Fauja. *A Brief Account of the Freedom Movement in Punjab.* Patiala: Punjabi University, 1972.

————. *Eminent Freedom Fighters of Punjab.* Patiala: Punjabi University, 1972.

————, ed. *Historians and Historiography of the Sikhs.* New Delhi: Oriental, 1978.

————, ed. *Who's Who [:] Punjab Freedom Fighters.* Patiala: Punjabi University, 1972.

Singh, Ganda. *The Sikhs and their Religion.* Redwood City, California: Sikh Foundation, 1974.

Singh, Gopal. *History of the Sikh People (1469–1978).* New Delhi: World Sikh University Press, 1979.

Singh, Gopal, ed. [Different from previous author.] *Punjab Past, Present and Future.* Delhi: Ajanta, 1994.

Singh, Gurcharan, and V. S. Suri. *Pir Budhu Shah: The Saint of Sadhaura.* Chandigarh: GGSF, 1967. 42 pp.

Singh, Harnam. *Tales of the Sikh History.* Patiala: LDP, 1971.

Singh, Khushwant. *A History of the Sikhs.* 2 vols. Princeton, New Jersey: Princeton University Press, 1963, 1966. Revised edition, Delhi: OUP, 1991.

Singh, Rajinder. *Five Hundred Years of Sikhism.* Amritsar: CKD, N.d.

Singh, Teja, and Ganda Singh. *A Short History of the Sikhs (1469–1765).* Bombay: Orient Longmans, 1950. Reprint, Patiala: Punjabi University, 1989.

The Eighteenth Century

Ahluwalia, M. L. *Life and Times of Jassa Singh Ahluwalia*. Patiala: Punjabi University, 1989. 48 pp.

Alam, Muzaffar. *The Crisis of Empire in Mughal North India: Awadh and the Punjab 1707–1748*. Delhi: OUP, 1986.

Banga, Indu. *Agrarian System of the Sikhs*. New Delhi: Manohar, 1978.

Data, Piara Singh. *Banda Singh Bahadur*. Delhi: NBS, N.d.

Deol, Gurdev Singh. *Banda Bahadur*. Jullundur: New Academic, 1972.

Gandhi, Surjit Singh. *Struggle of the Sikhs for Sovereignty*. Delhi: Gur Das Kapur, 1980.

Malik, Arjan Dass. *An Indian Guerilla War: The Sikh People's War, 1699–1768*. New Delhi: Wiley Eastern, 1975.

Nayyar, Gurbachan Singh. *Sikh Polity and Political Institutions*. New Delhi: Oriental, 1979.

Sachdeva, Veena. *Policy and Economy of the Punjab During the Late Eighteenth Century*. Delhi: Manohar, 1993.

Seetal, Sohan Singh. *Rise of the Sikh Power in the Panjab*. Jullundur: Dhanpat Rai, 1970.

———. *The Sikh Misals and the Punjab*. Ludhiana: Lahore Book Shop, 1981.

Singh, Bhagat. *History of the Sikh Misals*. Patiala: Punjabi University, 1993.

———. *Sikh Polity in the Eighteenth and Nineteenth Centuries*. New Delhi: Oriental, 1978.

Singh, Ganda. *Ahmad Shah Durrani: Father of Modern Afghanistan.* Bombay: APH, 1959.

————. *Life of Banda Singh Bahadur.* Amritsar: Khalsa College, 1935. Reprint, Patiala: Punjabi University, 1990.

————. *Sardar Jassa Singh Ahluwalia.* Patiala: Punjabi University, 1990.

Singh, Kirpal. *Life of Maharaja Ala Singh of Patiala.* Amritsar: SGPC, 1954.

Sinha, Narendra Krishna. *Rise of the Sikh Power.* Calcutta: University of Calcutta, 1936.

Maharaja Ranjit Singh and His Successors

There is an extensive bibliography dealing with the period of the most popular Sikh ruler of the Punjab, Ranjit Singh (1800–39), and the ten years of his successors. Because most of the works fall strictly within the area of History, as opposed to Religion, they have not been included here, apart from a few of particular importance and those which deal with figures of religious importance. For a fuller bibliography of the period see Joseph T. O'Connell, et al, eds., *Sikh History and Religion in the Twentieth Century* (Toronto: University of Toronto 1988), pp. 462–67; and Rajwant Singh, comp., *The Sikhs* (Delhi: Indian Bibliographies Bureau, 1990), pp. 113–24.

Ahluwalia, M. L. *Sant Nihal Singh alias Bhai Maharaj Singh: A Saint-Revolutionary of the 19th Century Punjab.* Patiala: Punjabi University, 1972.

————, and Kirpal Singh. *The Punjab's Pioneer Freedom Fighters.* New Delhi: Orient Longmans, 1963.

Alexander, Michael, and Sushila Anand. *Queen Victoria's Maharajah: Duleep Singh 1838–93.* London: Weidenfeld and Nicolson, 1980.

Bajwa, Fauja Singh. *Military System of the Sikhs During the Period 1799–1849.* Delhi: Motilal Banarsidass, 1964.

Banerjee, A. C. *The Khalsa Raj.* New Delhi: Abhinav, 1985.

Grewal, J. S. *Maharaja Ranjit Singh.* Amritsar: GNDU, 1982.

————. *The Reign of Maharaja Ranjit Singh: Structure of Power, Economy and Society.* Patiala: Punjabi University, 1981. 47 pp.

————, and Indu Banga, eds. *Maharaja Ranjit Singh and His Times.* Amritsar: GNDU, 1980.

Hasrat, Bikrama Jit. *Life and Times of Ranjit Singh: A Saga of Benevolent Despotism.* Nabha: author, 1977.

Saggar, Balraj. *Who's Who in the History of the Punjab (1800–1849).* New Delhi: NBO, 1993.

Singh, Bhagat. *Maharaja Ranjit Singh.* Patiala: Punjabi University, 1983.

————. *Maharaja Ranjit Singh and his Times.* New Delhi: Sehgal, 1990.

Singh, Fauja. *After Ranjit Singh.* New Delhi: Master, 1982.

————. *Some Aspects of State and Society under Ranjit Singh.* New Delhi: Master, 1982.

————, and A. C. Arora, eds. *Maharaja Ranjit Singh: Politics, Society and Economy.* Patiala: Punjabi University, 1984.

Singh, Harbans. *Maharaja Ranjit Singh.* New Delhi: Sterling, 1980.

Singh, Khushwant. *The Fall of the Kingdom of the Punjab.* Bombay: Orient Longmans, 1962.

————. *Ranjit Singh: Maharajah of the Punjab 1780–1839.* London: George Allen & Unwin, 1962.

Singh, Teja, and Ganda Singh, eds. *Maharaja Ranjit Singh: First Death Centenary Memorial.* Amritsar: Khalsa College, 1939.

Waheeduddin, Fakir Syed. *The Real Ranjit Singh.* Karachi: Lion Art Press, 1965.

Early British Interest and Administration

Bal, S. S. *British Policy Towards Punjab 1844–49.* Calcutta: New Age, 1971.

Banerjee, Himadri. *Agrarian Society of the Punjab (1849–1901).* New Delhi: Manohar, 1982.

Cunningham, J.D. *A History of the Sikhs from the Origin of the Nation to the Battles of the Sutlej.* London: John Murray, 1849. Reprint, New Delhi: S. Chand & Co., 1985.

Davis, Emmett. *Press and Politics in British Western Punjab 1836–1947.* Delhi: Academic, 1983.

Domin, Dolores. *India in 1857–59: A Study in the Role of the Sikhs in the People's Uprising.* Berlin: Akademie-Verlag, 1977.

Dua, J. C. *Eighteenth Century Punjab.* New Delhi: Radha, 1992.

Gordon, John H. *The Sikhs.* Edinburgh: William Blackwood, 1904. Reprint, Patiala: LDP, 1970.

Gough, Charles, and Arthur D. Innes. *The Sikhs and the Sikh Wars: The Rise, Conquest, and Annexation of the Punjab State.* London: Innes, 1897. Reprint, Patiala: LDP, 1970.

Grey, C. *European Adventurers of Northern India, 1785–1849.* Edited by H. L. O. Garrett. Lahore: Government Printing Press, 1929. Reprint, Patiala: LDP, 1970.

Hugel, Charles. *Travels in Cashmere and the Punjab, Containing a Particular Account of the Government and Character of the Sikhs.* Translated from the German with notes by Major T.B. Jervis. London: John Petheram, 1845. Reprint, Patiala: LDP, 1970.

Khurana, G. *British Historiography on the Sikh Power in Punjab.* New Delhi: Allied, 1985.

M'Gregor, W.L. *The History of the Sikhs.* 2 vols. London: James Madden, 1846.

Malcolm, John. *Sketch of the Sikhs.* London: John Murray, 1812.

Mehta, H. R. *A History of the Growth and Development of Western Education in the Punjab 1846–1884.* Lahore: Punjab Government Record Office, 1929. Reprint, Patiala: LDP, 1971.

Murray, William. *Political, Religious and Social Affairs of the Punjab and the Sikh Memoirs of Capt. William Murray.* New Delhi: Deep & Deep, 1976. *See entry under Prinsep, Henry T.*

Prinsep, Henry T. *Origin of the Sikh Power in the Punjab and Political Life of Maharaja Ranjit Singh.* Includes appendix "On the manner, rules, and customs of the Sikhs" by Captain W. Murray. (*See under Murray, William.*) Calcutta: Military Orphan Press, 1834. Reprint, Patiala: LDP, 1970.

Rose, H. A., comp. *A Glossary of the Tribes and Castes of the Punjab and North-West Frontier Province.* 3 vols. Lahore: Punjab Government Printing Press, 1919. Reprint, Patiala: LDP, 1970.

Sethi, Kamla. *Administration of Punjab: A Study in British Policy, 1875–1905.* Delhi: Renaissance, 1990.

Sharma, Inderjit. *Land Revenue Administration in the Punjab (1849–1901)*. New Delhi: Atlantic, 1985.

Singh, Ganda. *Indian Mutiny of 1857 and the Sikhs*. Delhi: Sikh Students Federation, 1960. 49 pp.

―――, ed. *Early European Accounts of the Sikhs*. Calcutta: Indian Studies Past and Present, 1962.

Singh, Hari. *Agrarian Scene in British Punjab*. New Delhi People's Publishing House, 1983.

Singh, Sukhpal. *Civil Service in the Punjab (1849–1947)*. Jalandhar: ABS Publications, 1987.

Steinbach, (Henry). *The Punjaub; Being a Brief Account of the Country of the Sikhs*. London: Smith, Elder and Co, 1845. New edition edited by W. H. McLeod, Karachi: OUP, 1976.

Thorburn, S. S. *The Punjab in Peace and War*. Edinburgh: Blackwood, 1904. Reprint, Patiala: LDP, 1970.

[Thornton, Thomas Henry]. *History of the Punjab and of the Rise, Progress & Present Condition of the Sect and Nation of the Sikhs*. 2 vols. London: W. H. Allen, 1846. Reprint, Patiala: LDP, 1970.

The Singh Sabha, The Gurdwara Reform Movement, and Independence, 1873–1947

Ahluwalia, M. L., ed. *Gurdwara Reform Movement, 1919–1925: An Era of Congress-Akali Collaboration: Select Documents*. New Delhi: Ashoka, 1985.

Ali, Imran. *The Punjab under Imperialism, 1885–1947*. Delhi: OUP, 1989.

All-India Sikh Gurdwaras Legislation: Statement of the Objectives and Reasons of the Proposed Bill and the Contents Thereof. Amritsar: SGPC, N.d.

Bajwa, Surinder Kaur. *Sikh Gurdwaras Act 1925*. Patiala: Punjabi University, 1971.

Bal, S. S. *Political Parties and the Growth of Communalism in Punjab 1920–47*. Chandigarh: CRRID, 1989.

Bal, Sukhmani. *Politics of the Central Sikh League*. Delhi: Books N' Books, 1990.

Barrier, N. Gerald. *Banned: Controversial Literature and Political Control in British India 1907–1947*. New Delhi: Manohar, 1976.

————. *Sikh Resurgence: The Period and its Literature*. Delhi: Manohar, 1969. 28 pp.

Bhatia, Shyamala. *Social Change and Politics in Punjab 1898–1910*. New Delhi: Enkay, 1987.

Darling, Malcolm Lyall. *At Freedom's Door*. London: OUP, 1949.

————. *The Punjab Peasant in Prosperity and Debt*. London: OUP, 1925. Reprint, with introduction by Clive J. Dewey, Columbia, Missouri: South Asia Books, 1978.

————. *Rusticus Loquitur, or the Old Light and the New in the Punjab village*. London: OUP, 1930.

————. *Wisdom and Waste*. London: OUP, 1934.

Deol, Gurdev Singh. *Role of the Ghadar Party in the National Movement*. Delhi: Sterling, 1969.

Dhillon, Gurdarshan Singh. *Character and Impact of the Singh Sabha Movement on the History of the Punjab*. Patiala: Punjabi University, 1973.

Effenberg, Christine. *The Political Status of the Sikhs during the Indian National Movement 1935–1947*. New Delhi: Archives, 1989.

Fox, Richard G. *Lions of the Punjab: Culture in the Making*. Berkeley, California: University of California Press, 1985.

Ghai, Prem Vati. *The Partition of the Punjab 1849–1947*. New Delhi: Munshiram Manoharlal, 1986.

Grewal, J. S., and Puri, H. K., ed. *Letters of Udham Singh*. Amritsar: Guru Nanak University, 1974.

Grover, D. R. *Civil Disobedience Movement in the Punjab (1930–34)*. Delhi: B. R. Publishing Corporation, 1987.

Indictment of Patiala. Bombay: All India States' People's Conference, 1939.

Javed, Ajeet. *Left Politics in Punjab 1935–47*. Delhi: Durga, 1988.

Jones, Kenneth W. *Socio-religious Reform Movements in British India*. Vol. III.1 of *The New Cambridge History of India*. Cambridge: CUP, 1989.

Josh, Bhagwan. *Communist Movement in Punjab (1926–47)*. New Delhi: Anupama, 1979.

Josh, Sohan Singh. *Hindustan Gadar Party: A Short History*. 2 vols. New Delhi: People's Publishing House, 1977–78.

Kapur, Rajiv A. *Sikh Separatism: The Politics of Faith*. London: Allen & Unwin, 1986.

Khanna, K. *Sikh Leadership and Some Aspects of Anglo-Sikh Relations*. Patiala: Punjabi University, 1969.

Khullar, K. K. *Shaheed Bhagat Singh*. New Delhi: Hem, 1981.

Mittal, S. C. *Freedom Movement in Punjab (1905–29)*. Delhi: Concept, 1977.

Mohan, Kamlesh. *Militant Nationalism in the Punjab 1919–1935*. New Delhi: Manohar, 1985.

Nabha, Kahan Singh. *Sikhs: We Are Not Hindus*. Translated by Jarnail Singh. Willowdale, Ontario: translator, 1984.

Nijjar, Bakhshish Singh. *History of the Babar Akalis*. Jalandhar: ABS Publications, 1987.

Oberoi, Harjot. *The Construction of Religious Boundaries: Culture, Identity and Diversity in the Sikh Tradition*. Delhi: OUP, 1994; Chicago: University of Chicago Press, 1994.

Oxen, Stephen. *The Sikhs and the Punjab Politics 1921–1947*. Vancouver: UBC, 1964.

Petrie, D. *Developments in Sikh Politics 1900–1911: A Report*. Amritsar: CKD, N.d.

Puri, Harish K. *Ghadar Movement: Ideology, Organisation and Strategy*. Amritsar: GNDU, 1983.

Rahbar, Hansraj. *Bhagat Singh and his Thought*. New Delhi: Manak, 1990.

Rai, Satya M. *Legislative Politics and the Freedom Struggle in the Panjab 1897–1947*. New Delhi: Indian Council of Historical Research, 1984.

———. *Punjabi Heroic Tradition 1900–1947*. Patiala: Punjabi University, 1978.

Sahni, Ruchi Ram. *Struggle for Reform in Sikh Shrines*. Amritsar: Sikh Itihas Research Board, 1964.

Saini, B. S. *The Social & Economic History of the Punjab 1901–1939*. Delhi: Ess Ess, 1975.

Sarsfield, Landen. *Betrayal of the Sikhs*. Lahore: Lahore Book Shop, 1946.

Sethi, G. R. *Sikh Struggle for Gurdwara Reform or The History of the Gurdwara Reform Movement*. Amritsar: Union Press, 1927.

Sharma, S. C. *Punjab: The Crucial Decade*. New Delhi: Nirmal, 1987.

Singh, Amar. *Memorandum of the Central Akali Dal*. Lahore: Westend, 1946.

Singh, Darbara. *The Punjab Tragedy, 1947*. Amritsar: Steno House Agency, 1949.

[Singh, Ganda]. *A History of the Khalsa College Amritsar*. Amritsar: Khalsa College, Amritsar, 1949.

Singh, Ganda, ed. *Some Confidential Papers of the Akali Movement*. Amritsar: SGPC, 1965.

————, ed. *The Singh Sabha and Other Socio-Religious Movements in the Punjab 1850–1925*. Vol. VII, Part I (April, 1973) of *The Panjab Past and Present*. Patiala: Punjabi University, 1984.

Singh, Gurbachan, and Lal Singh. *The Idea of the Sikh State*. Lahore: Lahore Book Shop, 1946.

Singh, Gurcharan. *Babbar Akali Movements*. Zira: Aman, 1993.

Singh, Gurmit. *Failures of Akali Leadership*. Sirsa: Usha Institute of Religious Studies, 1981.

Singh, Hari. *Punjab Peasant in Freedom Struggle*. New Delhi: People's Publishing House, 1984.

Singh, Iqbal. *Facts about Akali Agitation in Punjab*. Chandigarh: Fairdeal Press, 1960.

Singh, Kardar. *The Plight of the Sikhs*. Lahore: Servants of Sikh Society, 1944.

Singh, Khushdeva. *Love is Stronger than Hate: A Remembrance of 1947*. Patiala: Guru Nanak Mission, 1973.

Singh, Khushwant, and Satindra Singh. *Ghadar 1915: India's First Armed Revolution*. New Delhi: R & K Publishing House, 1966.

Singh, Kirpal. *The Partition of the Punjab*. Patiala: Punjabi University, 1972.

Singh, Manjit. *Late S. Khazan Singh: A Pioneer in the Akali Movement*. 2 vols. New Delhi: author. Vol. 1, 3rd edition, 1975. Vol. 2, 2nd edition, 1974.

Singh, Mohinder. *The Akali Movement*. New Delhi: Macmillan, 1978. Reprinted, with extra chapter, as *The Akali Struggle: a retrospect*. New Delhi: Atlantic, 1988.

Singh, Nahar, and Kirpal Singh, eds. *Struggle for Free Hindustan (Ghadr Movement)*. New Delhi: Atlantic, 1986.

Singh, Rup. *Tat Khalsa: The Purest of the Pure*. Lahore: Sikh Tract Society, 1917. 17 pp.

Singh, Teja. *The Gurdwara Reform Movement and the Sikh Awakening*. Jullundur: Desh Sewak, 1922. Reprint, Amritsar: SGPC, 1984.

Smith, V. W. *Akali Dal and Shiromani Gurdwara Parbandhak Committee*. Simla: Superintendent, Government Printing, 1922.

Talbot, Ian. *Punjab and the Raj 1849–1947*. New Delhi: Manohar, 1988.

Talib, Gurbachan Singh. *Muslim League Attack on Sikhs and Hindus in 1947*. Amritsar: SGPC, 1950.

————, comp. *Muslim League Attack on Sikhs and Hindus in the Punjab 1947*. New Delhi: Voice of India, 1991.

Tuteja, K. L. *Sikh Politics (1920–1940)*. Kurukshetra: Vishal, 1984.

Uprety, Prem Raman. *Religion and Politics in the Punjab in the 1920's*. New Delhi: Sterling, 1980.

Walia, Ramesh. *Praja Mandal Movement in East Punjab States*. Patiala: Punjabi University, 1972.

The Period Since Independence

Adhikari, Gangadhar M. *Sikh Homeland through Hindu-Muslim-Sikh Unity*. Bombay: Peoples Publishing House, 1945.

Aggarwal, J. C., and S. P. Agrawal, eds. *Modern History of Punjab*. Select documents. New Delhi: Concept, 1992.

Amnesty International. *India: Human Rights Violations in Punjab: Use and Abuse of the Law*. New York: Amnesty International, 1991.

Anand, Jagjit Singh, et al. *Punjabi Suba: A Symposium*. Delhi: National Book Club, 1967.

Arora, S. C. *President's Rule in Indian States: A Study of Punjab*. New Delhi: Mittal, 1990.

————. *Turmoil in Punjab Politics*. New Delhi: Mittal, 1990.

Bains, Ajit Singh. *Siege of the Sikhs: Violation of Human Rights in Punjab*. Toronto: New Magazine Publishing Company, 1988.

Bhalla, Bhushan Chander. *The Punjab belongs to the Sikhs*. Lahore: Modern, 1947.

Bhullar, Pritam. *The Sikh Mutiny.* New Delhi: Siddharth, 1987.

Brar, K. S. *Operation Blue Star: The True Story.* New Delhi: UBS, 1993.

Butani, D. H. *The Third Sikh War? Towards or Away from Khalistan?.* New Delhi: Promilla, 1986.

Chakravarti, Uma, and Nandita Haksar, eds. *Delhi Riots: Three Days in the Life of a Nation.* New Delhi: Lancer International, 1987.

Chopra, V. D., et al. *Agony of Punjab.* New Delhi: Patriot, 1984.

Deol, Gurdev Singh, ed. *Punjab Problem: An Academic Approach.* Amritsar: Sikh History Research Centre, 1989.

Deora, M. S. *Akali Agitation to Operation Bluestar.* Chronology of events. 2 vols. New Delhi: Anmol, 1991.

Dharam, S. S. *Internal and External Threats of Sikhism.* Arlington Heights, Illinois: Gurmat Publishers, 1986.

Dhillon, G. S. *India Commits Suicide.* Chandigarh: Singh and Singh, 1992.

Dogra, Bharat. *Punjab: Grass-roots Problems and Solutions.* New Delhi: Shahid Bhagat Singh Research Committee, 1988.

Duggal, K. S. *Understanding the Sikh Psyche: Reflections on the Current Punjab Crisis.* New Delhi: Siddharth, 1992.

Embree, Ainslie T. *Utopias in Conflict: Religion and Nationalism in Modern India.* Berkeley and Los Angeles, California: University of California, 1990.

Gossman, Patricia. *Punjab in Crisis.* Asia Watch Report. New York: Human Rights Watch, 1991.

IHRO. *Indo-US Shadow over Punjab*. London: International Human Rights Organisation, 1992.

Jafar, Ghani. *The Sikh Volcano*. New Delhi: Atlantic, 1988.

Jain, Harish, comp. *Report of Justice Ranganath Misra Commission of Inquiry*. Sirhind: Takshila, N.d.

Jeffrey, Robin. *What's Happening to India? Punjab, Ethnic Conflict, Mrs. Gandhi's Death and the Test for Federalism*. London: Macmillan, 1986.

Judge, Paramjit S. *Insurrection to Agitation: the Naxalite Movement in Punjab*. Bombay: Popular Prakashan, 1992.

Kanwal, Jaswant Singh. *The Other Zafarnamah: An Open Letter to Rajiv Gandhi*. Sirhind: Lokgeet, N.d.

Kapur, Anup Chand. *The Punjab Crisis: An Analytical Study*. New Delhi: S. Chand & Company, 1985.

Kaur, Harminder. *Blue Star over Amritsar*. Delhi: Ajanta, 1990.

Khosla, Shyam, et al. *Terrorism in Punjab: cause and cure*. Chandigarh: Panchnad Research Institute, 1987.

Kshitish. *Storm in Punjab*. Translated by Vinod Dhawan. New Delhi: The Word Publications, 1985.

Kumar, Parmod, et al. *Punjab Crisis: Context and Trends*. Chandigarh: CRRID, 1984.

Kumar, Ram Narayan, and Georg Sieberer. *The Sikh Struggle: Origin, Evolution and Present Phase*. Delhi: Chanakya, 1991.

Lal, Mohan. *Disintegration of Punjab*. Chandigarh: Sameer, 1984.

Maini, D. S. *Cry the Beloved Punjab*. New Delhi: Siddharth, 1986.

Narang, A. S. *Democracy Development and Distortion.* New Delhi: Gitanjali, 1986. Also published under the title *Punjab Accord and Elections Retrospect in Prospect.* New Delhi: Gitanjali, 1986.

Nayar, Kuldip, and Khushwant Singh. *Tragedy of Punjab: Operation Bluestar & After.* New Delhi: Vision Books, 1984.

Nijjar, B. S. *Indian Panjab.* Jalandhar: ABS Publications, 1985.

Rai, Satya M. *Partition of the Punjab: A Study of Its Effect on Politics and Administration 1947–56.* New York: APH, 1965.

———. *Punjab Since Partition.* Delhi: Durga, 1986.

Randhawa, M. S. *Out of the Ashes.* An account of the rehabilitation of refugees from West Pakistan in rural areas of East Punjab. N.p., 1954.

Reddy, G.K.C., ed. *Army Action in Punjab: Prelude and Aftermath.* New Delhi: Samata Era, 1984.

Sahota, Dharam Singh. *Sikh Struggle for Autonomy (1940–1992).* Garhdiwala: Guru Nanak Study Centre, 1993.

Samiuddin, Abida, ed. *The Punjab Crisis: Challenge and Response.* Delhi: Mittal, 1985.

Sarhadi, Ajit Singh. *Punjabi Suba: The Story of the Struggle.* Delhi: U. C. Kapur, 1970.

Sarin, Ritu. *The Assassination of Indira Gandhi.* New Delhi: Penguin, 1990.

Saxena, N. S., et al. *Punjab Tangle: The Different Perspectives.* New Delhi: Amrit, 1984.

Sidhu, Bhagwant Singh. *Sikhs at Crossroads.* Patiala: Des Raj, 1984.

Singh, Amrik, ed. *Punjab in Indian Politics: Issues and Trends.* Delhi: Ajanta, 1985.

Singh, Bhan, ed. *Facts about Punjabi Suba Agitation: A Collection of Memorandum Presented Before Das Commission.* Amritsar: Shiromani Akali Dal, 1960.

Singh, Darshan ('Canadian'). *Terrorism in Punjab.* Selected articles and speeches. Edited by Satyapal Dang. New Delhi: Patriot, 1987.

Singh, Devinder. *Akali Politics in Punjab (1964–1985).* New Delhi: NBO, 1993.

Singh, Gopal, ed. *Punjab Today.* New Delhi: Intellectual, 1987.

Singh, Gur Rattan Pal. *The Illustrated History of the Sikhs (1947–84).* Chandigarh: author, 1979.

Singh, Gurmit. *History of Sikh Struggles. 1946–1989.* 3 vols. New Delhi: Atlantic, 1989–91.

Singh, Hari. *Agricultural Workers' Struggle in Punjab.* New Delhi: People's Publishing House, 1980.

Singh, Harnam. *Sikh Memorandum to the Punjab Boundary Commission.* Lahore: author, 1947.

Singh, Hukum. *Plea for Punjabi-speaking State.* Amritsar: Shiromani Akali Dal, N.d.

Singh, Iqbal. *Punjab Under Siege: A Critical Analysis.* New York: Allen, McMillan and Enderson, 1986.

Singh, Jaswant. *Facts without Rhetoric: The Demand for Punjabi Suba.* New Delhi: Suba Press, 1960.

Singh, Kapur. *Some Documents on the Demand for the Sikh Homeland.* Chandigarh: All India Sikh Students' Federation, 1956.

Singh, Khushwant. *My Bleeding Punjab.* New Delhi: UBSPD, 1992.

————, et al. *The Punjab Story.* New Delhi: Roli Books International, 1984.

Singh, Kirpal, ed. *Select Documents on Partition of Punjab, 1947.* Delhi: NBS, 1991.

Singh, Mohinder. *Peasant Movement in PEPSU Punjab.* New Delhi: NBO, 1991.

Singh, Partap. *Khalistan: The Only Solution.* West Hills, California: author, 1991.

Singh, Patwant, and Harji Malik, eds. *Punjab: The Fatal Miscalculation.* New Delhi: Patwant Singh, 1985.

Singh, Sadhu Swarup. *The Sikhs Demand their Home Land.* Lahore: Sikh University Press, 1946.

Singh, Satinder. *Khalistan: An Academic Analysis.* New Delhi: Amar Prakashan, 1982.

Singh, Tara. *Save Hindi Agitation and Sikh View-point.* Delhi: Indian Union Press, N.d.

Stephens, Ian. *Among the Sikhs: An Overblamed People.* Calcutta: Statesman, 1948.

Surjeet, Harkishan Singh. *Deepening Punjab Crisis: A Democratic Solution.* New Delhi: Patriot, 1992.

Tully, Mark, & Satish Jacob. *Amritsar: Mrs. Gandhi's Last Battle.* Calcutta: Rupa, 1985.

Doctrine and Symbols

Doctrine: General

Bir, Ragbir Singh. *Bandagi Nama: Communion with the Divine.* Calcutta: Atam Science Trust, 1981.

Cole, W. Owen. *The Guru in Sikhism.* London: Darton, Longman & Todd, 1982.

Doabia, Harbans Singh. *Introduction to the Philosophy of Sikh Religion (based wholly on Divine Hymns) God, Maya and Death.* Chandigarh: Harbans Singh Satwant Kaur Charitable Trust, N.d.

Gill, Pritam Singh. *Trinity of Sikhism: Philosophy, Religion, State.* Jullundur: New Academic, 1973.

Jain, Nirmal Kumar. *Sikh Religion and Philosophy.* New Delhi: Sterling, 1979.

Kaur, Gurnam. *Reason and Revelation in Sikhism.* New Delhi: Cosmo, 1990.

Kaur, Rajinder. *Sikh Conception of Godhood.* Chandigarh: Panjab University, 1965.

Kohli, Surindar Singh. *Outlines of Sikh Thought.* New Delhi: Punjabi Prakashak, 1966.

———. *Real Sikhism.* New Delhi: Harman, 1994.

———. *The Sikh Philosophy.* Amritsar: Singh Brothers, 1992.

Lahori, Lajwanti. *The Concept of Man in Sikhism.* Delhi: Munshiram Manoharlal, 1985.

McMullen, Clarence O., ed. *The Nature of Guruship.* Batala: Christian Institute of Sikh Studies, 1976.

Mansukhani, Gobind Singh. *The Quintessence of Sikhism.* Amritsar: SGPC, 1958.

Massey, James. *The Doctrine of Ultimate Reality in Sikh Religion: A Study of Guru Nanak's Hymns in the Adi Grantha.* New Delhi: Manohar, 1991.

Puri, Gopal Singh. *Self-realisation and the Sikh Faith.* New Delhi: Falcon Books, 1994.

Sharma, Harbans Lal. *Concept of Jiva of Guru Nanak Against the Background of Different Indian Schools of Philosophy and Religions.* Patiala: Punjabi University, 1971.

Sikka, Ajit Singh. *Beacons of Light.* Ludhiana: Bee Kay, 1975.

————. *Facets of Guru Nanak's Thought.* Ludhiana: author, 1972.

————. *Philosophy of Mind in the Poetry of Guru Nanak: A Comparative Study with European Philosophy.* Ludhiana: Bee Kay, 1973.

Singh, Dharam. *Sikh Theology of Liberation.* New Delhi: Harman, 1991.

Singh, Godwin Rajinder. *Gur Parsad: Sikh Doctrine of Divine Grace, an Interfaith Perspective.* Kowloon, Hong Kong: Christian Conference of Asia, 1992.

Singh, Harnam. *Sikh Religion: Karma and Transmigration.* Jullundur: author, 1955.

Singh, Himmat. *Philosophical Conception of 'Sabda'.* Patiala: author, 1985.

Singh, Jodh. *A Few Sikh Doctrines Reconsidered.* Delhi: NBS, 1990.

Singh, Madanjeet. *Reflections of my Mind.* Delhi: Gurdas Kapur, 1973.

Singh, Narain. *Our Heritage.* Amritsar: CKD, N.d.

Singh, Nikky-Guninder Kaur. *The Feminine Principle in the Sikh Vision of the Transcendent.* Cambridge: CUP, 1993.

Singh, Nirbhai. *Philosophy of Sikhism: Reality and Its Manifestations.* New Delhi: Atlantic, 1990.

Singh, Partap. *Gurmat Philosophy.* Amritsar: Sikh Publishing House, 1951.

Singh, Prakash. *The Sikh Gurus and the Temple of Bread.* Amritsar: SGPC, 1964.

Singh, Pritam, ed. *Sikh Concept of the Divine.* Amritsar: GNDU, 1985.

Singh, Teja. *Sikh Religion: An Outline of Its Doctrines.* Amritsar: SGPC, 1958. 36 pp.

Singh, Wazir. *Philosophy of Sikh Religion: A Bunch of Eleven Studies.* New Delhi: Ess Ess, 1981.

―――. *The Sikh Vision: Problems of Philosophy and Faith.* New Delhi: Ess Ess, 1992.

Uberoi, Mohan Singh. *Sikh Mysticism: The Sevenfold Yoga of Sikhism.* Amritsar: author, 1964.

Ethics

Anand, Balwant Singh. *Guru Nanak: Religion and Ethics.* Patiala: Punjabi University, 1968.

Kohli, Surindar Singh. *Sikh Ethics.* Delhi: Munshiram Manoharlal, 1973.

Pannikar, K. M. *Ideals of Sikhism.* Lahore: Sikh Tract Society, 1924.

Singh, Avtar. *Ethics of the Sikhs.* Patiala: Punjabi University, 1970.

Singh, Nripinder. *The Sikh Moral Tradition: Ethical Perceptions of the Sikhs in the Late Nineteenth/Early Twentieth Century.* New Delhi: Manohar, and Columbia, Missouri: South Asia Publications, 1990.

Singh, Ranbir. *The Sikh Way of Life.* New Delhi: Indian Publishers, 1969.

Singh, Randhir. *Ethics of Sikhs.* Amritsar: SGPC, 1953.

Singh, Santokh. *Philosophical Foundations of the Sikh Value System.* New Delhi: Munshiram Manoharlal, 1982.

Singh, Trilochan. *Ethical Philosophy of Guru Nanak.* Calcutta: University of Calcutta, 1973.

Talib, Gurbachan Singh. *Study of the Moral Code of Guru Nanak's Teachings.* Chandigarh: Panjab University, 1970.

Symbols, Rituals, and Customs

Aggarwal, S. C. *Sketch of the Sikhs: Their Customs and Manners.* Chandigarh: Vinay, 1981.

Babraa, Davinder Kaur. *Visiting a Sikh Temple.* London: Lutterworth, 1981.

Bajwa, Ranjit Singh. *Semiotics of the Birth Ceremonies in Punjab.* New Delhi: Bahri, 1991.

Batth, Gurdev Singh. *Sikh Rehat Maryada.* Hong Kong: author, 1990.

Bedi, Sohinder Singh. *Folklore of the Punjab.* New Delhi: National Book Trust, 1971.

Bennett, Olivia. *Sikh Wedding.* London: Hamish Hamilton, 1985. 27 pp.

Cole, W. Owen, and Piara Singh Sambhi. *Baisakhi.* Oxford: Religious and Moral Education Press, 1986. 32 pp.

Doabia, Harbans Singh, trans. *Sacred Nitnem: The Divine Hymns of the Daily Prayers by the Sikhs*. Revised edition, Amritsar: Singh Brothers, 1976.

Jyoti, Surinder Kaur. *Marriage Practices of the Sikhs: A Study of Intergenerational Differences*. New Delhi: Deep & Deep, 1983.

Kapoor, Sukhbir Singh. *Rehras*. New Delhi: Sterling, 1993.

————. *Sikh Festivals*. Hove: Wayland, 1985.

McMullen, Clarence O., ed. *Rituals and Sacraments in Indian Religions*. Delhi: ISPCK, 1979.

Rama, Swami, trans. *Nitnem: Spiritual Practices of Sikhism*. Honesdale, Pennsylvania: Himalayan, 1989.

Singh, Chanda. *Hair and Health*. Kot Kapura: Human Hair Research Institute, 1956.

————. *Human Hair*. Kot Kapura: Human Hair Research Institute, 1954.

Singh, Gopal, trans. *The Sikh Prayer Book*. New York: World Sikh Centre, 1982.

Singh, Gurbakhsh. *Sri Rehras, Ardas and Sohila*. Text in Roman and Gurmukhi, English rendering in verse. Bombay: Veekay Weekly, N.d.

Singh, Jogendra. *Sikh Ceremonies*. Bombay: International Book House, 1941. Reprint, Chandigarh: Religious Book Society, 1968. Reprint, Ludhiana: Lahore Book Shop, 1989.

Singh, Kapur. *Parasharprasna or the Baisakhi of Guru Gobind Singh*. Jullundur: Hind Publishers, 1959. Revised edition edited by Madanjit Kaur and Piar Singh. Amritsar: GNDU, 1989.

Singh, Khazan. *Role in the Kirpan Struggle*. New Delhi: Manjit Singh, 1975.

Singh, Kirpal. *Sikh Symbols*. Gravesend: Sikh Missionary Society of UK, 1971.

Singh, Santokh. *Sword of the Khalsa*. Gangyal, Jammu: Gujral Printers, 1991.

Singh, Sher. *Thoughts on Forms and Symbols in Sikhism*. Lahore: Mercantile Press, 1927.

Singh, Shumsher, trans. *The Daily Sikh Prayer (Nitnem)*. Delhi: NBS, 1990.

Singh, Trilochan. *The Turban and the Sword of the Sikhs*. Gravesend: Sikh Missionary Society, 1977.

Suri, Paropkar Singh. *Rational Basis of Sikh Symbols*. Calcutta: author, 1957.

Talib, Gurbachan Singh. *Nitnem*. New Delhi: GNF, 1983.

Sacred Scripture and Other Religious Literature

The Adi Granth

Complete English Translations

Chahil, Pritam Singh, trans. *Sri Guru Granth Sahib*. 4 vols. New Delhi: translator, 1992.

Singh, Gopal, trans. *Sri Guru Granth Sahib*. 4 vols. Delhi: Gurdas Kapur & Sons, 1960–62.

Singh, Manmohan, trans. *Sri Guru Granth Sahib*. 8 vols. Amritsar: SGPC, 1969.

Talib, Gurbachan Singh, trans. *Sri Guru Granth Sahib*. 4 vols. Patiala: Punjabi University, 1984–1990.

Japji

Bedi, Gursharan Singh, trans. *The Psalm of Life: An English Translation of Guru Nanak's Japji Sahib in Verse*. Amritsar: Sikh Publishing House, 1950.

Bhave, Vinoba. *Commentary on Japuji: Guru Nanak's Great Composition*. English translation with notes and introduction by Gurbachan Singh Talib. Patiala: Punjabi University, 1973.

Chatterjee, Yatindra Mohan, trans. *Japji*. Calcutta: D. M. Library, 1946.

Chellaram, trans. *Jap ji*. New Delhi: NBSM, 1955.

Dhody, Chaman Lal, trans. *Japuji Sahib: The Chant Sublime*. New Delhi: Ess Ess, 1991.

Doabia, Harbans Singh, trans. *Sacred Jap ji*. Amritsar: Singh Brothers, 1974.

Ghai, O. P. *Jap ji*. New Delhi: Sterling, 1991.

Karamchandani, Pritam Das V. *Essay on Japji*. Poona: author, 1963.

———, trans. *Japji by Guru Nanak Sahib*. Bombay: D. N. Abhichandani, 1962.

Lal, P., trans. *Japji: Fourteen Religious Songs*. Calcutta: Writers' Workshop, 1967. 16 pp.

———, trans. *More Songs from the Japji*. Calcutta: Writers Workshop, 1969. 20 pp.

Layal, Naunihal Singh, trans. *Japji Sahib: Holy Inspired Writings of Guru Nanak*. New Delhi: author, 1961. 45 pp.

Majithia, Surinder Singh, and Y. G. Krishnamurty, trans. *Japji: The Universal Home*. Gorakhpur: Lady Parsan Kaur Charitable Trust, 1967.

Maunder, R. S., trans. *Message of Guru Nanak As Expressed in Jap Nissan*. Poona: author, 1965. 49 pp.

Peace, M. L., trans. *Japji: Immortal Morning Prayer*. Ferozepur: D. S. Bhalla, N.d. 38 pp.

Randhawa, G.S., trans. *Guru Nanak's Japuji*. Amritsar: GNDU, 1970. Revised edition, 1990.

———, and Charanjit Singh, trans. *Guru Nanak's Japji*. New Delhi: Navyug, 1970.

Singh, Darshan, trans. *Japuji Sahib: Context and Concerns of Guru Nanak*. Chandigarh: Panjab University, 1978.

Singh, Dewan. *Guru Nanak's Message in Japji*. Amritsar: Faqir Singh, 1972.

Singh, Gopal, trans. *Songs of Guru Nanak*. English translation of *Japji*. London: author, 1956.

Singh, Gurdial, trans. *Japji*. Delhi: GPC, 1969. 29 pp.

Singh, Gursaran, trans. *Guru Nanak's Japji: The Morning Prayer of the Sikhs*. Delhi: Atma Ram, 1972.

Singh, Harnam, trans. *The Japji*. New Delhi: Surindar Singh, 1957.

Singh, Iqbal, trans. *The Essence of Truth: Japji and Other Sikh Scriptures*. New York: Allen, McMillan and Enderson, 1986.

Singh, Jaswant, trans. *Japji or Guru Nanak's Conception of the Design of Existence*. Dehra Dun: translator, N.d.

Singh, Jodh, trans. *Japji translated into English*. Ludhiana: Lahore Book Shop, 1956.

Singh, Khushwant, trans. *Jupji: The Sikh Prayer*. London: Royal India, Pakistan and Ceylon Society, N.d. 23 pp.

Singh, Kirpal, trans. *Japji: The Message of Guru Nanak*. Delhi: Ruhani Satsang, 1959.

Singh, Mehar, trans. *Japji: The Morning Divine Service of the Sikhs*. New Delhi: Punjabi Sahit Kala Kendra, 1952.

Singh, Narain, trans. *Jap of the Nam: Guru Nanak's Japji*. Amritsar: translator, N.d.

Singh, Parkash, trans. *Guru Nanak and his Japji*. Amritsar: Singh Brothers, 1969.

Singh, Puran. *Japji of Guru Nanak and Internationalism of the Sikhs*. Amritsar: Shahid Sikh Missionary College, 1929. 23 pp.

————, trans. *Guru Nanak's Japji or the Morning Meditation, and Sohila Arti Bed Time Prayer*. Amritsar: CKD, 1969. 26 pp.

————, trans. *Japji Rendered into Beautiful English*. Lahore: Lahore Book Shop, 1945. 39 pp.

Singh, Sangat, trans. *Japji*. Delhi: Hind Pocket Books, 1974.

Singh, Sher, trans. *Japji or Sri Guru Nanak Devji's Master-Law*. Junagadh: Holy Publishers, 1950. 32 pp.

Singh, Shiv Dayal, trans. *Japji Sahib*. Lahore: Gulab Singh, 1937.

Singh, Sohan, trans. *The Seeker's Path: Being an Interpretation of Guru Nanak's Japji*. Bombay: Orient Longmans, 1959.

Singh, Surinderjit, trans. *Japuji: Translation and Transliteration*. Patiala: Punjabi University, 1986.

Singh, Teja, trans. *The Japji or Guru Nanak's Meditation*. Lahore: Sikh Tract Society, 1919. 5th edition, 1964.

Singh, Vir. *Sri Japji Sahib of Sri Guru Nanak Dev*. Translated into English by Gurbaksh Singh. Bombay: Veekay Weekly, 1968.

Sirmoore, Hira Lal, trans. *Shri Japji Sahib translated into English*. Patiala: translator, 1944. 47 pp.

Talib, Gurbachan Singh, trans. *Japuji: The Immortal Prayer-Chant*. New Delhi: Munshiram Manoharlal, 1977.

Varma, Sharad Chandra. *Guru Nanak and "The Logos of Divine Manifestation"*. Delhi: GPC, 1969.

Other English Translations

Chellaram, trans. *Barah Maha*. Sarproon: NBSM, 1965. 29 pp.

———, trans. *Hymns of Guru Tegh Bahadur*. New Delhi: NBSM, 1966.

Doabia, Harbans Singh, trans. *Sacred Asa di Var (alongwith the Chhants of Guru Ramdas)*. Amritsar: Singh Brothers, 1988.

———, trans. *Sacred Dialogues of Guru Nanak Dev Ji*. Amritsar: Singh Brothers, 1994.

———, trans. *Sacred Sukhmani*. Amritsar: author, 1979. 2nd edition, Amritsar: Singh Brothers, 1980.

Greenlees, Duncan. *Selections from the Adi Granth*. Adyar: Theosophical Publishing House, 1975.

Guru Granth Ratnavali. Text in Gurmukhi and Dev-nagari with English translation. Patiala: Punjabi University, N.d.

Kaur, Baljit. *Psalms of Hope: Poetic Exegesis of Bani of Shri Guru Tegh Bahadur*. Chandigarh: author, 1978.

Layal, Naunihal Singh, trans. *Asa di Var: Early Morning Prayer of Guru Nanak*. New Delhi: translator, 1968.

Loehlin, C. H., trans. *The Twelve Months by Guru Nanak*. Amritsar: SGPC, 1969.

Mansukhani, Gobind Singh, trans. *Hymns from the Holy Granth*. Delhi: Hemkunt Press, 1975.

Puri, L. R. *Teachings of the Gurus (as given in the Adi Granth Sahib)*. 4 vols. Beas: Radhaswamy Satsang, 1962–1965.

Rama, Swami, trans. *Sukhmani Sahib: Fountain of Eternal Joy*. Honesdale, Pennsylvania: Himalayan, 1988.

Sekhon, Sant Singh, trans. *Unique Drama: Translation of Benati Chaupai, Bachitra Natak and Akal Ustati*. Chandigarh: GGSF, 1968.

Shan, Harnam Singh, trans. *Guru Nanak in his Own Words*. Amritsar: CKD, 1970.

———, trans. *Sayings of Guru Nanak*. Amritsar: SGPC, 1969.

Sharma, Chandra Prakash. *Divine Symphony: Hymns of Guru Tegh Bahadur in English Verse*. Patiala: Purnima, 1976.

Sharma, G. L. *Anand Sahib*. Jalandhar: New Book Co., 1987.

Singh, Daljit, trans. *Asa-di-War*. Ludhiana: translator, 1984.

Singh, Harbans. *The Message of Sikhism*. Delhi: DSGMC, 1978.

Singh, Harbhajan, comp. *Gems of Thoughts from Guru Nanak Bani*. Amritsar: Dharm Parchar Committee, 1971.

Singh, Jodh, comp. *Gospel of Guru Nanak in his Own Words*. Patiala: LDP, 1969.

———, trans. *33 Swaiyas*. Translated into English. Ludhiana: Lahore Book Shop, 1953. 42 pp.

Singh, Jogendra, comp. *Thus Spoke Guru Nanak: A Collection of the Sayings of Guru Nanak*. 1st edition, London and Bombay: OUP, 1934. 2nd edition, Amritsar, CKD, 1967.

Singh, Khushwant, trans. *Hymns of Guru Nanak*. New Delhi: Orient Longmans, 1969.

Singh, Lou. *The Nitnem and the Sukhmani Sahib*. New Delhi: Sterling, 1980.

Singh, Manmohan, trans. *Hymns of Guru Nanak*. Patiala: Punjabi University, 1971.

————. *Life of Shri Guru Nanak, Japji and Asa de Var*. Dehradun: Jiwan Singh, 1972.

Singh, Narain. *Anand Sahib*. Amritsar: Bhagat Puran Singh, N.d.

Singh, Sher, trans. *Guru Nanak on the Malady of Man*. Delhi: Sterling, 1968.

Singh, Shumsher, trans. *Twelve Months by Sri Guru Nanak Dev ji and by Sri Guru Arjun Dev ji and Slokas (Couplets) by Sri Guru Tegh Bahadur ji*. Delhi: NBS, 1989.

Singh, Sohan, trans. *Asa di Var: The Ballad of God and Man by Guru Nanak*. Amritsar: GNDU, 1982.

Singh, Teja, trans. *Asa di Var or Guru Nanak's Ode in the Asa Measure*. Amritsar: SGPC, 1957.

————, trans. *The Holy Granth: Sri Rag to Majh*. Patiala: Punjabi University, 1985.

————, trans. *The Psalm of Peace: An English Translation of Guru Arjun's 'Sukhmani'*. Madras: OUP, 1938.

Singh, Trilochan, trans. *Hymns of Guru Tegh Bahadur: Songs of Nirvana*. Delhi: DSGMC, 1975.

————, et al, trans. *Selections from the Sacred Writings of the Sikhs*. London: George Allen & Unwin, 1960.

Singh, Wazir, ed. *The Sikh Prayer: Japji, Anand Sahib, Sukhmani*. Translated by Wazir Singh, G. S. Talib, and Teja Singh. Lucknow: Central Gurmat Parchar Board, 1982.

Song of Eternal Bliss: Anand. Bombay: Veekay Weekly, 1976.

Talib, Gurbachan Singh, trans. *Bani of Sri Guru Amar Das*. New Delhi: Sterling, 1979.

————, trans. *An Introduction to Sri Guru Granth Sahib*. Patiala: Punjabi University, 1991.

————, trans. *Selections from the Holy Granth*. Delhi: Vikas, 1975.

————, trans. *Thus Spake Guru Amar Das*. Patiala: Punjabi University, 1979.

Trumpp, Ernest, trans. *Adi Granth or the Holy Scriptures of the Sikhs*. London: Allen & Trubner, 1877. Reprint, New Delhi: Munshiram Manoharlal, 1970.

Tulsi, Baljit Kaur. *Psalms of Hope*. Chandigarh: SGTBCT, 1978.

————. *Revelation of Divine Bliss*. Chandigarh: SGTBCT, 1990.

Vaudeville, Ch. *Kabir*. Oxford: Clarendon, 1974.

————. *A Weaver called Kabir*. Delhi: OUP, 1993.

Historical and Exegetical

Anand, Balwant Singh. *Baba Farid*. New Delhi: Sahitya Akademi, 1975.

Arora, R. K. *The Sacred Scripture: Symbol of Spiritual Synthesis*. New Delhi: Harman, 1988.

Callewaert, Winand M., comp. *Index to the Sri Guru Granth Sahib.* In Devanagari with English introduction. 4 vols. New Delhi: Manohar, 1994.

————, and Peter G. Friedlander. *The Life and Works of Raidas.* New Delhi: Manohar, 1992.

Dhillon, N. S. *Pillars of Divine Philosophy: They Speak in the Holy Granth.* London, author, N.d.

Greenlees, Duncan. *The Gospel of the Guru-Granth Sahib.* Adyar: Theosophical Publishing House, 1952.

Grewal, Jagjit Singh. *Imagery in the Adi Granth.* Chandigarh: Punjab Prakashan, 1986.

Kaur, Gunindar. *The Guru Granth Sahib: Its Physics and Metaphysics.* New Delhi: Sterling, 1981.

Kaur, Madanjit, and Piar Singh. *Guru Arjan and his Sukhmani.* Amritsar: GNDU, 1992.

Kohli, Surindar Singh. *A Critical Study of the Adi Granth.* New Delhi: PWCIS, 1961. Reissued as *Guru Granth Sahib: An Analytical Study.* Amritsar: Singh Brothers, 1992.

————. *Sikhism and Guru Granth Sahib.* Delhi: NBS, 1990.

Sambhi, Piara Singh. *The Guru Granth Sahib.* 'Discovering Sacred Texts' series. Oxford: Heinemann, 1994.

Singh, Bachittar, ed. *Planned Attack on Aad Sri Guru Granth Sahib: Academics or Blasphemy?* Chandigarh: International Centre of Sikh Studies, 1994.

Singh, Daljeet. *Essays on the Authenticity of Kartarpuri Bir and the Integrated Logic and Unity of Sikhism.* Patiala: Punjabi University, 1987.

Singh, Daljit, comp. *Voice of the Gurus.* Lahore: Model Electric Press, 1934.

Singh, Darshan. *A Study of Bhakta Ravidas.* Patiala: Punjabi University, 1987.

Singh, Jodh. *Lectures on Sri Guru Granth Sahib.* Banaras: Banaras Hindu University, 1955.

Singh, Sutantar. *About Siri Guru Granth Sahib.* New Delhi: Young Sikh Cultural Association, 1978.

Singh, Taran. *The Ideal Man of the Guru Granth.* Patiala: Punjabi University, 1966. 14p.

Talib, Gurbachan Singh, ed. *Perspectives on Sheikh Farid.* Patiala: Baba Farid Memorial Society, 1975.

The Dasam Granth

Ashta, Dharam Pal. *The Poetry of the Dasam Granth.* New Delhi: Arun, 1959.

Bedi, B.P.L., trans. *Unto Victory: Letter from the Last Sikh Guru to the Last Moghul Emperor, Zafarnamah of Guru Gobind Singh Maharaj Address to Emperor Aurangzeb.* Persian text with English translation and notes. New Delhi: Unity Book Club of India, 1957.

Bedi, G. S., trans. *The Epistle of Victory: An English Translation of Zafarnama.* Amritsar: author, 1960.

Duggal, Devinder Singh, trans. *Fatehnama and Zafarnama.* Jullundur: Institute of Sikh Studies, 1980.

Loehlin, C. H. *The Granth of Guru Gobind Singh and the Khalsa Brotherhood.* Lucknow: Lucknow Publishing House, 1971.

Maghowalia, B. S., trans. *Bachittar Natak.* Hoshiarpur: translator, 1978.

Mansukhani, Gobind Singh, trans. *Hymns from the Dasam Granth.* New Delhi: Hemkunt, 1980.

Nath, Surendra. *Jap*. New Delhi: Gobind Sadan, 1991.

Nijhawan, P. K. *Sri Guru Gobind Geeta*. New Delhi: Army Education Store, 1985.

Peace, M. L. trans. *Guru Gobind Singh's Akal Ustat Translated into English verse*. Jullundur: author, 1963.

Rama, Swami, trans. *Sri Guru Gobind Singh: The Cosmic Drama (Bichitra Natak)*. Honesdale, Pennsylvania: Himalayan, 1989.

Singh, Brijindar, trans. *The Jap, or Thoughts on Godhead, with Shabads & Swayyas by Guru Gobind Singh*. Amritsar: translator, 1925.

Singh, Gopal, trans. *Thus Spake the Tenth Master*. Patiala: Punjabi University, 1978.

Singh, Kartar, trans. *The Epic of Chandi: Shri Guru Gobind Singh Ji*. Qadian: author, 1968. 39 pp.

Singh, Trilochan, trans. *Guru Gobind Singh's Jap: Meditational Prayer*. Delhi: GPC, 1968. 48 pp.

Tulsi, Baljit Kaur, trans. *Divine Effulgence of the Formless Lord*. A translation of *Jap Sahib*. Chandigarh: SGTBCT, 1985.

———, trans. *The Ramayana by Shri Guru Gobind Singh Ji*. Patiala: LDP, 1967.

General Religious Literature

Bedi, B.P.L. *The Pilgrim's Way: Diwan of Bhai Nand Lal Goya*. Translated from the Persian. Patiala: Punjabi University, 1969.

Callewaert, W. M., and P. G. Friedlander. *The Life and Works of Raidas*. New Delhi: Manohar, 1992.

Hawley, John Stratton, and Mark Juergensmeyer, eds. *Songs of the Saints of India*. New York: OUP, 1988.

Kaur, Kanwaljit, and Inderjit Singh, trans. *Rehat Maryada: A Guide to the Sikh Way of Life*. London: Sikh Cultural Society, 1969. 21 pp.

Kaur, Premka, comp. *Peace Lagoon: The Songs of Guru Nanak, Guru Amar Dass, Guru Ram Dass, Guru Arjan and Guru Gobind Singh*. San Rafael, California: Spiritual Community, 1974.

Lajwanti, Rama Krishna. *Panjabi Sufi Poets, 1460–1900*. London: OUP, 1938.

Loehlin, C.H. *The Sikhs and their Book*. Lucknow: Lucknow Publishing House, 1946.

————. *The Sikhs and their Scriptures*. Lucknow: Lucknow Publishing House, 1958.

Lorenzen, David N., ed. *Religious Change and Cultural Domination*. Mexico: El Colegio de Mexico, 1981.

Machwe, Prabhakar. *Namdev: Life & Philosophy*. Patiala: Punjabi University, 1968.

McLeod, W. H., trans. *The B40 Janam-sakhi*. Amritsar: GNDU, 1980.

————, trans. *The Chaupa Singh Rahit-nama*. Dunedin: University of Otago, 1987.

————. *Early Sikh Tradition: A Study of the Janam-sakhis*. Oxford: Clarendon, 1980.

Maghowalia, B.S., trans. An Extract from Diwan-i-Goiya [of Nand Lal]. Hoshiarpur: translator, 1979.

Mansukhani, Gobind Singh. *A Book of Sikh Studies*. Delhi: NBS, 1989.

————, trans. *Hymns from Bhai Gurdas's Compositions*. Amritsar: Singh Brothers, 1989.

Sagar, Sabinderjit Singh. *Historical Analysis of Nanak Prakash: Bhai Santokh Singh*. Amritsar: GNDU, 1993.

Schomer, Karine, and W. H. McLeod, eds. *The Sants: Studies in a Devotional Tradition of India*. Berkeley, California: Berkeley Religious Studies Series, 1987; Delhi: Motilal Banarsidass, 1987.

Singh, Attar, trans. *The Rayhit Nama of Pralad Rai or the Excellent Conversation of the Duswan Padsha and Nand Lal's Rayhit Nama or Rules for the Guidance of the Sikhs in Religious Matters*. Translated from the original Gurmukhi. Lahore: Albert Press, 1876.

————, trans. *Sakhee Book or the Description of Gooroo Gobind Singh's Religion and Doctrines*. Translated from Gooroo Mukhi into Hindi, and afterwards into English. Banaras: Medical Hall Press, 1873.

Singh, Fauja, ed. *Hukamnamas Shri Guru Tegh Bahadur Sahib*. Punjabi, Hindi, English. Patiala: Punjabi University, 1976.

Singh, Jodh. *Kabir*. Patiala: Punjabi University, 1971.

Singh, Manjit. *Gurbani and Science: A Study*. Delhi: Gurdas Kapur, 1973.

Singh, Narendra Pal. *Gleanings from the Masters*. Calcutta: Sikh Cultural Centre, 1965.

Singh, Nirbhai. *Bhagata Namadeva in the Guru Grantha*. Patiala: Punjabi University, 1981.

Singh, Ranbir. *The Sikh Way of Life*. New Delhi: India Publishers, 1968.

Singh, Sampooran. *Song of the Khalsa: The Song of the Pure Man of God.* Jodhpur: Faith Publishers, 1978.

Talib, Gurbachan Singh. *Baba Sheikh Farid Shakar Ganj.* New Delhi: National Book Trust, 1974.

————, ed. *Baba Sheikh Farid: Life and Teachings.* New Delhi: Baba Farid Memorial Society, 1973.

————, ed. *The Sikh-Sufi Quest for Harmony: A Symposium.* Patiala: Baba Farid Memorial Society, 1980.

Analysis and Apologetics

Inquiry and Analysis

Ahluwalia, Jasbir Singh. *Metaphysical Problems of Sikhism.* Chandigarh: Godwin, 1976.

————. *Sikhism Today: The Crisis Within and Without.* Chandigarh: GGSF, 1987.

————. *Sovereignty of the Sikh Doctrine.* New Delhi: Bahri Publications, 1983.

Cole, W. Owen. *Thinking about Sikhism.* London: Lutterworth, 1980.

————, and P. S. Sambhi. *Meeting Sikhism.* London: Longman, 1980. 49 pp.

Duggal, K. S. *Secular Perceptions in Sikh Faith.* New Delhi: National Book Trust, India, 1982.

Grewal, J. S. *Present State of Sikh Studies.* Batala: CISS, 1973.

McLeod, W. H. *The Evolution of the Sikh Community.* Delhi: OUP, 1975. Oxford: Clarendon, 1976.

————. *The Sikhs: History, Religion, and Society*. New York: Columbia University Press, 1989.

————. *Who is a Sikh? The Problem of Sikh Identity*. Oxford: Clarendon, 1989; New Delhi: OUP, 1989.

Mann, Jasbir Singh, and Harbans Singh Saraon, eds. *Advanced Studies in Sikhism*. Irvine, California: Sikh Community of North America, 1989.

————, and Kharak Singh, eds. *Recent Researches in Sikhism*. Patiala: Punjabi University, 1992.

Singh, Attar. *Secularism and Sikh Faith*. Amritsar: GNDU, 1973. 28 pp.

Singh, Darshan. *Western Perspective on the Sikh Religion*. New Delhi: Sehgal, 1991.

Singh, Gurdev, ed. *Perspectives on the Sikh Tradition*. Chandigarh: Siddharth Publications, 1986.

Singh, I.J. *Sikhs and Sikhism: A View with a Bias*. Columbia, Missouri: South Asia Books, 1994; New Delhi: Manohar, 1994.

Singh, Jagjit. *In the Caravan of Revolution: Another Perspective View of the Sikh Revolution*. Sirhind: Lokgeet Prakashan, 1988.

————. *Perspectives on Sikh Studies*. New Delhi: GNF, 1985.

————. *The Sikh Revolution: A Perspective View*. New Delhi: Bahri, 1981.

Singh, Jodh. *Some Studies in Sikhism*. Ludhiana: Lahore Book Shop, 1953.

Singh, Kharak, et al, eds. *Fundamental Issues in Sikh Studies*. Chandigarh: Institute of Sikh Studies, 1992.

Singh, Khushwant. *Need for a New Vision in India & Other Essays*. Edited by Rohini Singh. New Delhi: UBSPD, 1991.

———, and Bipan Chandra. *Many Faces of Communalism*. Chandigarh: CRRID, 1985.

Singh, Trilochan. *Ernest Trumpp & W. H. McLeod as Scholars of Sikh History, Religion & Culture*. Chandigarh: International Institute of Sikh Studies, 1994.

Apologetics

Caveeshar, Sardul Singh. *The Sikh Studies*. Lahore: National Publications, 1937.

Dhillon, Gurdarshan Singh. *Insights into Sikh Religion and History*. Chandigarh: Singh and Singh, 1992.

———. *Religion and Politics: The Sikh Perspective*. Chandigarh: author, 1989.

———. *Researches in Sikh Religion and History*. Chandigarh: Sumeet, 1989.

Dhillon, N. S. *Practical Sikhism*. London: author, 1980.

Gill, Pritam Singh. *Concept of Sikhism*. Jullundur: New Academic, 1979.

Guleria, J. S. *Rediscovering Religion*. New Delhi: PWCIS, 1983.

Johar, Surinder Singh. *The Message of Sikhism*. Delhi: DSGMC, 1982.

———. *The Universal Faith*. Delhi: NBS, 1987.

Josh, Mahinder Singh. *An Analytical Study of the Propagation of Sikh Thought*. New Delhi: Sikh Missionary College, N.d.

Kapoor, S. S. *Being a Sikh*. New Delhi: Hemkunt, 1990.

————. *Philosophy, Facts and Fundamentals of the Sikh religion*. New Delhi: Hemkunt, 1994.

Kaur, Sahib. *Sikh Thought*. New Delhi: author, 1990.

Majithia, Surinder Singh, and Y. G. Krishnamurty. *The Sikh Life-view*. Sardar Nagar: Lady Parsan Kaur Charitable Trust, 1963.

Maskeen, Sant Singh. *Lectures of Maskeen Ji*. Edited by Anokh Singh. Singapore: editor, 1977.

Peace, M. L. *Life and Light of Sikhism*. Jullundur: author, 1962.

Sahota, Sohan Singh. *The Destiny of the Sikhs*. Jullundur: Sterling, 1971.

Sambhi, Piara Singh. *Understanding your Sikh Neighbour*. London: Lutterworth, 1980.

Sethi, Amarjit Singh. *Universal Sikhism*. New Delhi: Hemkunt Press, 1972.

Singh, Ajit, and Rajinder Singh, eds. *Glimpses of the Sikh Religion*. Delhi: NBS, 1988.

Singh, Ardaman. *One Guru One Movement*. Patiala: Guru Nanak Mission, 1978.

Singh, Balkar, ed. *Essential Postulates of Sikhism*. Patiala: Punjabi University, 1988.

Singh, Dalip. *Universal Sikhism: An Aid to Moral Upliftment*. New Delhi: Bahari, 1979.

Singh, Daljeet. *Essentials of Sikhism*. Amritsar: Singh Brothers, 1994.

Singh, Gopal. *Religion and Society: A Collection of Essays by Dr. Gopal Singh*. Edited by Mohinder Singh. Delhi: Dr. Gopal Singh Memorial Foundation, 1991.

Singh, Gurbakhash. *Sikh Faith for the Youth*. Richardson, Texas: Sikh Study Circle DFW, 1990.

Singh, Harkishen, comp. *The Sikhs: Tenets & Tremors*. New Delhi: N.p., N.d.

Singh, Jodh. *Indifference to Religion and its Causes*. Lahore: Sikh Tract Society, 1929.

―――. *Miracle of Sikhism*. Ludhiana: Sahitya Sangam, 1970.

Singh, Kapur. *Sikhism: An Oecumenical Religion*. Edited by Gurtej Singh. Chandigarh: Institute of Sikh Studies, 1993.

―――. *Sikhism for Modern Man*. Edited by Madanjit Kaur and Piar Singh. Amritsar: GNDU, 1992.

Singh, Kartar. *Rekindling of the Sikh Heart*. Lahore: Lahore Book Shop, 1945.

Singh, Khushdeva. *Lasting Solution of Punjab Problems*. Patiala: Guru Nanak Mission, N.d.

Singh, Lou (Khalsa Angrez). *Is Sikhism the Way for Me?*. Selangor, Malaysia: New Approach Mission for Occidental Sikhism, 1985.

Singh, Mehervan. *Sikhism—Its Impact*. Singapore: Chopmen, 1973.

Singh, Puran, *The Spirit-Born People*. Peshawar: Zorawar Singh, 1929. Reprint, Patiala: Punjabi University, 1990.

―――. *Spirit of the Sikh*. Lahore: Uttam Chand Kapoor, N.d. [c.1930–31]. Reprint, 3 volumes, Patiala: Punjabi University, 1978–1981.

Singh, Rup. *Sikhism: A Universal Religion*. Amritsar: Coronation Printing Works, 1913. 38 pp.

Singh, Sarup. *Forgotten Panth*. Amritsar: Sikh Religious Book Society, 1954. 29 pp.

Singh, Taran, ed. *Sikh Gurus and the Indian Spiritual Thought.* Patiala: Punjabi University, 1981.

Singh, Teja. *Essays in Sikhism.* Lahore: Sikh University Press, 1944.

————. *Growth of Responsibility in Sikhism.* Lahore: Sikh Tract Society, 1919. 6th edition, Bombay: Forward, 1948.

Singh, Trilochan. *Responsibility of Sikh Youth in the Context of Human and Political Situation in the East and West.* New Delhi: Light & Life, 1981.

Vaswani, T. L. *In the Sikh Sanctuary.* Madras: Ganesh, 1922.

Sects and Other Religions

Sects

Ahluwalia, M. M. *Kukas: The Freedom Fighters of the Punjab.* Bombay: Allied, 1965.

Bajwa, Fauja Singh [Singh, Fauja]. *Kuka Movement: An Important Phase in Punjab's Role in India's Struggle for Freedom.* Delhi: Motilal Banarsidass, 1965.

Gargi, Balwant. *Nihangs: Knight Errants of the Guru.* Chandigarh: Punjab Tourism Department, 1975.

————. *Nirankari Baba.* Delhi: Thomson Press, 1973.

Gian Singh, Giani. *Namdhari Sikhs: A Brief Account as Narrated by Giani Gian Singh.* Translated by Haribhajan Singh. Sri Jiwan Nagar: Harbans Singh, 1988.

Jolly, Surjit Kaur. *Sikh Revivalist Movements: The Nirankari and Namdhari Movements in Punjab in the Nineteenth Century.* New Delhi: Gitanjali, 1988.

Sikhism and the Nirankari Movement. Patiala: Academy of Sikh Religion and Culture, 1990.

Singh, Ganda. *Sikhism and Nirankari Movement.* Patiala: Guru Nanak Dev Mission, 1978. 32 pp.

Singh, Gurmit. *Sant Khalsa. The Kuka Sikhs.* Sirsa: Usha Institute of Religious Studies, 1978.

Singh, Jaswinder, ed. *Kuka Movement: Freedom Struggle in the Punjab.* New Delhi: Atlantic, 1985.

———, comp. *Kukas of Note in the Punjab.* Sri Bhaini Sahib: Namdhari Darbar, 1985.

Singh, Nahar. *Short Account of the Kukas or Namdharis.* Ludhiana: author, N.d. 18 pp.

———, comp. *Gooroo Ram Singh and the Kuka Sikhs: Rebels against the British power in India.* Documents 1863–1880. 3 vols. New Delhi: Amrit Book Co, 1965–66; Sri Jiwan Nagar: Namdhari History Research Society, 1967.

———, and Kirpal Singh, eds. *Rebels against the British Rule.* Vol. 1: *Guru Ram Singh and the Kuka Sikhs.* Vol. 2: *Bhai Maharaj Singh.* New Delhi: Atlantic, 1989–90.

Webster, John C.B. *The Nirankari Sikhs.* Delhi: Macmillan, 1979.

Sikhism and Other Religions

Ahmed Shah, E. *Sikhism and the Christian Faith.* Lucknow: Lucknow Publishing House, N.d.

Ahuja, N. D. *Essence and Fragrance: A Comparative Study of Islam and Sikhism.* Chandigarh: International, 1975.

———. *Great Guru Nanak and Muslims.* Chandigarh: Kirti, 1974.

———. *Islam and the Creed of Guru Nanak.* Chandigarh: Vee Vee, 1972.

———. *The Muslim Attitude towards Nanak.* Chandigarh: Vee Vee, N.d.

———. *Muslim Sikh Relations: The Truth and the Case for Re-Appraisal.* Chandigarh: Vee Vee, N.d.

Archer, John Clark. *The Sikhs in Relation to Hindus, Muslims, Christians and Ahmadiyyas: A Study in Comparative Religion.* Princeton, New Jersey: Princeton University Press, 1946.

Birch, John M. *The Sikhs in Canada: A Christian Perspective.* Boring, Oregon: InterAct Ministries, 1993.

Cole, W. Owen, and P. S. Sambhi. *Sikhism and Christianity: A Comparative Study.* London: Macmillan, 1993.

Das, Sunil Kumar. *Sri Caitanya and Guru Nanak: A Comparative Study of Vaishavism and Sikhism.* Calcutta: Rabindra Bharati University, 1985.

Fremantle, Richard. *British Embracing Sikhism.* New Delhi: Sikh Information and Missionary Society, 1949.

Hira, Bhagat Singh. *Indian Religious Thought and Sikhism.* New Delhi: Bhagat Singh Hira, 1987.

———. *Semitic Religious Thought and Sikhism.* Delhi: NBS, 1992.

Kapoor, Sukhbir Singh. *The Ideal Man: The Concept of Guru Gobind Singh the Tenth Prophet of the Sikhs.* London: Khalsa College London Press, 1987.

Kohli, Surindar Singh. *Yoga of the Sikhs.* Amritsar: Singh Brothers, 1991.

Loehlin, C. H. *The Christian Approach to the Sikh*. London: Edinburgh House Press, 1966.

Pincott, Frederic. *Sikhism In Relation to Mohammadanism*. London: W. H. Allen & Co., 1885.

Puri, Gopal Singh. *Multicultural Society and Sikh Faith*. New Delhi: Falcon Books, 1992.

Santhanathan, S. M., et al. *Hindu-Sikh Conflict in Punjab: Causes & Cure*. Bangalore: Sri Guru Singh Sabha, 1983. 28 pp.

Seagrim, Dudley. *Notes on Hindus and Sikhs*. Allahabad: Pioneer Press, 1895. 31 pp.

Singh, Dalip. *Yoga and Sikh Teachings: Some Basic Questions*. New Delhi: Bahri, 1979.

Singh, Daljeet. *Sikh Ideology*. New Delhi: GNF, 1984.

———. *Sikhism: A Comparative Study of Its Theology and Mysticism*. New Delhi: Sterling, 1979.

Singh, Gurmit. *A Critique of Sikhism*. Sirsa: Ishar Singh Satnam Singh, 1964.

———. *Islam and Sikhism: A Comparative Study*. Sirsa: Usha Institute of Religious Studies, 1966.

Singh, Santokh. *Consciousness as Ultimate Principle*. New Delhi: Munshiram Manoharlal, 1985.

Singh, Trilochan. *Guru Nanak's Religion: A Comparative Study of Religions*. Delhi: Rajkamal, 1968. 34 pp.

Sobti, Harcharan Singh. *Studies in Buddhism and Sikhism*. Delhi: Eastern Book Linkers, 1986.

Thornton, D. M. *Parsi, Jaina and Sikh: Some Minor Religious Sects in India*. 1st edition, London: Religious Tract Society, 1898. Reprint, Delhi: Mittal, 1987.

Walji Bhai. *Hari Charitra or a Comparison Between the Adi Granth and the Bible*. Lodhiana: Lodhiana Mission Press, 1893.

Society

Sikh Society

Ahluwalia, Sadhu Singh. *Economic Conditions of the Sikhs*. Poona: Poona University, 1959.

Chopra, Kanchan. *Agricultural Development in Punjab: Issues in Resource Use and Sustainability*. Delhi: Vikas, 1990.

Duggal, K. S. *The Sikh People Yesterday and Today*. New Delhi: UBSPD, 1994.

Gill, Pritam Singh. *Heritage of Sikh Culture: Society, Morality, Art*. Jullundur: New Academic, 1975.

Hershman, Paul. *Punjabi Kinship and Marriage*. Edited by Hilary Standing. Delhi: Hindustan Publishing Corporation, 1981.

Ibbetson, Denzil. *Punjab Castes*. Lahore: Government Printing, 1916.

Izmirlian, Harry (Jr). *The Politics of Passion: Structure and Strategy in Sikh Society*. New Delhi: Manohar, 1979.

Jaspal, D. S. *Punjab: Provisional Population Totals*. Chandigarh: 1991.

Johar, R. S., and J. S. Khanna, eds. *Studies in Punjab Economy*. Amritsar: GNDU, 1983.

Juergensmeyer, Mark. *Religion as Social Vision: The Movement Against Untouchability in 20th-Century Punjab*. Berkeley,

California: University of California, 1982. Republished as *Religious Rebels in the Punjab*. Delhi: Ajanta, 1988.

Kaur, Jitinder. *Punjab Crisis: The Political Perceptions of Rural Voters*. Delhi: Ajanta, 1989.

Kaur, Madanjit. *Co-existence in a Pluralistic Society*. Amritsar: GNDU, 1991.

Kaur, Rajinder. *Sikh Identity and National Integration*. New Delhi: Intellectual, 1992.

Kaur, Upinder Jit. *Sikh Religion and Economic Development*. New Delhi: NBO, 1990.

Kessinger, Tom G. *Vilyatpur 1848–1968: Social and Economic Change in a North Indian Village*. Berkeley and Los Angeles, California: University of California, 1974.

Leaf, J. Murray. *Information and Behavior in a Sikh Village: Social Organization Reconsidered*. Berkeley, California: University of California, 1972.

Lekhi, R. K., and Joginder Singh. *Punjab Economy*. Ludhiana: Kalyani, 1986.

McMullen, Clarence O. *Religious Beliefs and Practices of the Sikhs in Rural Punjab*. New Delhi: Manohar, 1989.

Marenco, Ethne K. *Transformation of Sikh Society*. New Delhi: Heritage, 1976.

Pettigrew, Joyce. *Robber Noblemen: A Study of the Political System of the Sikh Jats*. London: Routledge and Kegan Paul, 1975.

Rao, Venkateswar. *Sikhs and India: Identity Crisis*. Hyderabad: Sri Satya, 1991.

Saberwal, Satish. *Mobile Men: Limits to Social Change in Urban Punjab*. New Delhi: Vikas, 1976.

Sikhism and Indian Society. Transactions of the Indian Institute of Advanced Study. Simla: IIAS, 1967.

Singh, G. B. *Transformation of Agriculture: A Case Study of Punjab.* Kurukshetra: Vishal, 1979.

[Singh, Ganda]. *History of the Khalsa College, Amritsar.* Amritsar: Khalsa College, 1949.

Singh, Harjinder. *Authority and Influence in two Sikh Villages.* New Delhi: Sterling, 1976.

Singh, Jodh. *Caste and Untouchability in Sikhism.* Amritsar: SGPC, 1976.

Singh, Lakshman. *Decay of Sikh Institutions: Sanatanis and the Sikhs.* Lahore: STS, 1916. 44 pp.

Singh, Nihal, ed. *Young Men's Sikh Association, 1931–56.* Silver Jubilee Prakashan, 1965.

Singh, Rattan. *Revolt of the Sikh Youth.* Lahore: Modern, 1948.

Singh, Wazir, ed. *Religious Pluralism and Co-existence.* Patiala: Punjabi University, 1986.

Virdi, Harbans Singh. *Sikh Olympians & Internationals.* Amritsar: SGPC, 1992.

―――. *The Sikhs in Sports.* Delhi: DSGMC, 1982.

Sikh Politics

Bajwa, Harcharan Singh. *Fifty Years of Punjab Politics (1920–1970).* Chandigarh: Modern, 1979.

Brar, J. S. *The Communist Party in Punjab: The Politics of Survival.* New Delhi: NBO, 1989.

Brass, Paul R. *Ethnicity and Nationalism: Theory and Comparison.* New Delhi: Sage, 1991.

————. *Language, Religion, and Politics in North India.* Cambridge: CUP, 1974.

Chaddah, Mehar Singh. *Are Sikhs a Nation?* Delhi: DSGMC, 1982.

Chand, Attar. *Jawaharlal Nehru and Politics in Punjab.* New Delhi: H. K. Publishers & Distributors, 1989.

Dhami, M. S. *Minority Leaders' Image of the Indian Political System: An Exploratory Study of the Attitudes of Akali Leaders.* New Delhi: Sterling, 1975.

Dilgir, Harjinder Singh. *Shiromani Akali Dal.* Chandigarh: Rachna, 1980.

Gandhi, Surjit Singh. *Perspectives on Sikh Gurudwaras Legislation.* New Delhi: Atlantic, 1993.

Gulati, Kailash Chander. *The Akalis Past and Present.* New Delhi: Ashajanak, 1974.

Kaur, Jitinder. *The Politics of Sikhs: A Study of Delhi Sikh Gurdwara Management Committee.* New Delhi: NBO, 1986.

Misra, Madhu Sudan. *Politics of Regionalism in India with Special Reference to Punjab.* New Delhi: Deep & Deep, 1988.

Narang, A. S. *Storm over the Sutlej: The Akali Politics.* New Delhi: Gitanjali, 1983.

Nayar, Baldev Raj. *Minority Politics in the Punjab.* Princeton, New Jersey: Princeton University Press, 1966.

Oren, Stephen. *Sikhs and the Punjab Politics 1921–1947.* Vancouver: University of British Columbia, 1964.

Puri, Nina. *Political Elite and Society in the Punjab*. New Delhi: Vikas, 1985.

Sandhu, Devinder Pal. *Sikhs in Indian Politics: Study of Minority*. New Delhi: Patriot, 1992.

Shourie, Arun. *Religion in Politics*. New Delhi: Roli Books, 1987.

Sidhu, Lakhwinder Singh. *Party Politics in Punjab*. New Delhi: Harman, 1994.

Singh, Dalip. *Dynamics of Punjab Politics*. New Delhi: Macmillan, 1981.

Singh, Gobinder. *Religion and Politics in the Punjab*. New Delhi: Deep & Deep, 1986.

Singh, Gurharpal. *Communism in Punjab*. Delhi: Ajanta, 1994.

Singh, Gurmit. *Gandhi and the Sikhs*. Sirsa: Usha Institute of Religious Studies, 1969.

Singh, Gurnam. *A Unilingual Punjabi State and the Sikh Unrest*. New Delhi: Super Press, 1960.

Singh, Harbans. *Nehru Family and the Sikhs*. New Delhi: B. R. Publishing Corporation, 1984.

————. *Sikh Political Parties*. New Delhi: Sikh Publishing House, n.d.

Singh, Hukam. *Sikh Problem and its Solution: An Elucidation*. Amritsar: Shiromani Akali Dal, N.d. [1951]. 49 pp.

Singh, Iqbal. *Facts about Akali Agitation in Punjab*. Chandigarh: Fairdeal Press, 1960.

Singh, Kehar, ed. *Perspectives on Sikh Polity*. New Delhi: Dawn, 1993.

Singh, Khazan. *Warning to the Panth*. Edited by Manjit Singh. New Delhi: editor, 1972. 27 pp.

Singh, Khushdeva. *Sikh Religion and Satyagraha*. Patiala: GGSF, 1972.

Singh, Sher. *Sikhism and Politics*. Ludhiana: Chardi Kala, N.d.

Singh, Sutantar. *Non-violence and the Sikhs*. Delhi: Rachna, 1975.

Wallace, Paul, and Surendra Chopra, eds. *Political Dynamics of Punjab*. Amritsar: GNDU, 1981. Revised edition, 1988.

Yadav, Kripal C. *Elections in Panjab 1920–1947*. New Delhi: Manohar, 1987.

Biography and Autobiography

Amrita Pritam. *Life and Times*. New Delhi: Vikas, 1989.

Anand, G. S., ed. *Dr. Balbir Singh Smriti Granth*. Dehradun: Dr. Balbir Singh Sahitya Kendra, 1976.

Archer, J. C. *John Clark Archer: A Chronicle*. Hamden, Connecticut: Cathaline Alford Archer, 1958.

Bakshi, S. R. *Bhagat Singh*. New Delhi: Anmol, 1990.

Barque, A. M., and Khosla, T. S. *Eminent Sikhs of Today*. Lahore: Barque, 1942.

Deol, Gurdev Singh. *Bhagat Singh: A Biography*. Patiala: Punjabi University, 1969.

———. *Shaheed-i-Azam Sardar Bhagat Singh*. Nabha: Deep Parkashan, 1978.

———. *Sir Sunder Singh Majithia*. Amritsar: Khalsa College, 1992.

Doabia, Harbans Singh. *Life Story of Baba Nand Singh Ji of Kaleran*. Amritsar: Singh Brothers, 1981.

———. *Life Story of Sant Attar Singh Ji (of Mastuana Sahib)*. Amritsar: Singh Brothers, 1992.

Duggal, K. S. *Giani Gurmukh Singh Musafir*. New Delhi: National Book Trust, India, 1982.

Ghai, Charan Dass. *God's Man: A Biography of Sant Fateh Singh*. Ludhiana: Lahore Book Shop, 1969.

Gopal, Madan. *Dyal Singh Majithia*. New Delhi: Publications Division, 1994.

Guleria, J. S. *Bhai Vir Singh: A Literary Portrait*. Delhi: NBS, 1985.

———, ed. *Bhai Vir Singh: The Sixth River of Punjab*. New Delhi: Guru Nanak Vidya Trust, 1972. 2nd edition, New Delhi: Bhai Vir Singh Sahitya Sadan, 1984.

Hira, Bhagat Singh. *The Great Sikh Saints*. Delhi: NBS, N.d.

Jalandhary, Surjeet. *Bhindranwale Sant*. Jalandhar: Punjab Pocket Books, 1984.

Jaspal, Partap Singh. *Eternal Glory of Baba Nand Singh Ji Maharaj*. New Delhi: author, 1992.

Johar, Surinder Singh. *Giani Zail Singh: a biography*. Jalandhar: Gaurav, 1984.

Josh, Harcharan Singh. *The Man on the Economic Wheel: A History of Punjab & Sind Bank and its Chairman Dr. Inderjit Singh*. Delhi: Preet, 1982.

Josh, Sohan Singh. *My Tryst with Secularism: An Autobiography*. New Delhi: Patriot, 1991.

Joshi, Chand. *Bhindranwale: Myth and Reality*. New Delhi: Vikas, 1984.

Kalia, D. R. *Sant Harchand Singh Longowal (1932–1985): A Martyr For Peace*. Jalandhar: New Age, 1985.

Kaur, Madanjit, ed. *Painter of the Divine: Sobha Singh*. Amritsar: GNDU, 1987.

Khosla, G. S. *Bhai Vir Singh: An Analytical Study*. New Delhi: Heritage, 1984.

Kirpal, Prem Nath, and Lajpat Rai Nair. *Dyal Singh Majithia: A Short Biographical Sketch*. Lahore: Bhupal Singh, 1935.

Lloyd, Sarah. *An Indian Attachment*. London: Harvill, 1984.

Mookerji, Radha Kumud. *Baba Kharak Singh Abhinandan Granth: 86th birthday commemoration Volume*. New Delhi: Baba Kharak Singh Abhinandan Committee, N.d.

Parkash, Ram. *Giani Zail Singh: Life and Work*. New Delhi: Panchsheel, 1984.

Pavate, D. *My Days as Governor*. Delhi: Vikas, 1974.

Safeer, Pritam Singh. *A Study of Bhai Vir Singh's Poetry*. New Delhi: Bhai Vir Singh Sahitya Sadan, 1985.

Singh, Basant Kumari. *Reminiscences of Puran Singh*. Patiala: Punjabi University, 1980.

Singh, Darbara. *Ten Eminent Sikhs*. Amritsar: Literature House, 1982.

Singh, Durlab. *Sikh Leadership*. Delhi: Sikh Literature Distributors, 1950.

————. *The Valiant Fighter: A Biographical Study of Master Tara Singh*. Lahore: Hero Publications, 1942.

Singh, Ganda, ed. *Bhai Vir Singh: Birth Centenary Volume.* Reprint, Patiala: Punjabi University, 1984.

Singh, Gurcharan, and Manjit Inder Singh, eds. *Professor G. S. Talib: A Perspective.* Delhi: Professor Talib Memorial Trust, 1987.

Singh, Harbans. *Bhai Vir Singh.* New Delhi: Sahitya Akademi, 1972.

————, ed. *Bhai Vir Singh Abhinandan Granth.* New Delhi: Bhai Vir Singh Abhinandan Samiti, 1954.

————, and N. Gerald Barrier, eds. *Essays in Honour of Dr Ganda Singh.* Patiala: Punjabi University, 1976.

Singh, Harnam. *Life of Baba Dip Singh Sahib.* Lahore: Sikh Tract Society, 1924. 39 pp.

Singh, Lakshman. *Bhagat Lakshman Singh: Autobiography.* Edited by Ganda Singh. Calcutta: Sikh Cultural Centre, 1965.

————. *Sikh Martyrs.* Madras: Ganesh, 1923.

Singh, Mohinder. *Sardar-i-Azam Master Tara Singh Ji: Life of Master Tara Singh.* Amritsar: Panthic Tract Society, 1950.

Singh, Mohinder, ed. [Different from previous author.] *Prof. Harbans Singh Commemoration Volume.* New Delhi: Prof. Harbans Singh Commemoration Committee, 1988.

Singh, Parkash. *Continuing Influence of Bhai Vir Singh.* Amritsar: Singh Brothers, 1972.

Singh, Partap. *Biography: Sardar Hukam Singh.* New Delhi: author, 1989.

Singh, Randhir. *Autobiography of Bhai Sahib Randhir Singh.* Translated by Trilochan Singh. Ludhiana: Bhai Sahib Randhir Singh Publishing House, 1971.

Singh, Trilochan. *Our Leader Today: Maharaja Yadvindra Singh of Patiala*. Patiala: Panthic Durbar, 1948. 48 pp.

Syngal, Munna Lal. *Patriot Prince, or the Life Story of Maharaja Ripudaman Singh of Nabha Who Died as Martyr*. Ludhiana: Doaba House, 1961.

Talib, Gurbachan Singh. *Sewa Singh Thikriwala: A Brief Sketch of His Life and Work*. Patiala: Punjabi University, 1971. 31 pp.

————, and Attar Singh, eds. *Bhai Vir Singh: Life, Times & Works*. Chandigarh: Panjab University, 1973.

————, and Harbans Singh, eds. *Bhai Vir Singh: Poet of the Sikhs*. New Delhi: Motilal Banarsidas, 1976.

Gurdwaras and Sacred Cities

Ahluwalia, Jasbir Singh, and H. S. Dilgir, eds. *Sri Akal Takht: A Symbol of Divine Sovereignty*. Chandigarh: GGSF, 1994.

Arshi, P.S. *The Golden Temple: History, Art and Architecture*. New Delhi: Harman, 1989.

Bajwa, Fauja Singh [Singh, Fauja]. *Guide to Sikh Shrines and Historical Places in Delhi*. New Delhi: DGPC, 1953.

Bali, Jang Bahadur. *Sis Ganj: The Story of the Historical Sikh Shrines of Delhi*. New Delhi: Swarn, 1967.

Bawa, J. S. *The Heritage of Amritsar*. Amritsar: Faqir Singh, 1977.

Datta, V. N. *Amritsar Past and Present*. Amritsar: Municipal Committee, 1967.

Dilgeer, Harjinder Singh. *The Akal Takht*. Jullundur: Punjabi Book Company, 1980. Republished as *Glory of the Akal Takht*, 1984.

Gandhi, Surjit Singh. *Perspectives on Sikh Gurdwaras Legislation.* New Delhi: Atlantic, 1993.

Gauba, Anand. *Amritsar: A Study in Urban History (1840–1947).* Jalandhar: ABS Publications, 1988.

Grewal, J. S., and Indu Banga, eds. *Studies in Urban History.* Amritsar: GNDU, c. 1978.

Janjua, H.S. *Sikh Temples in the U.K. and the People Behind Their Management.* London: Jan Publications, 1976.

Johar, Surinder Singh. *The Heritage of Amritsar.* Delhi: Sundeep, 1978.

———. *The Sikh Gurus and their Shrines.* Delhi: Vivek, 1976.

Kaur, Madanjit. *Golden Temple: Past and Present.* Amritsar: GNDU, 1983.

Khan, Khan Mohammad Waliullah. *Sikh Shrines in West Pakistan.* Karachi: Department of Archaeology, Government of Pakistan, 1962.

Randhir, G. S. *Sikh Shrines in India.* New Delhi: Publication Division, Government of India, 1990.

Sandhu, Ranvinder Singh. *The City and its Slums: A Sociological Study.* A study of Amritsar. Amritsar: GNDU, 1989.

Sahi, J.S. *Sikh Shrines in India and Abroad.* Faridabad: Common World, 1978.

Shankar, Sondeep, and Mohinder Singh. *The Golden Temple.* Hong Kong: Guidebook, 1992.

Shergill, N.S. *Sikh Gurdwaras and Sikh Organisations Abroad.* Southall: author, 1980.

Singh, Baghel. *Sri Hemkunt Sahib.* Ludhiana: PWCIS, 1987.

Singh, Fauja. *City of Amritsar: A Study of Historical, Cultural, Social and Economic Aspects.* New Delhi: Oriental, 1978.

————. *City of Amritsar: An Introduction.* Patiala: PIU, 1977.

Singh, Ganda. *History of the Gurdwara Shahidganj, Lahore from its Origin to November 1935.* Amritsar: author, 1935.

Singh, Gurcharan. *The Place of Supreme Sacrifice: Gurdwara Fatehgarh Sahib Sirhind.* Amritsar: SGPC, N.d.

Singh, Gurmukh. *Historical Sikh Shrines.* Amritsar: Singh Brothers, 1994.

Singh, Harbans. *City of Joy: Siri Anandpur Sahib.* Amritsar: SGPC, 1966. 16 pp.

————. *Heritage of the Golden Temple.* Amritsar: SGPC, N.d. 28 pp.

Singh, Hazara. *History and Guide to the Golden Temple.* Amritsar: Partap Singh Sunder Singh, 1938.

Singh, Jagjit. *Temple of Spirituality or Golden Temple, Amritsar.* Tarn Taran: Sikh Religious Tract Society, 1935.

Singh, Kashmir. *Law of Religious Institutions: Sikh Gurdwaras.* Amritsar: GNDU, 1989.

————. *Sikh Gurdwaras Legislation.* Amritsar: Singh Brothers, 1991.

Singh, Mehar. *Sikh Shrines in India.* New Delhi: Publication Division, Government of India, 1975. 50 pp.

Singh, Narinderjit. *Around the Golden Temple.* Amritsar: JSKS, 1977.

Singh, Patwant. *The Golden Temple.* New Delhi: Time Books, 1988.

————. *Gurdwaras in India and around the World*. New Delhi: Himalayan, 1992.

Singh, Sunder. *Guide to the Darbar Sahib of the Golden Temple of Amritsar*. Amritsar: author, 1905.

Singh, Trilochan. *Historical Sikh Shrines in Delhi*. New Delhi: DGPC, 1967.

Sodhi, Hazara Singh. *History and Guide to the Golden Temple*. Amritsar: PSSS, 1938.

Art, Literature, and Music

Ahluwalia, Jasbir Singh. *Punjabi Literature in Perspective: A Marxist Approach*. Ludhiana: Kalyani, 1973.

Aijazuddin, F. S. *Pahari Paintings and Sikh Portraits in the Lahore Museum*. Karachi and Delhi: OUP, 1977.

Archer, W.G. *Paintings of the Sikhs*. London: HMSO, 1966.

Arshi, P. S. *Sikh Architecture*. New Delhi: Intellectual, 1986.

Bedi, Joginder Singh. *Modern Punjabi Poets and their Vision*. Chandigarh: Raghbir Rachna, 1987.

Bedi, K. S., and S. S. Bal, eds. *Essays on History, Literature, Art and Culture*. Presented to Dr. M. S. Randhawa. New Delhi: Atma Ram, 1970.

Hans, Surjit, ed. *B-40 Janamsakhi Guru Baba Nanak Paintings*. Amritsar: GNDU, 1987.

Joshi, Mohinder Singh, and Gurmukh Singh Jeet, eds. *Contemporary Punjabi Short Stories*. New Delhi: PWCIS, 1984.

McLeod, W.H. *Popular Sikh Art*. Delhi: OUP. 1991.

Maini, Darshan Singh. *Studies in Punjabi Poetry*. New Delhi: Vikas, 1979.

Manasvi. *Sikh History and Culture: Reflections in Indian Fiction*. New Delhi: Harman, 1993.

Mansukhani, Gobind Singh. *Indian Classical Music and Sikh Kirtan*. New Delhi: Oxford & IBH, 1982.

Marg: a magazine of the arts. Vol. XXX, no. 3. Homage to Amritsar. Bombay: Marg Publications, 1977.

Marg: a magazine of the arts. Vol. XXXIV, no. 1. Maharaja Ranjit Singh. Bombay: Marg Publications, 1981.

Narang, C. L. *History of Punjabi Literature 850–1850 A.D.* Delhi: NBS, 1987.

Roopa-Lekha. Vol. XXXIX, no. 1. Portraits of the Sikh Gurus by Sikh artists. New Delhi: All India Fine Arts and Crafts Society, c.1970.

Sandhu, Gulzar Singh. *Punjabis, War and Women*. Edited by Marcus Franda. New Delhi: Heritage, 1983.

Shackle, C. *An Introduction to the Sacred Language of the Sikhs*. London: SOAS, University of London, 1983.

Shamsher, Jogindar. *The Overtime People*. Punjabi writers of Great Britain. Jalandhar: ABS Publications, 1989.

Sikh Sacred Music. New Delhi: Sikh Sacred Music Society, 1967.

Singh, Attar. *Secularization of Modern Punjabi Poetry*. Chandigarh: Punjab Prakashan, 1988.

Singh, Daljit. *Sikh Sacred Music*. Ludhiana: Sikh Sacred Music Society, 1967.

Singh, Darshan. *Sikh Art and Architecture*. Chandigarh: Panjab University, 1986–87.

Singh, G. S. Sohan. *Revealing the Art of G. S. Sohan Singh*. Amritsar: author, 1971.

Singh, Harbans. *Aspects of Punjabi Literature*. Ferozepore Cantt: Bawa, 1961.

Singh, Harbans. [Different from previous author.] *Mahindi, and Other Stories*. Delhi: Navyug, 1984.

Singh, Pritam, ed. *The Voices of Dissent*. Jalandhar: Seema, 1972.

Singh, Puran. *Walt Whitman and the Sikh Inspiration*. Patiala: Punjabi University, 1982.

Singh, Vir. *Bijai Singh*. Translated by Devinder Singh Duggal. New Delhi: Hemkunt, 1983.

———. *The Epic of Rana Surat Singh*. Translated by Gurbachan Singh Talib. Chandigarh: Panjab University, 1986.

———. *Rana Bhabor*. Translated by Amar Singh Malik. Dehradun: Dr. Balbir Singh Sahitya Kendra, 1982.

———. *Sundri*. Translated by Gobind Singh Mansukhani. New Delhi: Hemkunt, 1983.

Sobti, Harcharan Singh. *The Sikh Psyche: A Study of the Fictional Writings of Bhai Vir Singh*. Delhi: Eastern Book Linkers, 1990.

Srivastava, S. P. *Art and Cultural Heritage of Patiala*. Delhi: Sundeep, 1991.

Tasneem, N. S. *Studies in Modern Punjabi Literature*. New Delhi: Avishkar, 1980.

The Army

Anderson, R. H. *History of the 45th Rattrays Sikhs, 1914–21*. London: Stifton Praed and Co., 1925.

Bamford, P. G. *1st King George V's Own Battalion, the Sikh Regiment, the 14th King George's Own Ferozepore Sikhs, 1846–1946.* Aldershot: Gale and Bolden, 1948.

Barstow, A. E. *Sikhs: A Handbook for the Indian Army.* Calcutta: Government of India Publications Branch, 1928. Reprint, Delhi: B. R. Publishing Corporation, 1985.

Bingley, A. H. *Sikhs.* Calcutta: Government Printing, 1918. Reprint, Patiala: LDP, 1970.

Birdwood, F. T. *Sikh Regiments in the Second World War.* Norwich: Jarrod and Sons, N.d.

Brander, H. R. *32nd Sikh Pioneers: A Regimental History.* 2 vols. Calcutta: SGP, 1906.

Falcon, R. W. *Handbook on Sikhs for the Use of Regimental Officers.* Allahabad: Pioneer Press, 1896.

Gupta, Hari Ram. *Soldierly Traditions of the Sikhs up to 1849.* New Delhi: Sirjana, N.d. 41 pp.

History of the 1st Punjab Cavalry. Lahore: Civil and Military Gazette Press, 1887.

History of the 1st Sikh Infantry, 1866–1886. Calcutta: Thacker, Spink and Co., 1887.

History of the 2nd Punjab Cavalry, 1849–86. London: Kegan Paul and Co., 1888.

MacMunn, George F. *The Armies of India.* London: A. & C. Black, 1911.

———. *History of the Sikh Pioneers.* London: Sampson Low, 1936.

Macrae, H. St.G.M. *Regimental History of the 45th Rattray's Sikhs.* Glasgow: Robert Markhose and Co., 1953.

May, C. W. *History of the 2nd Sikhs 12th Frontier Force Regiment 1846–1933.* Jubbulpore: Mission Press, 1933.

Shearer, J. E. *History of the 1st Battalion 15th Panjab Regiment, 1857–1937.* London: Aldershot, Gale & Polden, 1937.

Shirley, S. R. *History of the 54th Sikh Frontier Force previously designated 4th Sikhs Punjab Frontier Force, 1846 to 1914.* London: Aldershot, Gale & Polden, 1915.

Sikh Portrait of Courage. Delhi: GPC and Khalsa Defence Council, N.d.

Sikhs Outside the Punjab

General Abroad

Bahadur Singh, I.J., ed. *The Other India: The Overseas Indians and Their Relationship with India.* New Delhi: Arnold-Heinemann, 1979.

Barrier, N. Gerald, and Verne A. Dusenbery, eds. *The Sikh Diaspora: Migration and Experience beyond Punjab.* Columbia, Missouri: South Asia Books, 1989; New Delhi: Chanakya, 1989.

Kondapi, C. *Indians Overseas 1838–1949.* New Delhi: Indian Council of World Affairs, 1951.

Kurian, George, and Ram P. Srivasatva, eds. *Overseas Indians: A Study of Adaptation.* New Delhi: Vikas, 1983.

United Kingdom

Agnihotri, Rama Kant. *Crisis of Identity: The Sikhs in England.* New Delhi: Bahri, 1987.

Aurora, G.S. *The New Frontiersmen: A Sociological Study of Indian Immigrants in the United Kingdom.* Bombay: Popular Prakashan, 1967.

Beetham, David. *Transport and Turbans: A Comparative Study in Local Politics.* London: OUP, 1970.

Bhachu, Parminder. *Twice Migrants: East African Settlers in Britain.* London: Tavistock, 1985.

Bidwell, Sidney. *The Turban Victory.* Southall: Sri Guru Singh Sabha Gurdwara, N.d.

Butler, D.G. *Life among the Sikhs.* London: Edward Arnold, 1980.

Chandan, Amarjit. *Indians in Britain.* New Delhi: Sterling, 1986.

Cole, W. Owen. *A Sikh Family in Britain.* Oxford: Religious Education Press, 1973.

Desai, Rashmi. *Indian Immigrants in Britain.* London: OUP, 1963.

De Souza, Allan. *The Sikhs in Britain.* London: Batsford, 1986.

DeWitt, John. *Indian Workers' Associations in Britain.* London: OUP, 1969.

Fitzgerald, Kitty, comp. *Speaking for Ourselves: Sikh Oral History.* Manchester: Manchester Sikh History Project, 1986.

Ghuman, P.A.S. *Cultural Context of Thinking: A Comparative Study of Punjabi and English Boys.* Windsor: NFER, 1975.

Helweg, A.W. *Sikhs in England: The Development of a Migrant Community.* Delhi: OUP, 1979. Revised edition, 1986.

Henley, Alix. *Caring for Sikhs and their Families: Religious Aspect of Care.* London: Department of Health and Social Security and King Edward's Hospital Fund for London, 1984.

James, Alan G. *Sikh Children in Britain*. London: OUP, 1974.

Kalra, S.S. *Daughters of Tradition: Adolescent Sikh Girls and Their Accommodation to Life in British Society*. Birmingham: Third World Publications, 1980.

Kaur, Jasbir, and Kulwinder Kaur. *Young Sikh Girls in Britain*. London: British Council of Churches, N.d.

Madan, Raj. *Colored Minorities in Great Britain*. Westport, Connecticut: Greenwood Press, 1979.

Marsh, Peter. *Anatomy of a Strike*. London: Institute of Race Relations, 1967.

Nesbitt, Eleanor. *'My Dad's Hindu, my Mum's side are Sikhs': Issues in Religious Identity*. Warwick: National Foundation for Arts Education, 1991.

Shan, Sharan-Jeet. *In My Own Name*. London: Women's Press, 1985.

Singh, Ramindar. *The Sikh Community in Bradford*. Bradford: Bradford College, 1978. 44 pp. Revised edition published as *Immigrants to Citizens*, 1992.

Tinker, Hugh. *The Banyan Tree: Overseas Emigrants from India, Pakistan and Bangladesh*. Oxford: OUP, 1977.

Watson, James L., ed. *Between Two Cultures: Migrants and Minorities in Britain*. Oxford: Basil Blackwell, 1977.

North America

Ashworth, Mary. *Immigrant Children and Canadian Schools*. Toronto: McClelland and Stewart, 1975.

Blaise, Clark, and Bharati Mukherjee. *The Sorrow and the Terror: The Haunting Legacy of the Air India Tragedy*. Markham: Penguin Books Canada, 1987.

Buchignani, Norman, and Doreen M. Indra. *Continuous Journey: A Social History of South Asians in Canada.* Toronto: McClelland and Stewart, 1985.

Chadney, James G. *The Sikhs of Vancouver.* New York: AMS Press, 1984.

Chandra, K. V. *Racial Discrimination in Canada.* San Francisco: R & E Research Associates, 1973.

Gibson, Margaret A. *Accommodation without Assimilation: Sikh Immigrants in an American High School.* Ithaca, New York: Cornell University, 1988.

Hardwick, Francis C., ed. *From Beyond the Western Horizon: Canadians from the Sub-Continent of India.* Vancouver: Tantalus Research, 1974.

Hawley, John Stratton, and Gurinder Singh Mann, eds. *Studying the Sikhs: Issues for North America.* Albany: SUNY, 1993.

Hirabayashi, Gordon, and K. Victor Ujimoto. *Visible Minorities and Multiculturalism: Asians in Canada.* Toronto: Butterworth, 1980.

Jacoby, Harold S. *A Half-century of Appraisal of East Indians in the United States.* Stockton, California: College of the Pacific, 1956. 35 pp.

Jain, Sushil K. *East Indians in Canada.* Windsor: Canadian Bibliographic Center, 1970.

Jensen, Joan M. *Passage from India: Asian Indian Immigrants in North America.* New Haven, Connecticut: Yale University Press, 1988.

Johnston, Hugh. *The Voyage of the Komagata Maru: The Sikh Challenge to Canada's Colour Bar.* Delhi: OUP, 1979.

Judge, Paramjit S. *Punjabis in Canada: A Study of Formation of an Ethnic Community.* Delhi: Chanakya, 1993.

Kanungo, Rabindera, ed. *South Asians in the Canadian Mosaic.* Montreal: Kala Bharati, 1984.

Kashmiri, Zuhair, and Brian McAndrew. *Soft Target: How the Indian Intelligence Service Penetrated Canada.* Toronto: James Lorimer & Co., 1989.

La Brack, Bruce. *The Sikhs of Northern California 1904–1975.* New York: AMS Press, 1988.

Leonard, Karen Isaksen. *Making Ethnic Choices: California's Punjabi Mexican Americans.* Philadelphia: Temple University, 1992.

Mulgrew, Ian. *Unholy Terror: The Sikhs and International Terrorism.* Toronto: Key Porter Books, 1988.

Narula, Surinder Singh. *Koma Gata Maru.* Ludhiana: Central, 1985.

Pollock, Sharon. *The Komagata Maru Incident.* A play. Toronto, Playwrights Canada, 1978.

Rosenstock, Janet, and Dennis Addair. *Multiracialism in the Classroom: A Survey of the Interracial Attitudes in Canadian Schools.* Don Mills, Ontario: Fulcrum Press, 1973.

Singh, Gurdit. *Voyage of the Kamagata-Maru or India's Slavery Abroad.* Calcutta: author, N.d.

Singh, Jane, et al. *South Asians in North America.* Berkeley, California: Center for South and Southeast Asian Studies, University of California, 1988.

Singh, Kesar. *Canadian Sikhs and the Komagata Maru Massacre.* Surrey, British Columbia: author, 1989.

Singh, Sohan. *Tragedy of Komagata Maru.* New Delhi: People's Publishing House, 1975.

Unna, Warren. *Sikhs Abroad: Attitudes and Activities of Sikhs Settled in the USA and Canada.* Calcutta: Statesman, 1985. 34 pp.

Williams, Raymond Brady. *Religions of Immigrants from India and Pakistan.* New York: CUP, 1988.

Other Abroad

Chowdhary, Hardip Singh, and Anup Singh Choudry, comp. *Sikh Pilgrimage to Pakistan.* London: Gurbani Cassette Centre, 1985.

de Lepervanche, Marie M. *Indians in a White Australia.* Sydney: George Allen & Unwin, 1984.

Ghai, Dharam P., ed. *Portrait of a Minority: Asians in East Africa.* Nairobi: OUP, 1965.

Kalra, Balwant Singh. *Brief History of Sikh Gurdwaras in Thailand.* Bankok: author, N.d. 14 pp.

McLeod, W. H. *A List of Punjabi Immigrants in New Zealand 1890–1959.* Hamilton: Country Section of the Central Indian Association, 1984.

———. *Punjabis in New Zealand.* Amritsar: GNDU, 1986.

———. *Punjab to Aotearoa: Migration and Settlement of Punjabis in New Zealand 1890–1990.* With S.S. Bhullar. Hamilton: New Zealand Indian Association Country Section (Inc.), 1992.

Mangat, J. S. *A History of the Asians in East Africa.* Oxford: Clarendon, 1970.

Parkash, Ved. *The Sikhs in Bihar.* Patna: Janaki, 1981.

Sarna, Jasbir Singh. *Sikhs in Kashmir.* Delhi: NBO, 1993.

Sidhu, Manjit Singh. *The Sikhs in Kenya.* Chandigarh: Panjab University, N.d.

Singh, Gajraj. *The Sikhs of Fiji.* Suva: South Pacific Social Sciences Association, N.d. [1976–77].

Tinker, Hugh. *Separate and Unequal: India and the Indians in the British Commonwealth 1920–1950.* London: Hurst, 1976.

Tiwari, Kapil N., ed. *Indians in New Zealand: Studies of a Sub-Culture.* Wellington: Price Milburn, 1980.

Vaid, K. N. *The Overseas Indian Community in Hong Kong.* Hong Kong: Center of Asian Studies, University of Hong Kong, 1972.

Principal Sources for Sikhism in Punjabi

Adi Sri Guru Granth Sahib Ji. Sri Damdami Bir. Various printed editions. Standard pagination 1430 pp.

Bhangu, Ratan Singh. *Prachin Panth Prakash.* 1st edition, Amritsar: Vazir Hind Press, 1914. 4th edition, Amritsar: Khalsa Samachar, 1962.

Dasam Sri Guru Granth Sahib Ji. Various printed editions. Standard pagination 1428 pp.

Gurdas Bhalla (Bhai Gurdas). *Varan Bhai Gurdas.* Edited by Hazara Singh and Vir Singh. Amritsar: Khalsa Samachar, 1962.

Jaggi, Ratan Singh. *Janam Sakhi Bhai Bala.* Amritsar: Guru Nanak University, 1974.

———, ed. *Varan Bhai Gurdas: Shabad Anukramanika ate Kosh.* Patiala: Punjabi University, 1966.

Kohli, Surindar Singh, ed. *Janamasakhi Bhai Bala.* Chandigarh: Panjab University, 1975.

Nabha, Kahn Singh. [Singh, Kahn, or as Singh, Kahan.] *Gurushabad Ratanakar Mahan Kosh.* 1st edition in 4 vols. Patiala: Punjab State Government, 1931. 2nd edition, revised with addendum, in 1 vol. Patiala: LDP, 1960.

————, ed. *Guramat Maratand.* 2 vols. Amritsar: SGPC, 1962.

————, ed. *Guramat Prabhakar.* 4th ed. Patiala: LDP, 1970.

————, ed. *Guramat Sudhakar.* 4th ed. Patiala: LDP, 1970.

Nihang, Kaur Singh, comp. *Guru Shabad Ratan Prakash.* Line Index of the Adi Granth. Patiala: LDP, 1963. Original edition entitled *Sri Guru Sabad Ratan Prakash,* Peshawar, 1923.

Padam, Piara Singh, ed. *Rahit Name.* Patiala: author, 1974.

Photozincograph Facsimile of the *Colebrooke Janam-sakhi.* Dehra Dun: Survey of India, 1885.

Sikh Rahit Marayada. 1st ed. Amritsar: SGPC, 1950 and numerous editions thereafter.

Singh, Bhagavant 'Hari Ji'. *Dasam Granth Tuk-tatakara.* Patiala: Punjabi University, 1969.

Singh, Ganda, ed. *Bhai Nand Lal Granthavali.* Malacca: Sant Sohan Singh, 1968.

————, ed. *Hukamaname.* Patiala: Punjabi University, 1967.

————, ed. *Sri Gur Sobha.* Patiala: Punjabi University, 1967.

Singh, Guracharan, ed. *Adi Granth Shabad-anukramanika.* 2 vols. Patiala: Punjabi University, 1971.

Singh, Koir (also spelt Kuir). *Gurabilas Patashahi 10.* Edited by Shamsher Singh Ashok. Patiala: Punjabi University, 1968.

Singh, Piar, ed. *Janam Sakhi Sri Guru Nanak Dev Ji.* The B40 Janam-sakhi. Amritsar: GNDU, 1974.

Singh, Randhir, ed. *Shabadarath Dasam Granth Sahib.* 3 vols. Patiala: Punjabi University, 1985–88.

Singh, Sahib. *Sri Guru Granth Sahib Darapan.* 10 vols. Jullundur: Raj, 1962–64.

Singh, Santokh. *Nanak Prakash* and *Suraj Prakash.* 13 vols. Edited by Vir Singh and comprising: vol. 1, *Sri Gur Pratap Suraj Granthavali di Prasavana,* being Vir Singh's Introduction; vols. 2–4, *Sri Gur Nanak Prakash;* vols. 5–13, *Sri Gur Pratap Suraj Granth.* Amritsar: Khalsa Samachar, 1927–35.

Singh, Sukha. *Gurbilas Patshahi 10.* Edited by Gursharan Kaur Jaggi. Patiala: LDP, 1989.

Singh, Taran, ed. *Guru Nanak Bani Prakash.* 2 vols. Patiala: Punjabi University, 1969.

[Principally Teja Singh]. *Shabadarath Sri Guru Granth Sahib Ji.* Text and commentary on the Adi Granth. N.p.: 1936–41.

Singh, Vir. *Santhya Sri Guru Granth Sahib.* 7 vols. (incomplete). Amritsar: Khalsa Samachar, 1958–62.

[Vir Singh]. *Sri Guru Granth Kosh.* 3 vols. Amritsar: Khalsa Samachar, 1950.

————, ed. *Panj Granthi Satik.* 3rd ed. Amritsar: Khalsa Samachar, 1966.

————, ed. *Puratan Janam-sakhi.* Amritsar: Khalsa Samachar, several editions.

Sohan. *Sri Gur Bilas Patshahi 6.* Edited by Indar Singh Gill. Amritsar: Pramindar Singh Soch, 1968.

Journals

Abstracts of Sik Studies. Semiannual. Chandigarh: Institute of Sikh Studies, and Santa Ana, California: Center of Sikh Studies. 1991–

The Guru Gobind Singh Journal of Religious Studies. Quarterly. Chandigarh: GGSF, 1994–

International Journal of Punjab Studies. Semiannual. London: Sage. 1994–

Journal of Regional History. Annual. Amritsar: Department of History, GNDU. 1980–

The Journal of Religious Studies. Biennial. Patiala: Department of Religious Studies, Punjabi University. 1969-

Journal of Sikh Studies. Semiannual. Amritsar: Department of Guru Nanak Studies, GNDU, 1974–

Khera: Journal of Religious Understanding. Quarterly. New Delhi: Bhai Vir Singh Sahitya Sadan. 1981–

The Missionary. Quarterly. Delhi: Sikh Missionary Society. 1959–63.

The Panjab Past and Present. Biennial. Patiala: Department of Punjab Historical Studies, Punjabi University. 1967–

Proceedings of the Punjab History Conference. Annual. Patiala: Department of Punjab Historical Studies, Punjabi University. 1965–

The Punjab Journal of Politics. Biennial. Amritsar: Department of Political Science, GNDU. 1977–

The Sikh Review. Monthly. Calcutta: Sikh Cultural Centre. 1952-

Studies in Sikhism and Comparative Religion. Biennial. New Delhi: GNF, 1982–

ABOUT THE AUTHOR

W. H. McLeod is a New Zealander and teaches in his home country at the University of Otago in Dunedin. He took an MA from the University of Otago and a PhD from the School of Oriental and African Studies in London. For nine years he taught in the Punjab and there developed a life-long interest in the Sikhs. He returned to teach History in the University of Otago in 1971 and since then has paid frequent visits to the Punjab. All of his books and most of his published articles concern Sikh history, religion and sociology. The books include *Gurū Nānak and the Sikh Religion* (1968), *The Evolution of the Sikh Community* (1976), *Early Sikh Tradition* (1980), and *Who is a Sikh?* (1989), all of them published by the Clarendon Press in Oxford. Several other books have also been published, including *The Sikhs: History, Religion, and Society* which was issued by Columbia University Press in 1989. His *Textual Sources for the Study of Sikhism* was re-issued by the University of Chicago Press in 1990 and *Sikhism* is forthcoming from Penguin Books.